PAINTING ◦ COLOR ◦ HISTORY

COLLECTION PLANNED AND DIRECTED BY
ALBERT SKIRA

GERMAN PAINTING

From Dürer to Holbein

TEXT BY OTTO BENESCH

To My Wife

Translated from the German by H. S. B. Harrison

★

Distributed in the United States by
THE WORLD PUBLISHING COMPANY
2231 West 110th Street, Cleveland 2, Ohio

PRINTED IN SWITZERLAND

Until now the classical period of German painting, from the end of the fifteenth to the middle of the sixteenth century, has been considered mainly in terms of the work of a few great artists and their schools, or treated as a survey of the various regional groups or clans that flourished particularly in South Germany and along the Rhine. Such an approach may be valid for the second half of the fifteenth century because of the great variety of the artistic scene in Central Europe at that time; but when we come to the sixteenth century we find—what has been overlooked—that the art of the period has an overall unity and that the features common to the movement as a whole are more important than the individual achievements of any regional group. Such had already been the case in the fourteenth century, up to the end of the "international style"; so it was again in the sixteenth century. Although the period is dominated by the great figures of Dürer, Gothardt-Neithardt, Burgkmair, Cranach, Altdorfer, Baldung, Holbein, and Huber, these masters, despite their variety and individuality, were united by a single overriding impulse just as much as their Italian contemporaries were. Dominated by the religious and spiritual ideas of the period, they reflect them in visual terms. It would, however, be inadequate to call this period the "Age of the Reformation," as some art historians have done, for the reform of the Christian faith was only one *theme in the great fugue of the time, which also witnessed a revival of medieval fervour. It might, with equal justification, be considered as a period characterized by the search for a new philosophy of life, both magic and scientific, an attempt to represent both the macrocosmic and the microcosmic, to formulate a new conception of Man, and to achieve perfection of form.*

The paintings dealt with in the following pages were almost all executed on wood, like those of the Late Gothic period. The South German painters preferred coniferous woods (spruce, fir, larch, Scotch pine), while the North Germans, like the Netherlandish masters, had a preference for oak. Whereas the earlier artists had painted in pure tempera, those of the period considered here had a new technique at their disposal—that of oil painting, employing the mixture of oil and tempera introduced by the Van Eycks.

Technically, therefore, German painting in the period of Dürer remained closely linked with the Late Gothic. The technique of oil painting on canvas—which was already employed in Italy, mainly by the Venetians—was not unknown to German painters, most of whom had been to Italy, but they did not take it up, feeling it to be inappropriate to their aims. They used canvas exclusively for paintings in watercolour ("painted fabrics"), only a few of which have survived.

Vienna, November 1964   *Otto Benesch*

THE text of this book is an expanded version of a lecture course on "German Painting in the Age of Dürer," which my husband gave at the University of Vienna in 1959 and 1960. This text was completed, with the addition of the last two pages, on the day before his death (November 16, 1964). It is thus his final contribution to the history of art.

For having given most useful information while I was preparing the posthumous publication of this book, I wish to thank Dr Peter Halm, Director of the Graphische Sammlung, Munich, Dr Jan Lauts, Director of the Staatliche Kunsthalle, Karlsruhe, and Hofrat Dr Ernst Trenkler of the Austrian National Library in Vienna. My thanks are also due to Director Dr Erwin M. Auer, Kunsthistorisches Museum, Vienna, for his great help in procuring photographic material.

At the Albertina, scene of my husband's activities first as Curator, then as Director, the library and collection were placed at my disposal and my work was facilitated in every way; at the Austrian National Library I met with the most courteous and ready response in consulting the relevant literature. To both institutions I should like to express my particular thanks. I am also indebted to members of the Austrian Ministry of Education for their understanding in regard to my work.

Mr Albert Skira has been more than a publisher—he has been a friend. For the painstaking care lavished on the book and the handsome form given to it, I should like to extend my thanks both to him and to his collaborator Mr Lauro Venturi.

Vienna, December 1965   Eva Benesch

Contents

Albrecht Dürer (1471-1528). Self-Portrait, 1498. (20½×16⅛″) Prado, Madrid.

Chiliasm

1490-1500

We might ask: Who or what is a godlike or godly man? Answer: One who is inspired or illuminated by the eternal or godlike light and burns with eternal or godly love—that is a godly or godlike man.

Theologia Teutsch, Augsburg 1518, Chapter XXXIX (first printed edition from an incunabulum of 1497).

IN certain periods, the creative impulse has manifested itself through a variety of artists working on a wide front. This was the case in German painting in the fourteenth and fifteenth centuries, when a wealth of fascinating works, mostly anonymous, were produced in almost every German-speaking territory. In contrast to this are the periods dominated by a few outstanding artistic figures. In these periods, creative achievement is concentrated in a few regions and towns and confined to a handful of artists whose names are renowned throughout the world. At such times it seems as if the creative forces of a whole nation are concentrated at a few focal points, where they reach unrivalled heights. This was the case in Germany in the first half of the sixteenth century.

At that time, other European countries that had earlier thrown up a wealth of creative talent, such as France and the Netherlands, showed only a high general level of artistic culture, and it was in Germany and Italy that the great individual figures and towering achievements of the High Renaissance were found. In Italy, this artistic movement was centred on Florence, Rome, and Venice, while in the North the focal points were the cities and duchies of South Germany, Austria, and Switzerland. In Italy, this period represented the culmination of a process that began with the artistic revolution of about 1400; in Central Europe, its beginnings coincided with a revolutionary break with the old, declining world of the Middle Ages and the advent of a completely new era of thought. The new movement accordingly had an especially strong impact in the North, and the peak period of German Renaissance art is called the "Age of Dürer" after the man who expressed this impact most vigorously in visual terms.

At the turn of the century, round about 1500, artistic life in Germany was undergoing a profound change. This was not the result of a gradual process, as in Italy, but marked a drastic breach with the past. It was made all the more abrupt and violent by the fact that the medieval spirit, in the form of Late Gothic, still lived on at the very threshold of the new era, whereas in Italy it had been laid to rest by the fathers of the Renaissance about 1410, reappearing only feebly and intermittently during the rest of the Quattrocento.

The historical and geographical disposition of southern Germany during the second half of the fifteenth century—with its ancestral estates and their specific types of artistic expression corresponding to the variations in the spoken language—remained unchanged in the sixteenth century. We can thus still distinguish the Franconian, Swabian, Alemannic, and

Bavarian schools of art. To classify the German art of the sixteenth century according to these schools would, however, be the equivalent of classifying that of the period around 1400 by provinces, and would falsify the overall picture. In the sixteenth century, the overriding importance of certain outstanding figures deprived the regional divisions of their meaning, just as the influence of the great movements had done about 1400. Young people from every region flocked to Dürer's workshop, and the mature masters took to new surroundings as easily as they had done at the time of the "international style."

This was to some extent due to the fact that ducal patronage played a decisive role, much as it had done at the end of the fourteenth century, whereas in the later fifteenth century the artist had been wholly dependent on communal patronage. In addition, the growth of modern commerce on an international scale, which had helped promote printing and book production in the fifteenth century, did much to increase the dissemination of graphic art. Since many leading artists, besides being painters, were also draftsmen and print-makers, this served to spread the renown of their achievements in painting. Ducal rule was no longer merely the expression of a local feudalism as it had been at the end of the Middle Ages, but came to represent a modern conception of government and political thought on a European scale.

Albrecht Dürer developed out of the Late Gothic art of Nuremberg, his native city. He was born on May 21, 1471. Like Michelangelo, he belonged to the great creative generation of the seventies that was produced by the new era and borne along by it. While the German masters who preceded him, even those whose names we know, are obscure, poorly documented figures, Dürer was aware of the historical significance of his work and personality. He not only carefully signed all his work, but kept a family chronicle, began a memorial book, kept a diary during his journey to the Netherlands, and wrote numerous letters that have been preserved. He wrote poetry and left a considerable body of scientific writings on the theory of art and mathematics, in which he created a new language much as Luther did in the realm of religion. He wrote of the life and death of his parents, treating them as people whose destiny fitted into the medieval concepts of heaven and earth, whose life in this world was directed towards the next. To them death meant liberation from the narrow needy existence that was the lot of even the most highly skilled medieval craftsman.

Thus, in the Uffizi portrait of 1490, Dürer depicts his father as a godfearing man with a calm, reserved face, offset by dark clothes, his bearing devout, almost timid, ready at any moment to answer the call from the Almighty, his strong capable fingers holding his rosary. Dürer inherited much of his ancestors' devout nature, as can be seen from his poetry. When he writes of their death, however, he reveals a capacity for human experience and a depth of emotion that show him to be a very different man from those of the pious generation to which his father belonged.

Apart from his own writings, the most important source for our knowledge of Dürer's life is the tribute to Anton Kress written by his friend Dr Christoph Scheurl. Albrecht Dürer the Elder, a goldsmith of Hungarian origin, had intended his son to follow him in the family craft. The boy learned to draw in his father's workshop—an early example of his genius is the *Self-Portrait* he drew at the age of thirteen—and he may also have learnt to handle the engraver's needle there, but his chief ambition was to become a painter. His father therefore wrote in 1484 to his professional colleague Martin Schongauer, of Colmar, who had become a noted painter-engraver. As it turned out, Schongauer had moved and Dürer was apprenticed instead to Michael Wolgemut.

Though powerful in their way, Wolgemut's sombre, gnarled portraits probably had little appeal for Dürer. The vigour and drama of his woodcuts would have made a greater impression; Wolgemut was just then working on the illustrations for the *Weltchronik* and the

Schatzbehalter. The precious enamelling of Pleydenwurff's panels, carefully modelled on the work of Rogier van der Weyden, would have appealed to Dürer, as would the luminous colours of the *Augustinian, Landauer,* and *Strache Altarpieces*, whose anonymous masters probably made no less impression on him than did his own teacher. The small *St Christopher* in the Dessau Museum—thought to be a youthful work by Dürer—shows a definite kinship with the portrayal of the saint in the *Augustinian Altarpiece*, yet clearly reveals the difference between the younger and the older master. Dürer's painting is filled with *Sturm und Drang*, with brooding tension and unrest. The same is true of his earliest drawings, dating back to his Nuremberg years. But he was beckoned away from his early surroundings by the wider horizons of the Upper Rhine, the homeland of the great Schongauer, whom he must have seen as the most modern, most advanced artist of the day, standing head and shoulders above his German contemporaries.

However, when Dürer, who had left Nuremberg in 1490, arrived in Colmar in 1492, Schongauer was dead; he had spent his last years in Alt-Breisach working on his most powerful legacy to mankind, the fresco of the *Last Judgement* in the cathedral. We may assume that Dürer, who was received in Colmar by the master's brothers, saw this monumental work —the culminating achievement of a genius who had made his way up from copperplate engravings based on the goldsmith's craft and small, minutely detailed paintings to monumental works in the grand manner.

A young painter in his twenties like Dürer could not fail to be stirred by Schongauer's art which held the seeds of the future and confirmed his own sense of a turning-point in human affairs, the decline of one epoch and the beginning of another. Schongauer's influence was not confined to the field of graphic art, although he had absolute mastery in it. Between 1490 and 1492, Dürer showed himself to be a prolific wood-engraver and draftsman, illustrating Sebastian Brant's *Ship of Fools*, the *Knight of the Tower*, and the *Comedies* of Terence for publishers in Basel; his style was derived from Schongauer rather than from what he had learnt at home, although his apprenticeship to the wood-engraver's craft in Nuremberg undoubtedly contributed to it. In painting, Schongauer had an equally great influence, even outside his own narrow circle of pupils (which included Burgkmair). His capacity for achieving subtle effects in his pictures and frescoes as well as in his engravings influenced a whole generation of artists between Basel and Strasbourg, establishing a school. True to its role as a centre for significant movements in art, the Upper Rhine once more gathered together the best talents from the German-speaking world in the critical time at the close of the century.

That Dürer spent most of his Upper Rhine period in Basel can be concluded from the vast amount of graphic work he produced there. In 1492, he left this intellectual and artistic centre and went by way of Colmar to Strasbourg where we find him in 1493. Most of his painting during his early travels appears to have been done in these two towns. The paintings by Schongauer and his school that he saw in Colmar must have had a decisive influence on him. From them he would have learnt the strictest control and discipline of form, together with harmony of colour and light—for, despite their Late Gothic decorativeness and grace, they had a certain freshness and strength. Here there was none of the cramped and crabbed uncertainty of the Nuremberg school. That the narrow, hard, and stolid people depicted by Wolgemut, Hans Traut, Jakob Elsner and the other Nuremberg painters had been superseded by a superior, more sophisticated generation can be seen from the fine *Portrait of a Young Man* (1491) in the Metropolitan Museum.

Ernst Buchner and Friedrich Winkler have identified this portrait as the work of a young artist who co-operated with Dürer on altarpieces dedicated to the Passion and to St Dominic. Panels from these altarpieces are to be found in the Darmstadt Museum and the Munich Pinakothek. In them the work of two different artists can clearly be distinguished, and the

Albrecht Dürer (1471-1528).

The Man of Sorrows, c. 1493-1494. (11¾×7½″) Staatliche Kunsthalle, Karlsruhe.

more vigorous of the two was most probably the youthful Dürer. The *Death of St Dominic* contains the splendid figure of a young monk, who kneels in the foreground, an aspersorium in his hand—this figure is worthy of Dürer. The use of dark outlines is reminiscent of Dürer's drawings in his Upper Rhine period, while the full, rich orchestration of colour is of a type unknown to the school of Wolgemut. The tender, delicately painted *Lamentation* might perhaps be by the same hand as the New York *Portrait of a Young Man*, but the tragic seriousness, the brooding tension—the dark eyes draw us with a strange power—suggest that here too Dürer made a decisive contribution.

The *Man of Sorrows*, a small picture in the Staatliche Kunsthalle, Karlsruhe, can claim sole authorship by Dürer. This exquisite panel was intended for private prayer and devotion; Pleydenwurff had painted a similar one for the Count of Löwenstein. It may also have given pleasure to the cultured onlooker as one of those cabinet pictures that were being produced in increasing numbers alongside the great altarpieces. In this painting the theme of the Saviour who has gone through the agony of the Passion—he is holding the instruments of the Passion and is already marked by their wounds—is merged with that of Christ as the Man of Sorrows resting by the wayside. He is crouching in the entrance to the tomb, his large eyes turned in sorrow on the onlooker. The profound sadness of his expression seems to say "Tua culpa!"—its burning intensity can scarcely be contained within the framework of the old iconographic conventions. It testifies to that individuality of conception to which Dürer's works owe their greatness.

Here we are standing at the threshold of a new epoch in matters of faith, a revival of the mystical tradition of the late fourteenth century. The intensity of feeling we find in Dürer's painting is also encountered in the words of the *Theologia Teutsch*, a widely read work by an anonymous Sachsenhausen mystic: "Lo, sin is such suffering to God and hurts him so much that God himself sought martyrdom and bodily death so that men might thereby conquer sin."

Dürer strove for a new truth and directness not only in his religious paintings but also in his portraits. Since earliest youth he had scrutinized his own features repeatedly in his drawings. While the portraits he painted of his master and his master's wife in Strasbourg have been lost, the *Self-Portrait* on vellum (Louvre) has survived. Dürer painted it in 1493 to send home as a record of his development, or perhaps to forward his courtship. In it we see the man as he was, with all his youthful uncouthness—one might even call it ugliness—yet full of daring, gallantry, and purity of intention. Such naturalism is a kind of ethical challenge, the expression of an uncompromising love of truth, similar to the mature Dürer's search for canons of perfection.

Dürer returned to Nuremberg in 1494, round the time of his birthday, and married Agnes Frey, whose features often appear in her husband's drawings and paintings. In conformity with the bourgeois conventions of the time, the match had been arranged by the couple's fathers, who belonged to the same trade. By the autumn of the same year Dürer was on his way to Italy. An outbreak of the plague—that recurrent scourge of medieval cities—which drove all the wealthier people from the town has been suggested as the reason for this early departure. In fact, the real reason was a personal one. On the Upper Rhine, if not in Nuremberg itself, Dürer had come into contact with Italian works of art in the form of prints by Mantegna and his circle. He was so deeply impressed by them that he made careful drawings of them, a proof that he considered them an achievement that he himself could as yet realize only fumblingly and uncertainly. We must visualize Dürer in Venice not as the busy creative artist of the Upper Rhine period but as a man who was observing and learning. In his own creative work—sketches for engravings—he continued the apprenticeship that had started on the Upper Rhine, but he also copied and drew from nature. Gentile Bellini's paintings and the bronze and marble sculptures of the Italian masters were a revelation to him, as were the lively artist's models of the South and the Venetian women who walked across the Piazza in velvets and brocades.

The great *painter* who had always been hidden in Dürer the draftsman was revealed in the watercolours he made on his journey through the Tyrol and the Italian Alps. As works of art, they are the most significant result of his first Italian journey and show the coming to terms of a Promethean artist with the visible world, his immeasurable delight at its unsuspected marvels. The watercolour, now in the Louvre, of the town and fortress of Arco on Lake Garda was painted on his return journey in 1495 and demonstrates not only a new awareness of the organic structure of rock, soil, vegetation, and human handiwork, but also a new sensitivity to colour in the deep violet shadows on the cliff face and the silvery blues of the olive trees. In its period, it is equalled only by Leonardo's landscape drawings, but these were carefully based on scientific research, whereas in Dürer's case we have the amazing phenomenon of an original artistic creation with nothing premeditated about it. Dürer's passionate interest in landscape is shown by the series of watercolours he continued to produce after his return from Italy. These were painted in the surroundings of Nuremberg and include the remarkable *Pond in the Woods* (British Museum, London) with its glowing dawn colours. Dürer did not exercise his great gifts as a landscape painter *a prima vista* after the 1490s because he became absorbed in other things, but he broke the ground for others, especially the masters of the Danube School.

Despite the medieval narrowness of its fifteenth-century painters, Nuremberg was a modern progressive town, not so much in the artistic sphere like Basel or Strasbourg as in its economic organization and intellectual life. The city's printers and merchants had connections all over the world, and the fact that Dürer was the godson of Anton Koberger, the printer and publisher, may have smoothed his way both in Basel and Venice.

In Italy Dürer had confined himself mainly to observing and learning, but on his return home his creative energy overflowed. In Nuremberg the organization of the craftsmen's guilds was not excessively strict. The sons of Nuremberg masters were not obliged to enter an existing workshop, but allowed to work independently. This is what Dürer did, depending for his livelihood on his graphic work—copper engravings and woodcuts which he issued himself in single sheets or in series, instead of disposing of them to publishers of illustrated books. His prints were circulated not only among connoisseurs and artists, who soon imitated and exploited them, but also among the people, who bought them at fairs and religious festivals. Like the artists of the Late Gothic period, Dürer was not above offering his works in the market-place.

While Dürer's chief works in the later 1490s were predominantly graphic, he nevertheless made tremendous strides in his painting. Thus he became an artist of a completely new type, a "painter-engraver," able to express himself with equal mastery in both media and to enrich his graphic work by means of his knowledge of painting. The watercolours to which we now attach so much importance and value were for him no more than a pastime, something he painted for his own pleasure. His whole ambition as an artist lay elsewhere, but to realize it he needed a patron. The young Dürer found one in Frederick the Wise, Elector of Saxony, a connoisseur of the arts and an energetic promoter of religious reform.

The wealth of creative achievement in Renaissance Germany was made possible only by the patronage of provincial rulers eager to enhance their own glory by supporting the arts. Although the divisions and conflicting interests in the country paralysed it politically and handicapped the Imperial government, this state of affairs was a blessing for German art. Frederick the Wise was as important a factor in Dürer's life at this period as the Emperor

Albrecht Dürer (1471-1528). View of Arco, 1495. Watercolour. (8⅝×8⅝″) Cabinet des Dessins, Louvre, Paris.

Maximilian was to be in his maturity. During a four-day stay in Nuremberg in April 1496 he commissioned a portrait from the artist, probably sitting for a drawing, on which the painting (Staatliche Museen, Berlin) was based. Executed in size- and water-colours on canvas, it was intended for the private collection of a connoisseur. The figure is powerfully rendered and the compelling gaze of the large eyes has an almost frightening intensity. This portrait has a grandeur and inner tension of a kind unknown to Dürer's predecessors. The painter did not aim at creating a conventional likeness but at expressing the prince's personality; to do this, he did not attempt a psychological characterization but stressed the spiritual side of the subject. In Italy he may have seen portraits by Mantegna and Antonello da Messina that employed a similar combination of strong realism and imposing calm.

Dürer employed a similar technique in several other works commissioned by the Elector, notably in the *Wittenberg Altarpiece* (Gemäldegalerie, Dresden), which shows the Virgin and Child on the central panel and St Anthony and St Sebastian on the (later) wings, and in *Hercules Killing the Birds of Stymphalus* (1500, Germanisches Nationalmuseum, Nuremberg). The last-mentioned is a "studied" type of painting, in which the artist is trying out his skill, together with his knowledge of southern art and of humanist themes. The art of Pollaiuolo and of Mantegna and his followers is here combined with the hard, steely German manner. In the Elector's castle was a room containing four scenes from the life of Hercules; the Nuremberg picture was one of these. There were similar rooms in the Castles of Ferrara and Mantua, and the German patrons were anxious to keep up with the Italian ones. It is possible that Dürer's friend, the erudite humanist Willibald Pirckheimer, helped him to master the classical subject, but the painting is wholly imbued with personal feeling and the figure of Hercules is similar to his own. In an evening landscape the classical hero,

Albrecht Dürer (1471-1528). Lot and his Daughters Fleeing from Sodom and Gomorrah, c. 1497.
(19⅝×15½″) Reverse of the Haller Madonna.
National Gallery of Art, Washington, D.C. Samuel H. Kress Collection.

armed with a Turkish bow and quiver, is shown fighting phantasmal transparent forms that hover above a veritable *mappa mundi*. A new cosmic sense of space mingles strangely with the haunting colours of a northern twilight.

Frederick the Wise combined a humanistic patronage of art with a medieval devoutness and filled his churches and chapels with pious donations. Dürer played a leading part in the decoration of the Schlosskirche at Wittenberg, and painted the large panel known as the *Sorrows of the Virgin* (Alte Pinakothek, Munich), which was surrounded by scenes of suffering from the *Life of the Virgin* (Gemäldegalerie, Dresden). Unlike the paintings executed for the prince personally, these works show no trace of Mantegna's style. The Munich panel and a pendant, now lost, depicting the *Joys of the Virgin* were intended for the ordinary church-goer and so had to be easily understandable and make the same universal impression as a sermon. There is accordingly nothing muted or discreet about them (as there is in the "painted fabrics"), but a glowing eloquence expressed in flowing enamel-like colour. They carry on the Late Gothic manner, the tradition of Schongauer, and show a direct continuity with the panels painted in the Upper Rhine region. Surging upwards in the characteristic S-shaped curve of the Late Gothic style, the Virgin is far from being a static Italianate figure. Nevertheless, even if we knew nothing of the circumstances in which it was painted, this picture could never be ascribed to Dürer's journeyman years. It may be considered as a vast synthesis expressing in powerful accents the diverse aspects of the northern genius. In it, the Late Gothic style takes on an unaccustomed grandeur and urgency. The curving forms betray an inner tension that matches the tragic quality of the figure with the sword. The religious pathos of the medieval world is here endowed with a new depth of expression reflecting the mood of a tense and troubled age. The Dresden panels, which were painted with the help of an assistant, have the almost theatrical narrative quality of Dürer's earlier illustrations for books.

The difficulty of dating some of Dürer's works raises the question of his development, which was far from being single-minded, regular, or continuous. In this he resembled most artists of genius. Particularly where his drawings and paintings are concerned, a number of confusing problems arise. His progress may best be followed from certain central points— rather than a single one—and seen as a radial process in which the various tendencies some-times coincide and sometimes diverge. His travels as a journeyman in the Upper Rhine region had aroused certain impulses that were not fully clarified until he went to Italy, although they had nothing to do with Italian art. The years immediately following his return to Germany saw their transformation into achievement. These impulses mingled with the Late Gothic heritage handed down by Schongauer and led to a transitional phase that was full of significance for the future—the phase of the great cycles of woodcuts and the religious paintings for Wittenberg and Nuremberg.

As well as carrying out princely commissions, Dürer accepted assignments from some of the patrician families of Nuremberg. For the Haller family, he painted the *Madonna and Child* (National Gallery, Washington), a work so Venetian in its colour and gusto that it used to be ascribed to Bellini. A preparatory brush study (Cologne), however, has such an empha-tically northern and Late Gothic air that it has wrongly been attributed to the Upper Rhine period. A miniature on vellum (formerly Koenigs Collection, Haarlem), dating from the same period, places the Holy Family in a Late Gothic setting of branches, although the wealth of forms recalls Vivarini and Crivelli. On the back of the Haller Madonna is a painting of *Lot and his Daughters* fleeing from the destruction of Sodom; executed in transparent water-colours, it conjures up an eerie vision of the end of the world. This painting dates from the time when Dürer was working on the *Apocalypse* (1498) since the townscape in the woodcut of the *Whore of Babylon* is derived from it. A historical painting on an Old Testament theme was in itself unusual at that time. The figures are small, bewildered townsfolk, and there is something rather touching about them, but the real subject of the picture is the cataclysm from which they are fleeing. The towns of Sodom and Gomorrah stand on the coast, the second some distance behind the first. A gigantic mushroom cloud—like that of an atomic explosion—billows over each town. The fire that consumes them is no ordinary one, but a phenomenon beyond human understanding. Opening and spreading above the doomed towns like fantastic blossoms are fountains of grey and black, fiery tongues of yellow and red. A quarter of a century later Dürer drew a *Dream Vision* of a vast cataclysm in which similar imagery appears. In the lurid light shed by the fire, the cliff is transformed and seems to glow from within like molten glass. So powerfully is the painter shaken by his apprehension of disaster that the most familiar things take on a hallucinatory quality.

Dürer was haunted by such fantasies, and his sense of the impending end of all things reached its climax in the woodcuts of the *Apocalypse*. Such works are, however, something more than the expression of a personal vision; they record like a seismograph the tense and sombre mood of the time.

Like most of the leading artists of his time in Germany, Dürer was the product of what is known in social history as an urban culture. Italy had led the way, and the North was following its example. The feudal and religious culture of the Middle Ages underwent a transformation in the new urban society with its increasingly independent middle class—to which Dürer, as an artist, belonged—and its proletariat, who soon recognized the similarity between their lot and the unrelieved serfdom of the peasantry. This development paved the way for social upheavals. The Dolcinists in Italy and the Taborites in Bohemia had already manifested their discontent in no uncertain terms. The most devastating outbreak of this kind was the Peasants' War in Germany, which had been foreshadowed by the Bundschuh insurrections in Alsace. The period preceding these open outbreaks was fraught with disquiet. The Imperial reform that was meant to lead Germany out of the political wilderness led only to fresh disunity. Wars between the various German provinces, the threat from the Turks, hunger, scourges such as plague and syphilis (the subject of a caustic print by Dürer): all combined to feed the smouldering fire.

The first warning of the coming storm took the form of the religious phenomenon known by historians as "chiliasm": the belief that Christ was about to return to earth and reign for a thousand years. Mass religious hysteria of this kind is often a symptom of impending social revolution. People grew restless and uneasy, and there was a vogue for pilgrimages to such wonder-working shrines as the Bleeding Host of Wilsnack, to the town piper Hans Böhaim at Niklashausen in the Tauber Valley, to the Schöne Maria in Regensburg. Another manifestation of religious hysteria was the phenomenon of "showers of crosses," in which splashes of mud on women's clothes were taken as having symbolic significance. Dürer drew one such "cross" in his memorial book. Showers of crosses, meteors, comets: all these were grist to the mill of contemporary astrologers like Johannes Lichtenberger, who interpreted them as signs of divine judgement. Although such movements collapsed as rapidly as they arose, they nevertheless left a deep impression on men's minds. This background helps to explain much of Dürer's work in the 1490s.

The chiliastic mood of the *Apocalypse* is found again in the woodcuts of the *Large Passion*. In his devotional pictures for churches undertaken at the behest of various Nuremberg patrician families, in an occasional epitaph or a pious memento mori which he was called upon to paint, Dürer was inspired by the same deep inner fervour rather than by an interest in composition and the portrayal of the human form, though this was also present. Both paintings of the *Lamentation of Christ*—made at the turn of the century, the first for the Holzschuher family (Germanisches Nationalmuseum, Nuremberg), the second for the Glimm family of goldsmiths (Alte Pinakothek, Munich)—were modelled on the *Lamentation* in the *Large Passion*. The composition is built round the great body of Christ, in which Dürer displayed all his new-found

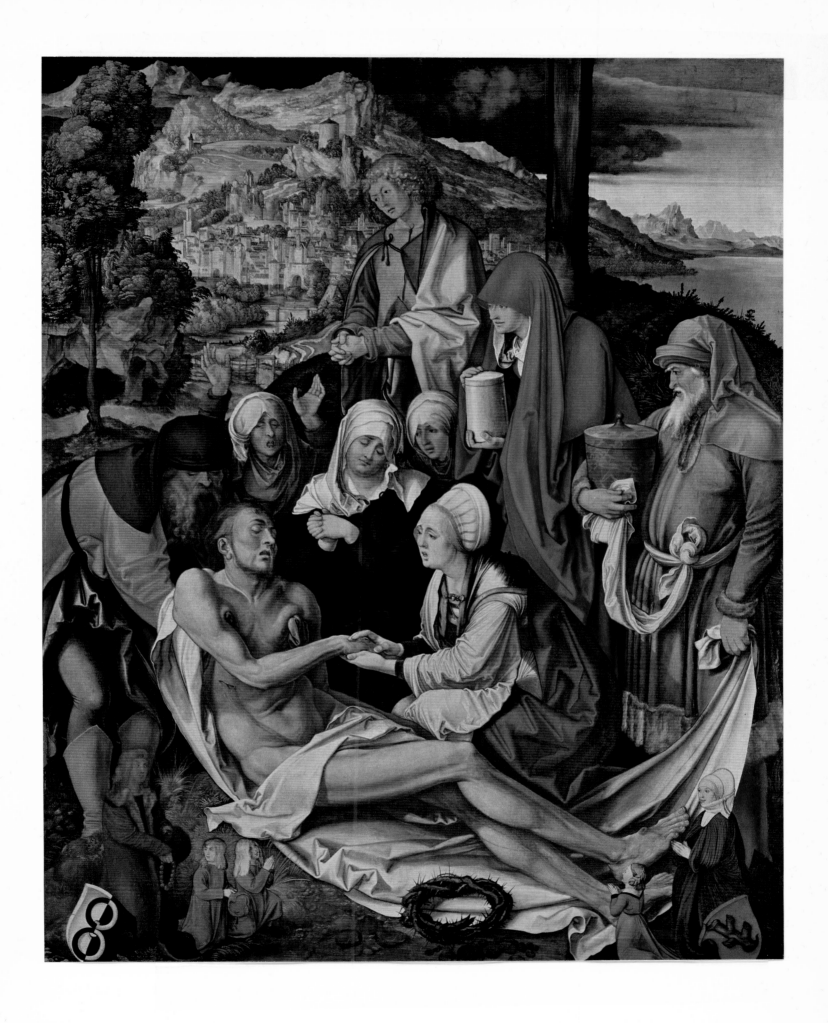

Albrecht Dürer (1471-1528).
The Lamentation of Christ, c. 1500. (59¾×47¾″) Alte Pinakothek, Munich.

mastery of the human form, and transposed to an idealized plane where human emotion takes the form of timeless, solemn mourning and not—as in the *Apocalypse*—of terror. Its deep seriousness is akin to that of similar paintings by Dürer's teacher Wolgemut, but where the latter was narrow and morose Dürer is generally universal and sublime. The understanding of the cosmos he had gained in his magnificent landscapes, together with his new-found knowledge of the human body, also stood him in good stead for this type of painting. But here, for the sake of compactness and greater solemnity, Dürer deliberately refuses to apply his knowledge of the rational disposition of bodies in space. He lifts the onlooker into another world, and heightened colours are used to intensify the effect.

Fra Bartolommeo was attempting similar things in Florence at about the same time. Dürer—such was the polarity of the German art of the period—was striving not only for a new realism, but for a new idealism. Developments that had taken a century and a half in Italy were compressed into half a century in Germany. Apparently irreconcilable elements were combined into a single whole, even in the work of one and the same man—not in terms of a higher harmony as in Italy, but with all their strongly irrational contrasts maintained. Nevertheless, those contrasting features were fundamentally linked by a new concept of life that embraced both the real and the ideal, combining medieval metaphysics with the new tendencies in thought and art.

In Italy, Dürer not only entered a new world of art, but gained a more direct and frank approach to human relations. This helped him to achieve greater verisimilitude in his portraits, as can clearly be seen by comparing the *Portrait of the Artist's Father* painted in 1497 (National Gallery, London) with that painted in 1490 (Uffizi, Florence). The later picture is more relaxed and has none of the self-conscious piety of the earlier one. The artist's eye perceives a greater intellectual alertness and openness of character in the subject, while doing justice to the wisdom and reserve born of age and experience. Here, Venice seems to have played a part— Giovanni Bellini rather than Mantegna.

In portraiture we find the earliest evidence of the new humanistic spirit from the South, of an awareness of the value of the individual. The finest testimony of this, however, is the *Self-Portrait* in the Prado (1498), which has a special place among Dürer's masterpieces not only as a great work of art but as a document of historical significance. It expresses a new conception of man, of the artist and his relationship with the world. In the *Self-Portrait* of 1493 in the Louvre, Dürer is still the journeyman painter. In the later portrait, he is the member of an intellectual elite, to which formerly only scholars belonged. He had gained social distinction in Italy, and here he carries it for the first time into the social environment of the North. The Late Gothic craftsman—a standing which was still typical of the generation of Dürer's teachers—has vanished. But the composition of the picture continues to show traces of the Late Gothic style.

The schema of the Prado *Self-Portrait* owes something to Memling: the half-length figure, framed by Gothic walls, stands behind a ledge on which the arms and hands are resting. The hands are not clasped in prayer or holding a religious object, as was often the case in portraits by painters from the Netherlands, but are folded, expressing something of the artist's satisfaction in this self-scrutiny. Dürer has "got himself up" to look his best both in his own eyes and those of the world. Nevertheless, he still shows something of the naivety that was such a deeply rooted trait of his character. His pleasure in himself has something childish about it, and this is emphasized by the words written on the wall: "I painted this in my own likeness—I was twenty-six years old." The colours are clear and luminous and have an impressive harmony. The dominant black and white of the jerkin are set off by the tobacco-brown of the cloak and the light grey of the buckskin gloves. The painter's delight in colours comes out in the blue and white cord of the cloak and the mauve of the cap. Beyond the open window, a landscape—obviously the mountains of the Tyrol—stretches into the pale blue distance. We are reminded of Leonardo's study of the Tuscan landscape between Vinci and Pistoia (1473, Uffizi, Florence). These are no idealized imaginary crags such as formed the background for the Late Gothic paintings of Nuremberg and the Upper Rhine; we can see the tellurian folds of the mountains, the geological formation of the earth's crust, as first recorded by Leonardo. Together with the human figure, this landscape conjures up that sense of the cosmic first introduced into northern thought by Nicolaus Cusanus, a great philosopher who influenced Leonardo himself, Dürer being the first northern artist to give expression to his ideas and teaching.

The portrait of an eighteen-year-old Nuremberg girl belonging to the Fürleger family (1497) is almost in the nature of a pendant to the Prado self-portrait; the canvas in the Heugel Collection in Paris is perhaps the original of the Fürleger portrait. This fresh and lively work makes those of the other Nuremberg portraitists of Dürer's time and earlier seem almost freakish. The same young woman appears again in a Madonna-like *Half-length Figure* in the Städelsches Kunstinstitut, Frankfurt.

From 1499 date the portraits of the Nuremberg patricians Hans and Niclas Tucher (the latter is lost) and the companion pieces of their wives Felicitas and Elsbeth (Weimar and Kassel). Although small, these paintings make a monumental impression. The narrow embrasure emphasizes the rounded modelling of the heads so that the setting and even the landscape appear flat and merely ornamental beside them. Dürer's art is increasingly concentrated not just on the human being, but on the human being in relation to the universe. From the same year dates the portrait of the Lindau merchant *Oswolt Krel* (Pinakothek, Munich), a strong-minded, aggressive gentleman who is shown in front of a vermilion curtain; on the left, we glimpse slender trees in a meadow under a glowing evening sky. Dürer suggests the personality of the subject in a way that would have been impossible for the old Nuremberg masters. In depicting individual characteristics, he hardly goes beyond his predecessors; indeed he rather emphasizes the common humanity of his subjects. Nevertheless, he succeeds in laying bare their souls. The small *Portrait of his Brother Hans* (a tailor), dating from 1500 (Pinakothek, Munich), conveys an amazingly clear and forceful idea of the sitter's character. The head is set firmly within the narrow frame and stands out luminously against the background of unrelieved black, chosen so as not to distract attention from the essentials.

A similar technique is used in the famous *Self-Portrait* (Pinakothek, Munich), also dating from 1500, in which the painter is portrayed as a half-length figure squarely facing the onlooker. The magnificently modelled right hand fingering the fur of the cape is Gothic in its expressiveness. Painted in the lofty, Late Gothic spirit of the *Apocalypse*, it offers a contrast to the softness of the face, which Dürer touched up in his later years. It appears that he kept this painting among his personal possessions until his death. The face, framed by a wreath of curls (Dürer referred to himself humorously in a poem as the "hairy, bearded painter"), stands out against a background of unfathomable blackness, creating an impression of unique solemnity. In this self-portrait, the artist seems to be making a definite analogy with the Vera Ikon, the image of Christ. Is this a form of self-worship, of megalomania? This is hardly likely, since Dürer always humbly accepted his genius as a gift vouchsafed by God. The painting is the expression of a religious and ethical attitude: he identifies himself not only with the Saviour as the revealer of a higher truth that for Dürer, the artist, became an artistic truth, but also with the Saviour who suffered. In a moving drawing of his final period (Kunsthalle, Bremen), he depicts himself in the guise of the Man of Sorrows. From the late medieval teachings of Thomas à Kempis, Dürer drew the conclusion that he had to imitate the Saviour both in doctrine and in suffering. The portrait reflects this sense of dedication and stands as a symbol of a unique turning-point in history—of the emergence of the faith that Dürer served with his art.

In the 1490s, the masters of the younger generation, born around 1470, were not the only painters at work. Several of their seniors were still active, including Michael Pacher, Bartolomäus Zeitblom, the Housebook Master, and Dürer's teacher Michael Wolgemut who continued to paint until well into the sixteenth century. These artists of the declining Late Gothic period are not within the scope of this book; on the other hand, we must consider those born in the decade before Dürer, who were at the height of their powers round about 1500 and paved the way for the artists of the new century. They belong to a transitional period that was on the whole an organic part of the new age, though their work has stronger links with the past than that of such masters as Dürer who made a decisive break with it.

The most important artists of the transitional generation did not come from Nuremberg, but from Swabia. We must now turn away from the rough Franconian landscape sketched by Dürer, with its picturesque quarries, rounded hilltops, and pinewoods, from the undulating countryside surrounding Nuremberg to the smiling sunlit cornfields of Upper Swabia with the Alps on the far horizon. This land of scattered abbeys and churches was the setting for the dazzling city of Augsburg, gateway to the Italian Renaissance and the styles and culture of the South and a cosmopolitan centre of European thought. It was only in the sixteenth century that Augsburg came to hold this position. Previously it had not had the significance of Nuremberg and had been overshadowed in intellectual and artistic matters by the city of Ulm—a showcase of Late Gothic culture, where busy printers and publishers redefined and popularized medieval culture at the very threshold of the new age. Ulm also took the lead in the sphere of painting and sculpture, but lost it to Augsburg at the end of the century. The Swabian temperament is one of poise and composure, lacking the violence and sombre menace of the Franconian temperament that Dürer inherited from his predecessors and the Nuremberg *genius loci*. The Swabian painters in the second half of the fifteenth century were measured, lyrical rather than dramatic, and had a secret hankering after the calm and classical. They were also masters of colour, unlike the painters of Nuremberg, who were preoccupied with form. Their aims were colour balance, harmony, and unity.

The most important Swabian artist at the end of the fifteenth century was Hans Holbein the Elder. He came from a family of tanners—believed to have originated in Uri in central Switzerland—who had settled in Ravensburg, moving to Augsburg in the middle of the fifteenth century. With Hans Holbein the Elder they became a family of painters, most of them outstanding and some very great indeed. Hans Holbein the Elder must be included among the very great ones, although his fame has been eclipsed by that of Hans Holbein the Younger. He was born about 1460-1465. His earliest known work is the *Death of the Virgin* (Museum of Fine Arts, Budapest), painted—probably in the eighties—as a memorial picture for the Preu family. This work continues the tradition of the older Augsburg painters such as the Master of 1477 and Thoman Burgkmair, combining figures that hark back to those of the early fifteenth century and a surprisingly perceptive observation of human qualities in a somewhat uncertain whole. It would appear that the engravings of the Housebook Master and Schongauer were not unknown to the artist. The composition is packed with figures and lacks spatial recession, for Holbein mastered this only later, under Netherlandish influence.

An altarpiece dated 1490 was probably painted for the Church of Sts Ulrich and Afra at Augsburg, since the outside of the wings depicts the burial of these two saints. The fine *Death of the Virgin* in Basel originally formed the inner side of the left wing. The harshness of the Budapest painting on the same theme here gives way to deep, rich colours and subtle, flowing brushwork. The Apostles and the Virgin are arranged in a semicircle in the tall narrow panel. The figures are huddled together as if they were cramped for space. The Virgin is half sitting, half kneeling. Her eyes are almost closed, her slender hands barely grasp the candle, her skin has the brownish-grey pallor of the dying. The flatness of the picture is emphasized by the splendour of her clothes, with their large pattern of black on gold in the encircling deep blue of the mantle. St John is supporting her—his attitude resembles that of the disciple catching the swooning Virgin in the paintings by Rogier van der Weyden and Robert Campin. He, too, has a cloak that billows in the wind, despite the stillness of the death-chamber. To the right, the figure of St Peter, who is shielding the Virgin and supporting her on the other side, is composed in a single flat, elastic curve. The fiery red of St John's cloak contrasts with the less vivid pink of St Peter's. The disk-shaped haloes have a flattening effect on the figures of the saints and hide those behind them, as in a painting of the Trecento.

The *Death of the Virgin* is painted with a wonderful delicacy and tenderness. The heads are as alive as if they were actual portraits, a characteristic of Holbein's religious paintings that contributes greatly to their warmth and humanity. The colours glow out of the shadows and then shade off again in a warm twilight zone; this was the principle of chiaroscuro as practised at the beginning of the fifteenth century. Together with the emphatic solemnity of the composition, it is indicative of a deliberate return to the classicism and scale of the art of that period—a sort of secret Renaissance preceding the appearance of Italian Renaissance forms in German painting.

The same secret classicism on the eve of the Italian Renaissance—in Swabia it prepared the way for Renaissance art—is noticeable in the work of the great woodcarver Gregor Erhart with whose brother, Michel Erhart, Holbein went into partnership in 1493. As a result Holbein moved for a short time to Ulm, where the two artists worked on the *Altarpiece of the Virgin* for the Benedictine Abbey of Weingarten. The wings painted by Holbein (now in Augsburg Cathedral) clearly show the influence of this contact with the school of Ulm, and in particular with the quiet, rather solemn verticalism of Zeitblom's style. Meanwhile Holbein had been to Cologne and the Low Countries. The figure of a woman in the *Presentation* is modelled on one in Van der Weyden's *Columba Altarpiece*. The fact that he reverted to Van der Weyden, although the latter's style had long been transformed by Schongauer and super-seded in Germany, again shows how his search for a new ideal led him back in spirit to the masters of an earlier period. In Italy, Perugino and the Umbrians took a similar path. The figures seem to float over the steeply sloping ground (Holbein adopted the empirical perspective of the Flemings), and their treatment shows no trace of the Late Gothic conception of form. Their solemnity is akin to that of the contemporary Bruges painters, of Hans Memling and Gerard David.

In 1494 the artist was again living in Augsburg where he married Thoman Burgkmair's daughter, the sister of the great Hans Burgkmair. Round about this time Gregor Erhart too moved to the more forward-looking town. In 1499 Holbein was again mentioned as a citizen of Ulm. He must have had a restless temperament, and he seems to have been a shy man who wanted to escape from the harsh realities of life. He probably paid more than one visit to the Netherlands, where he came into contact with the works not only of Rogier van der Weyden but also with those of Hugo van der Goes whose *Monforte Altarpiece* he sketched. From the changes in his style at the end of the century we may assume that he also knew the works of Hieronymus Bosch.

In the late 1490s Konrad Mörlin, the Abbot of the Benedictine Monastery of Sts Ulrich and Afra, commissioned from Holbein an *Altarpiece of the Passion*, the panels of which— now in the Donaueschingen Gallery—enclosed a carved Crucifixion. They are painted as grisailles with natural flesh-tones, as were some works by Van der Weyden and his school (Ludwig Baldass has pointed out the link with the *Cambrai Altarpiece*). For the first time a note of drama is found in Holbein's work. A presentiment of the impending tragedy weighs on the Saviour as he kneels on the Mount of Olives surrounded by the sleeping disciples. He is also shown being pushed, pulled, and beaten by a row of tormentors, who are

Hans Holbein the Elder (c. 1460/1465-1524). The Death of the Virgin, 1490. (54×28″)
Inner Side of the Left Wing of the Afra Altarpiece of Augsburg. Kunstmuseum, Basel.

deliberately depicted as repulsive creatures with demoniacal faces. Here we can recognize the influence of Hieronymus Bosch, whose work Holbein must have seen in the Netherlands, and especially of those mature paintings in which Bosch turned from full-length to half-length figures, concentrating on the facial expressions and treating the figures themselves more or less as puppets. Bosch, too, used the archaic techniques of early fifteenth-century art. The spindly limbs of Christ's tormentors are directly reminiscent of his work. Like Dürer's *Apocalypse*, Holbein the Elder's great altarpieces reflect the general tension that prevailed at the end of the century.

Between 1500 and 1501, Holbein painted one of his most important works, the double-shuttered altarpiece for the Dominican Church in Frankfurt, which was dedicated to the Virgin

Hans Holbein the Elder (c. 1460/1465-1524). The Arrest of Christ, 1500-1501. (65⅜ × 59¼")
Outer Wing of the Altarpiece for the Dominican Church of Frankfurt. Städelsches Kunstinstitut, Frankfurt.

and the Passion of Christ. When the wings were opened, the altarpiece measured some twenty feet wide. An undertaking on this scale required a whole team of assistants like those employed on the great folding altarpieces of the Late Gothic period. This kind of teamwork belonged to an earlier day and presents a contrast with the practice of Dürer, who at that time had no more than one or two assistants. Holbein's brother Sigmund and the young artist Leonhard Beck, who later was often employed by the Emperor for his publications, are mentioned by name in the records, but there must have been several anonymous helpers. Here Holbein himself chose those parts of the altarpiece in which his mastery of portraiture could have the widest possible scope, painting the genealogical tree of the Dominicans and the Saviour on the weekday side of the wings, and the events preceding the Passion on the predella. He loved drawing, and jotted down portraits of all kinds of people in his sketchbooks, later working their features into his religious paintings. Out of St Dominic's breast sprouts a tree with circular branches bearing portraits of the great schoolmen and mystics of the Order. They are so lifelike that they must be based on actual portrait studies of members of the Order.

The Sunday side of the altarpiece achieves a greater intensity and pathos than any of Holbein's earlier or later works. H. A. Schmid has pointed out the uncertain posture and movements of his figures: this seems to make the evil ones even more crawlingly repulsive and emphasizes the helplessness and pathos of the good. In Dürer's work, evil still has something heroic about it, whereas good has to suffer but will ultimately triumph by its steadfastness. The *Arrest of Christ* in the Frankfurt altarpiece presents a Bosch-like scene of frenzied action against a backcloth of night. The figures have a convulsive, maniacal quality. A torchbearer and a halbardier with protruding eyes leer at the Saviour, while the young St John is paralysed with horror. His face a mask of hypocrisy, Judas sidles up to Christ, and the soldiers—whose spotted armour suggests the plague-stricken bodies of demons—carry out their duties with automatic gestures. The nightmarish atmosphere of the scene led Schmid to conclude that the young Grünewald may have been one of the assistants in Holbein's workshop.

The tense mood of the period is again expressed in Holbein's *Basilica of Santa Maria Maggiore* (1499, Staatliche Gemäldegalerie, Augsburg). This painting is linked with the religious custom of the Jubilee, which met with a fervent response at this chiliastic time. From 1300 on, plenary indulgences were granted at the turn of each century to all who made the pilgrimage to Rome, and great crowds were thus set in motion, moving southwards from Northern Europe. By papal dispensation, the nuns of the Convent of St Catherine in Augsburg could grant the same indulgence to those who prayed in front of pictures of the Roman basilicas. A series of paintings of the seven main basilicas was accordingly executed by leading Augsburg painters at the behest of the prosperous nuns of this wealthy foundation. As the pictures had to be fitted into the ogival arches of the chapter-house walls, a Gothic form was demanded. The delicate interlacings of the Gothic arches created an abstract architectural framework permitting several other scenes to be grouped round the picture of the basilica: a *Coronation of the Virgin*, a *Nativity*, and a *Martyrdom of St Dorothy*. The idealized handling of these paintings, with their slender figures dressed in flowing clothes, is close to the "soft style" that flourished in Prague and Cologne. The angels disport themselves with a jubilance that anticipates Grünewald's *Concert of Angels* in the Isenheim Altarpiece.

Just as Holbein the Elder in his earlier phase was connected with Ulm, another noteworthy Swabian contemporary of his, Bernhard Strigel of Memmingen in Allgäu, was a child of the pre-Alps. He belonged to a family of painters who produced altarpieces for places as far afield as the Swiss Alpine valleys. In his later development, which we shall discuss below, there are strong links with Austria. When Bartholomäus Zeitblom was working as painter and Gregor Erhart as carver on the magnificent high altar for Blaubeuren, Strigel was one of their assistants. Curt Glaser considers that the fine Pfullendorf *Altarpiece of the Virgin* (now divided between the museums of Frankfurt and Sigmaringen) may have been one of

Strigel's early works, while B. Bushart thinks it an anonymous work of the school of Zeitblom. In it, Zeitblom's severity has been softened and enriched in the style of a younger generation. The Memmingen *Altarpiece of the Magi* and the votive diptych painted for Hans Funk (Pinakothek, Munich) are definitely known to be early works by Strigel. The latter illustrates two of his characteristics: the way he harked back to the art of the early fifteenth century (the Master of the Sterzing Altarpiece, the Master of the Dietenheim Panels of the Virgin) and his great talent for portraiture.

All these masters flourished in the transitional period between two centuries, fully committed to the new one, yet unable to make as radical a break with the old one as Dürer had done. Instead, they sought to carry over some of the old values of atmosphere and expression into the new manner and thus to enhance it—in itself a modern trait.

Hans Holbein the Elder (c. 1460/1465-1524).
The Basilica of St Paul (detail), 1504. Staatliche Gemäldegalerie, Augsburg.

The Search for the New Form and the Microcosm

> The mind of an artist is full of images which he might be able to produce. So that if a man making fit use of this art, and naturally disposed thereto, were allowed to live many hundred years, he would be capable, thanks to the power given to man by God, of pouring forth and producing every day new shapes of men and other creatures the like of which was never seen before nor thought of by any other man.
>
> Dürer, *Four Books on Human Proportions.*

As the sixteenth century began, Dürer was in his thirtieth year; he stood on the threshold of his maturity. If he had continued to develop in the spirit of the *Apocalypse* and the *Large Passion*, he would have become a great but onesided master of emotional expression, rather like Grünewald. But he broke with the older art forms, and his genius took unexpected new turnings. He was not satisfied to build on a single achievement and follow one line of development, like the Holbeins and Burgkmair; he was always attempting something new, his aim being to develop an all-round artistic personality. He worked *on himself* and continued to learn and study, creating a human ideal that was to be the aspiration of all German intellectuals right up to the time of Goethe and the idealist philosophers.

Dürer had been in contact with Italian art. He was, however, not content to accept set formulas; instead he strove to discover the underlying laws of nature for himself. He seized on every natural object—however crude, ugly, or wild—that interested him and reproduced it unadorned, revealing its force and power, creating a beauty *sui generis* that diverged from the southern concept of beauty. He sought the *law* of form, its inherent truth. To him art and nature were identical, as is shown by his oft-quoted remark: "For in truth art is implicit in nature, and whoever can extract it has it." Whatever he saw became an artistic vision which he had to render truthfully, for it was part of his ethical creed that the artist was the servant of truth. The large copperplate engraving of *Nemesis* executed at the beginning of the century, is virtually a symbol of his artistic aims. The proportioned, yet natural unit of the large form is set against the equally natural variety of the visible world which Dürer, with unflagging passion and curiosity, sought to render in all its profusion. This engraving illustrates the two opposing tendencies that were to decide the future development of his art.

While in his early watercolours he had been preoccupied with the cosmic fullness of the landscape, he now became fascinated by subjects such as the *Great Piece of Turf* (1503, Albertina, Vienna), whose microscopic detail in its own way also conveys a sense of the cosmic. Further watercolours of flowers and plants carry the same message. A famous watercolour in the Albertina (1502) is a faithful portrayal of a denizen of this plant world, a young *Hare*. In the Late Gothic period plants were already used as accessories in religious paintings, while illustrated books on plants and herbs were produced for students of botany. The branches and scrolls in Late Gothic engravings and carved altars were already peopled with animals. But they lack the power, depth, and pantheistic feeling of Dürer's studies from nature.

At the end of the Middle Ages, a growing subjectivity in religious feeling led to an increased interest in the cult of the Virgin. The eternal validity of the Holy Family had constantly to be reaffirmed. It was believed that the devout should be so deeply concerned with the members of the Holy Family as to experience them—like Christ's Passion—ever anew, seeing them as real people involved in real events. The cult of the Virgin was related to the ideal of happy motherhood, as can already be seen in Late Gothic paintings. In the watercolour *Virgin with Many Animals* (Albertina, Vienna), however, Dürer goes beyond his predecessors. He shows the Mother of God as mistress of the whole universe, of all the animals and plants that—as his studies of them testify—fascinated him so much. Here, however, they are not a subject in themselves, but are used to enhance the sense of jubilation. As the Psalmist has it, "Let the heavens rejoice, and let the earth be glad" with the Virgin. An idyllic, objective element is mingled with the religious one. There is still an echo of the old flower and animal symbolism of the Middle Ages, but it would be going too far to attempt to interpret, in terms of medieval religious analogy or symbolism, every detail of a picture that is primarily an expression of the artist's joy in life.

During this decade, Dürer made a great many portrayals of the Virgin. These reflect not only a religious tendency of the time, but Dürer's desire to deepen and humanize. Round about the years 1502-1504, he produced most of his delightful series of woodcuts of the *Life of the Virgin*. A modest little panel representing the *Virgin and Child* (Kunsthistorisches Museum, Vienna), dated 1503, is reminiscent of similar panels by Martin Schongauer and Holbein the Elder, in which, however, the intimacy of the treatment is still accompanied by a certain solemnity and ceremoniousness. There is none of this in Dürer's panel, which endows the Virgin with the warmth and feeling of any loving mother.

During the 1490s Dürer was not much troubled by problems of perspective. Empirical perspective had predominated in the Netherlands and Germany throughout the fifteenth century. Although Netherlandish and German painters came into contact with the Italians, they did not accept their scientific perspective since it had no relevance to the type of work they were doing. It was adopted in a few rare instances in which it had some meaning—for example, in the spatial recession of Michael Pacher's compositions. However, as Dürer's approach to his pictures became more subjective, the scientific treatment of space came all at once to assume a certain importance for him; he set himself to render the picture space, together with the figures and objects contained in it, from the subjective point of view of a specific observer. This was in line moreover with his subjective approach to religious experience. The series of woodcuts of the *Life of the Virgin* is an important illustration of this development. But Dürer's finest and most intimate rendering of space in terms of scientific perspective is to be found in a copperplate engraving, *The Nativity* (1504). Here he conjures up the enchanted atmosphere of the ruined courtyard of an old castle, an abandoned building in which the Holy Family has sought shelter. This is a genre scene of delightful intimacy, full of the magic of Christmas night.

The *Nativity* engraving was a by-product of Dürer's work on a similar scene, also set amid ruins, for the central panel of the altarpiece he was painting for the Paumgartner family. This commission was an offering to the Church of St Catherine in memory of the donors' parents. The central panel and the folding wings are in the Pinakothek at Munich, while the stationary wings—painted by the young Baldung and showing Sts Catherine and Barbara—are in the parish church at Schwabach, near Nuremberg. St George and St Eustace stand on either side as guardians of the central panel. Set against a dark background, the powerful figures of the two saints are clad in scarlet, grey, and dark green, a colour scheme with a martial ring to it, in contrast to the exultant tonalities of the central panel. The two figures express the sense of responsibility of the Christian warrior, which was later celebrated in the engraving of *Knight, Death, and the Devil*. Despite their concentrated power, the two saints

Albrecht Dürer (1471-1528). The Paumgartner Altarpiece, 1503.
The Nativity (centre) with St George (left) and St Eustace (right).
(Central panel 61⅛×49⅝″, folding wings 61⅞×24″) Alte Pinakothek, Munich.

are freely deployed in space; indeed, the pose of St George has something of an antique *contrapposto*. They are the forerunners of the bronze figures which Dürer and Peter Vischer later designed for the Emperor's tomb. According to an old tradition, the models for the warrior saints were the brothers Stephan and Lucas Paumgartner.

The severity of the side panels admirably sets off the brilliant colours of the central panel with the *Nativity*. Its background consists of architectural features resembling those in the *Life of the Virgin* and the *Nativity* engraving. A derelict building, in which Romanesque forms are employed for ancient Roman ones, symbolizes the decline of the old world. The new age that is dawning with the birth of the Holy Child is symbolized by a yellowish-violet light that radiates over the rich green of the landscape from the light-blue sky. The figures set within the crumbling walls form a colourful group. Mary and Joseph are kneeling opposite one another in a slight diagonal that is echoed by the angle of the wooden roof. The blue and carmine of their garments frame the joyous tableau of the Holy Child and the little angels.

Dürer's characteristic palette here seems to have achieved its full range. It is bright and luminous, and even uses the changeable tones (e.g. the light blue and carmine in the figure of the young shepherd) that were later to constitute the palette of the Mannerists. The forms are not modelled in layers of colour, as with the Venetians, but drawn with the brush in the manner of the Gothic panel painters. The absolute beauty of Dürer's colours has something marvellous and fairylike about it; at the same time there is a certain naivety in the painter's delight in their jewel-like glitter. Despite the severity of the perspective, we find here the same sense of joyous bustle and intimacy as in the *Life of the Virgin*. There is no trace of the cold, bloodless idealism so often found in the Italian masters of the High Renaissance.

The achievement of perfect proportion in the delineation both of objects in space and of the human body was one of the preoccupations of the Italian Renaissance painters. Work to this end was started as early as 1400 by artists who were also scientists. Once the new style had been created, the artists sought a theoretical justification for it in the literature of the ancient world. It would be wrong to say that in Italy the study of Vitruvius brought about a new art and a new conception of art, for Vitruvius was read only after the event. On the other hand, a new type of visual art was created in emulation of the Ancients, through a renewed study of nature.

In the North things happened the other way round. The humanist scholars were the first on the scene, and they were keenly aware of classical antiquity. When Terence's comedies were published in Ulm, they were illustrated by Late Gothic woodcuts. The illustrations in German editions of the classical authors showed no trace of the spirit of the ancient world. When the Vienna humanist Conrad Celtes published the Latin poems of Hrosvitha, with dedicatory woodcuts by Dürer, he emphasized—with the pride and self-confidence of the northern scholar—the fact that classical learning had flourished much longer in Germany than in Italy. Though the way for the artistic Renaissance in the North was prepared by a native movement at the end of the fifteenth century, it never freed itself entirely from its scholarly ancestry.

Albrecht Dürer (1471-1528). The Adoration of the Magi, 1504. (38⅝×44⅛″) Uffizi, Florence.

When Dürer was investigating the rules governing the representation of space and the human body, he expected great things from the science of the Italians. In 1506 he wrote to Pirckheimer from Venice that he intended to ride to Bologna to take lessons in "secret perspective" (the teacher was probably Leonardo's friend Fra Luca Pacioli). Such knowledge was regarded by Dürer as something arcane. Even before his second journey to Italy he hoped that the Venetian painter Jacopo de' Barbari, who turned up in Nuremberg in 1500, would reveal to him the secret knowledge of the Ancients concerning the structure of the human body, but he was disappointed. In a draft for the preface to his own treatise on human proportions, he wrote: " . . . but I could not get from him the reason why he used his art thus . . . then I tried Vitruvius, who says a little about the human form. So, after the two abovementioned, I searched according to my own ideas."

Since neither Jacopo de' Barbari nor Vitruvius could give him the key to the hidden knowledge of the Ancients, he attempted to rediscover it for himself. This was a tremendous undertaking, and not without a certain tragic side to it. There was an inherent contradiction between this didactic approach and Dürer's intuitive creativeness. "For a good painter has full figures inside his head," he wrote. While the constructed figures that have been identified in Dürer's paintings, engravings, and drawings sometimes have an academic coldness, we must not forget all the ardour and emotion of the intellectual effort involved in their creation. By his own efforts, Dürer caught up in a few years with the work of a whole century in Italy. This impressive achievement finally conquered even the Italians, leading to the triumph of Dürer's art in Italy at the beginning of the High Renaissance, and to a growing influence of the North upon the South.

As early as 1500 Dürer began to draw figures "to measure." One of the most important landmarks in his search for human proportions was a pen drawing of *Apollo* (British Museum), which he modelled on one of the figures from Mantegna's *Bacchanalia*. Into its outlines he fitted successive versions of a figure construction based on Vitruvius' norms. These efforts culminated in the masterly copperplate engraving of *Adam and Eve* (1504). It is typical of Dürer's work that this in turn became the starting-point for a fresh series of developments.

To a great painter like Dürer it was self-evident that construction alone could not lead to a genuine classicism. In the same year, he produced his most joyful and positive painting, full of southern warmth and German fervour, a work truly classic in its simplicity, the altarpiece of the *Adoration of the Magi* (Uffizi, Florence) painted for Frederick the Wise. For three years, the Elector's territories had been visited by the plague, and this may have been the reason for the donation, since the Magi were considered as protectors against the plague. So were Lazarus and Job, who appear on the wings of an altarpiece belonging to the Jabachs, a Cologne banking family (now in the Pinakothek, Munich, the Wallraf-Richartz Museum, Cologne, and the Städelsches Kunstinstitut, Frankfurt). It has been suggested by Hans Kauffmann that the wings of the *Jabach Altarpiece* may have belonged originally to the *Adoration of the Magi*, and this conjecture is supported by the fact that St Joseph is missing from the latter painting, but appears beside St Joachim on the inside of the left wing of the *Jabach Altarpiece*. This theory has recently been questioned, but the Jabach panels must certainly have belonged to a work commissioned by Frederick the Wise, since their provenance from the Schlosskirche at Wittenberg has been proved.

The *Adoration of the Magi* is composed diagonally, like Leonardo's famous painting on the same theme in the Uffizi, of which Dürer may have heard, since he too included groups of horsemen in the background. At this time Dürer—again following in Leonardo's footsteps—had begun to study the proportions of horses in a number of drawings. As in the *Paumgartner Altarpiece*, the setting consists of a ruin with arched gateways, the perspective having been worked out in preliminary sketches. Despite the incidental details—flowers growing in the clefts of the stonework and small animals like those in the Albertina watercolour—the structure is careful and deliberate. The disposition of the figures conforms to the strictest canons of classicism. They are contained in an isosceles triangle whose base is the lower frame of the picture, with the figure of the Virgin and the standing King forming the left side, while the steps, together with the Moorish King, form the right. The overgrown ruins mark the apex. The figure of the Virgin is also contained in a triangle. The architecture and landscape lend emphasis to the figures: a vaulted pillar to that of the Virgin, a wall to that of the standing King, the mountains to that of the Moor. Each element is firmly linked with the next, and all are carefully interrelated—the essence of a highly classical composition.

Nevertheless, there is a diagonal movement in depth of a kind that would later become so significant a feature of the Baroque. Thus, unlike certain Italian works of the High Renaissance, the *Adoration of the Magi* has nothing frigid or static about it; everything is alive and flowing. Here we again encounter Dürer's special technique, which is midway between drawing and goldsmith's work. Dark outlines drawn with the brush are filled in with gem-like sparkling colour. This technique was followed not only by the school of Dürer but by many other South German painters in the sixteenth century. The brilliant harmony of red, blue, and emerald green, accompanied by a slaty violet, is answered by the glowing warmth of the walls and the cheerful green and blue of the landscape.

For another large altarpiece, the *Crucifixion*, commissioned by Frederick the Wise, Dürer only prepared the sketches, leaving the execution to his pupil Hans Leonhard Schäufelein, for in the summer of 1505 he made his second journey to Venice. Again the plague may have provided the immediate reason for his departure, for with the warm weather it had returned to ravage Nuremberg. A charcoal drawing (British Museum, London) gives us a fascinating insight into Dürer's mood at the time. It shows King Death riding on a nag and mouthing the words *"Memento mei!"*—an uncannily convincing vision. There was a duality in Dürer's temperament just as there was a polarity in the aims of his art: the life-affirming man of the Renaissance, full of the spirit of experiment and invention, was constantly confronted by the thoughts of death and the next world that haunted the imagination of the northerner, bound as he still was by medieval traditions. This was an ever-present feature of German artistic and intellectual life—it comes out most movingly in Dürer.

We know a great deal about Dürer's second stay in Venice from his correspondence with Pirckheimer. His position was very different from what it had been during his first visit eleven years before. He was no longer an unknown artist, but a famous master who was not only fêted abroad but an object of envy and hostility. Doge and Patriarch, patricians and nobles, scholars and artists sought him out and visited his studio. The Doge offered him a fixed annual income if he would settle in Venice. He was flattered but also maligned: "I also have many enemies here who copy my things in churches and wherever they can find them. Then they run down my work, saying that it is not in the classical manner and is therefore no good." Friends warned him against accepting dinner invitations from fellow-artists, because poisoning at that time was a sure means of solving problems—and not only political ones. But he got on very well with Giovanni Bellini, of whom he wrote: "He is very old and still the best at painting." A memorable sentence in the same letter runs: "And the things I liked so much eleven years ago, I now don't like at all." This has been taken to refer to Jacopo de' Barbari, but probably refers to the Mantegna-style works that Dürer had outgrown. Bellini's late phase, with its almost classical balance, now appealed to him most. The new Florentine art had not yet reached Venice to any appreciable extent.

Several portraits have survived from the year 1505, the loveliest being that of the *Venetian Girl* in the Kunsthistorisches Museum in Vienna. Never again did Dürer paint a portrait so full of feminine charm. He dispensed with the finishing touches, and this makes the

Albrecht Dürer (1471-1528). Portrait of a Venetian Girl, 1505. (13¾×10¼″) Kunsthistorisches Museum, Vienna.

painting all the more attractive. Here he abandoned the characteristic hardness of the Nuremberg portraits, imitating the manner of Carpaccio and Bellini. The delicately modelled form, painted in warm golden tones, stands out luminously against the dark background. This small panel was probably a gift to the woman portrayed.

The same date is found on the *Self-Portrait* of almost the same size in the Kremsier Museum. Its relaxed handling—again the finishing touches have been omitted—immediately shows its relationship to the *Venetian Girl* in Vienna. Like Dürer's two portraits of the Fürleger girl (Städelsches Kunstinstitut, Frankfurt, and Heugel Collection, Paris), the Kremsier *Self-Portrait* belonged to the collection of King Charles I of England. In the Viennese lottery inventory of 1670, it figures as *"Un ritratto d'Alberto Dürer."* It is not a "dressed-up" portrait like that in Madrid, nor an idealized one like that in Munich, but shows Dürer as he was in real life—as Giulio Campagnola painted him in a contemporary fresco at the Scuola del Carmine in Padua and Marco Marziale in his *Supper at Emmaus* at the Accademia in Venice. That thoughtful, penetrating gaze holds us already in the early self-portrait drawing in the University Library at Erlangen.

The *Portrait of a Woman* in the Berlin Museum—which has, without foundation, been taken to be a likeness of Dürer's wife Agnes—depicts a German woman who lived in Venice. Here the use of atmosphere goes beyond Giovanni Bellini, and achieves an effectiveness reminiscent of Giorgione and the early Titian. The warm brownish tint of the flesh is enveloped by the soft blue atmosphere of the lagoon. The lock of hair seems to be stirring in a light breeze from the sea—for this is a genuine outdoor portrait of a type that does not recur in Dürer's later work, except in the sketchbook he kept in the Netherlands. The golden jewellery and the bright embroidery on the dress relate it to the *Venetian Girl* in Vienna.

Writing to Pirckheimer on January 6, 1506, Dürer reported that he had been commissioned by the German merchant community in Venice to paint an altarpiece that had to be ready one month after Easter. The Fondaco dei Tedeschi on the Grand Canal was the social and business centre for the rich merchants from Nuremberg and Augsburg. The Fuggers, Tuchers, and Imhoffs all had representatives in the town, and Dürer was in touch with them, since they dealt with his mail and banking transactions. They were cultivated men, with an interest in the arts. When they were forbidden to face the new Fondaco building with marble, they decided on a much more effective form of decoration—frescoes, which they commissioned from Giorgione and the young Titian. For the altarpiece of their nearby church of San Bartolommeo al Rialto, they naturally turned to the most famous of German painters. The work was completed within five months, as is proudly stated on the inscription held in the painting by the figure of Dürer himself. This altarpiece (now in the National Gallery in Prague)—a Venetian *pala* and not a German folding altarpiece—is Dürer's chief work in the realm of pure painting. It is only because of its poor state of preservation that it now takes second place to the *Adoration of the Magi* in the Uffizi, but what remains of it is so radiantly beautiful that it surpasses all his other paintings. The damage—parts that were torn out—is fairly easily recognizable, and the parts that have remained intact have an undiminished splendour.

The inspiration for the altarpiece was the cult of the rosary, traditionally founded by St Dominic and enthusiastically revived during the second half of the sixteenth century. In 1476 Jacobus Sprenger, a Dominican and the author of the notorious *Hexenhammer* ("Witch's Hammer"), founded the Brotherhood of the Rosary. It became a frequent theme of contemporary woodcuts, in which men and women, headed by the Emperor and the Pope, are shown assembled round the throne of the Mother of God and receiving rosaries from her hand. A branch of this brotherhood seems to have grown up in the German colony in Venice —thus the altarpiece depicts the *Feast of the Rose Garlands*. The composition matches the solemn, yet festive nature of the subject. The Virgin is shown enthroned under a baldachin, and the triangular central composition is symmetrically completed by the kneeling figures of the Pope (Julius II) and the Emperor (Maximilian I). The lute-playing angel at the Virgin's feet recalls those in paintings by Bellini and Carpaccio. This altarpiece was modelled mainly on Venetian works—for example, the *Madonna of Doge Antonio Barbarigo* by Giovanni Bellini (1488) in San Pietro Martire at Murano.

Similar compositions had existed in German Late Gothic painting, an example being the picture by Friedrich Herlin in the town hall at Nördlingen. They go back to Van der Weyden's altarpiece of the *Adoration of the Magi* for the church of St Columba at Cologne (now in the Munich Pinakothek). While the subject demanded a return to such time-honoured sources, these were probably not the only ones. Reference has already been made to Leonardo's *Adoration of the Magi* in connection with Dürer's altarpiece on the same theme. Although there is no evidence to show that Dürer ever visited Florence, he must at least have been familiar with copies and drawings of that celebrated work. Dürer's dramatic sense, combined with a

Albrecht Dürer (1471-1528). The Feast of the Rose Garlands, 1506. (63⅞×77⅝") National Gallery, Prague.

certain festive excitement, gives new life to this type of composition, which in the hands of his predecessors was solemn and stiff—this too may be due in some measure to Leonardo's influence. The Virgin is shown placing a garland on the head of the Emperor, who expresses his deep emotion by folding his hands, while the Holy Child leans over to crown the Pope and further garlands are distributed by St Dominic and the angels. Their gestures provide various counterpoints to the main theme, while among the kneeling worshippers there is a general movement and inclination towards the centre. All ranks of life, both ecclesiastical and lay, are represented, and the picture includes many portraits of members of the German colony in Venice. Dürer and a friend—Pirckheimer or the Augsburg scholar Peutinger—stand thoughtfully in the background.

When working on this painting, Dürer used a procedure that differed from his normal one and also from that of the Italians. After making some preliminary sketches—which have not survived—he laid in the ground of the panel in one week, then went straight on to the actual painting. This was similar to the method of the northern panel painters who sketched out their compositions in grisaille on the priming coat of gesso, then put in the colours straight away. Dürer, however, worked in part from large detailed studies drawn on blue Venetian paper; some of these have been preserved in the Albertina and other collections, and they are among his finest drawings. For the Italians the next step would be the use of a squared cartoon, which would be copied section by section in the final work. Dürer is not known to have used such cartoons, though some of Leonardo's, Fra Bartolommeo's, Michelangelo's, and Raphael's have survived. It is probable that he skipped this stage, and that his phenomenal sureness of touch enabled him to transfer his studies to the panel directly.

There is no doubt that in the *Feast of the Rose Garlands* Dürer reached his zenith as a painter. Despite the renewed impact of the great Venetians, he stuck to his own basic colour principles, retaining his delight in the absolute—idealized rather than realistic—beauty of colour, derived from the observation of nature, yet intensified and heightened. Dürer was not a colourist in the manner of the Venetians, whose profound sense of atmosphere prepared the way for the outdoor painters of the nineteenth century. He nevertheless knew how to endow his brilliant colours with a smooth flowing quality, and it was in Venice that he developed an atmospheric translucency unknown in the North. Inspired to new heights by the atmosphere and spirit of Venice, he outstripped his Venetian contemporaries, producing a work that was closer to the strict, monumental compositions of the Florentines. This was new, even in Venice, and created a great stir. The local artists stood abashed before his genius. He could report proudly to Pirckheimer: "And so I have silenced all the painters who said I was good at engraving, but that in painting I did not know how to handle colours. Now everyone says that they have never seen more beautiful colours."

In the same year, 1506, he produced the *Virgin with the Goldfinch* (Staatliche Museen, Berlin), an epitome of all that he had learned from Italian art. The subject and composition can be traced back to Bellini's *Madonna degli Alberetti*. Wearing a radiant blue dress in the latest Venetian style, the Virgin sits in front of a carmine curtain, with a wonderful landscape sparkling in the background. Her beauty is Germanic in type, and she has the gentle, abstract quality of an idealized conception. It is the children who bring life to the picture—the Christ Child playing with the bird poised on his arm and the infant St John bringing him lilies-of-the-valley. This motif was repeated by Titian in his *Virgin with the Cherries*.

Christ among the Doctors (Thyssen-Bornemisza Collection, Lugano) is an extraordinary piece of work, which Dürer seems to have undertaken as a form of relaxation while working on the larger picture. Completed in five days, this collection of head studies of old men against a dark background recalls certain half-length figures by Mantegna and Bellini. It is intended to give the impression of a throng pressing around the fair-haired young Christ, but is more in the nature of a *collage* of separate sketches. Here Dürer was not so much interested in the composition as in a series of character studies, which range from the dignified to the grotesque. The hands are as significant and as eloquent as the heads. The detailed preparatory drawings for this work, which are closely related to those for the *Feast of the Rose Garlands*, have been preserved and are greatly superior to the painting. They include magnificent studies of hands, which aptly illustrate Robert Vischer's phrase about the "antediluvian granite content in Dürer's genius." It is hardly likely that Dürer should have made such careful preparation for a quick experimental painting; it is much more probable that the painting is an attempt to bring the individual studies together in a single picture.

What induced him to try this experiment? As we have mentioned, Dürer was aware of Leonardo's researches, and he may have known of his drawings of grotesque heads, which seem to emerge from the narrow spaceless confines of a world of shadows and were recorded as specimens of the abnormal—"*viso fantastico*," Leonardo noted beside the address of one of his models. While in the *Feast of the Rose Garlands* and the *Virgin with the Goldfinch* Dürer was completely preoccupied with the search for ideal form, here, in *Christ among the Doctors*, he was concerned with the abnormal, the freakish, the excessive deviation from the norm. This experiment, like everything he undertook, was significant for his future work, since it paved the way for the character studies in the *Heller Altarpiece*.

Besides these major works, Dürer produced a few incidental portraits in Venice: the *Portrait of an Unknown Young Man* (1506, Hampton Court), whose features had already appeared in the *Feast of the Rose Garlands*; another portrait in the Kunsthistorisches Museum in Vienna (1507), on the reverse side of which is the loosely painted half-length figure of an ugly old woman symbolizing Avarice and reminiscent of Giorgione's *Vanitas ("Col Tempo")* in the Accademia in Venice—obviously an artist's revenge for non-payment of his fee. In 1507, the last year of his stay in Venice, he painted the half-length portrait on vellum of a fresh young girl with reddish-gold curls, dressed in boy's clothes (Berlin).

Dürer's travels in Italy did not take him beyond Bologna. He would have liked to join the Emperor Maximilian on his projected journey to Rome, but this venture was stopped by the Republic. He wrote to Pirckheimer about the preparations for the war that Venice was planning in alliance with France and the Pope against the Emperor. This time he found it hard to leave the South and wrote to Pirckheimer: "Oh, how I shall yearn for the sun. Here I am a gentleman, at home a parasite." By February 1507 he was back in Nuremberg.

When we consider Dürer's second Venetian journey in the light of his achievements in the South, we realize that it responded to a deep inner need. He would have had to undertake it, whatever the outward circumstances. He had come so far on his own account that he was now able to profit to the full from the teaching of the South. In consequence the way was cleared for him in his search for form. At the same time, this second journey of Dürer's to Venice was in some ways decisive for the whole development of art in Italy itself. The great minds of the period were stirred. The Italians recognized in Dürer's art something which they deeply needed and sought, but which only the great Northerner could give them. Transcending national frontiers, the art of the leading masters converged to form one mighty structure, which Wölfflin has summed up in the simple phrase "classical art."

At the beginning of the sixteenth century great events followed closely upon one another. Each year brought important artistic developments both in the South and the North, and they had mutual repercussions. The history of art in such a period cannot be dealt with in a series of monographs, nor can we follow each individual figure from the start to the finish of his career, for to do so would be to disrupt the overall sequence of events. We must therefore turn from Dürer and examine the work of his contemporaries in the German-speaking lands.

41

Hans Holbein the Elder (c. 1460/1465-1524). The Basilica of St Paul, 1504. (83⅞×130⅞″)
Staatliche Gemäldegalerie, Augsburg.

The large altarpiece which Hans Holbein the Elder executed in 1500-1501 for the Dominican Church in Frankfurt opened new horizons for the Late Gothic painting of the Augsburg school. Here the Swabian altarpiece loses some of its staidness and tranquillity, and gains much in expressive power, in structural design, in sweep and boldness of composition. This trend was confirmed in the subsequent development of Holbein himself.

The faithful continued their donations to the chapter house of St Catherine's Convent in Augsburg. Holbein's *Basilica of Santa Maria Maggiore* and his epitaph for the nuns of the Vetter family (1499) were followed in 1502 by another epitaph for the Walther family (Staatliche Gemäldegalerie, Augsburg). The framework formed by the Gothic arches divides the picture surface into three parts; the tall central panel contains the *Transfiguration of Christ*. The group on the mountain peak seems to be receding and to hover with medieval solemnity over that of the troubled apostles. The main emphasis is on the apostles, who twist and turn in frenzied ecstasy, their figures forming a vast curve. While idiom and style are Late Gothic, the strongly emotional expression and the compelling sense of atmosphere are already modern. The darkness between the figures is there not so much to suggest space as to set off the slow crescendo of the colours. That the painter was obviously striving to create an idealized effect can be seen by the flat arrangement reminiscent of a stained-glass window—another technique with which Holbein was familiar. The Renaissance of 1500 consisted not only in a rediscovery of the antique and the classical but also in the revival of certain medieval styles, in particular the solemn, highly expressive style of the art of around 1300 and 1400. There was a parallel development in Italy: Fra Bartolommeo and Michelangelo harked back to Duccio and Giotto, to Ghiberti, Quercia and Masaccio.

In 1502 Georg Kastner, the Abbot, commissioned the great altarpiece for the church of the Cistercian Monastery of Kaisheim, on which Gregor Erhart worked as sculptor and Holbein as painter. The wings depicting the *Life of the Virgin* on the inside and the *Passion of Christ* on the outside and the predella (Pinakothek, Munich) must be seen in the context of the altarpiece as a whole, in order to appreciate the intricacy of the composition, both in form and colouring. The panels are tall and narrow, the long-limbed figures slender and graceful. The linear harmony of the individual figures and of the work as a whole is extremely subtle.

The *Basilica of St Paul* (1504, Staatliche Gemäldegalerie, Augsburg), painted for St Catherine's Convent, is perhaps the most mature, the noblest, and the most moving of the works of Holbein's Augsburg period. Like the other paintings in the Basilica series, it was painted on the wall within the framework of a Gothic arch (the left and right corners were detached but a fragment showing the donor Veronika Welser was preserved). The Gothic tracery divides the surface of the picture into three parts like the stage for a mystery play; the central part depicts the nave of the church in which the saint is preaching. The effect is no longer flat, as it was in the earlier panels, but three-dimensional, depth being added by a skilful use of chiaroscuro. The splendid figure of the seated woman listener, seen from behind, has some of the charming intimacy of the Dutch school about it. In the foreground on the right we have the leave-taking of Sts Peter and Paul, on the left the martyrdom of St Paul. His body lies huddled on the floor, with the severed head close by; the places where the head has struck the floor are indicated by three blood-stains. The painting glows with warm colour, the basic tones being deep madder, ruby red, purple, golden brown, moss green, and greenish blue. With these are mingled brighter tones such as golden yellow and a light blue-green.

The apex of the painting shows *Christ crowned with Thorns*—this is like the sculptural group at the top of an altar shrine. The right-hand section of the picture shows the miracle that occurred during the burial of St Paul, when his body turned towards his severed head. The arches in the background show that Holbein was familiar with Dürer's *Paumgartner Altarpiece* and *Adoration of the Magi*. On the left are the *Conversion* and *Baptism of St Paul*. In the *Conversion* the form of the falling horse is antique in character and conception; it is in fact directly derived from Nicola Pisano's relief on the Arca di San Domenico in Bologna —a proof that Holbein had visited Italy as well as the Netherlands. It is significant that what he brought back from the South was not a motif from the new art of the Renaissance but one derived from thirteenth-century art. His predilection for this period can also be seen in his small Madonna panels, such as the *Madonna of Oberdorf* (1493). In Holbein the Elder, the idealized mythical past stands side by side with the realistic present: he depicts himself pointing out the miracle to his sons Hans the Younger and Ambrosius.

Besides the great altarpieces—including the *Hohenburg Altarpiece* (1509, National Gallery, Prague)—Holbein produced single panels on such themes as the Virgin and Child and Christ as the Man of Sorrows and the Saviour of the World. These are imbued with that warm humanity and ardent faith that were so characteristic of his art. From the *Votive Portrait of Burgomaster Ulrich Schwarz and his Family*, we can see his complete mastery of portraiture. Here he depicts a large family for whom Christ and the Virgin are interceding, turning away the wrath of God (Städtische Kunstsammlungen, Augsburg). Ulrich Schwarz had been beheaded. The lively portraits of the individual members of the family were obviously based on a series of those masterly silverpoint drawings in which Holbein took such pleasure. In this we can recognize the modern-minded painter who stood in the forefront of his period.

During the 1490s Holbein the Elder held undisputed sway in Augsburg. With the coming of the new century, however, the painters of Dürer's generation began to achieve maturity and Holbein was increasingly overshadowed by the younger masters who took their place beside him. The most outstanding of these was Hans Burgkmair the Elder, who personifies Augsburg painting at the period of its greatest brilliance, when it was beginning to be influenced by the achievements of the Italian Renaissance. Burgkmair adapted these achievements to the German genius more fluently, if less deeply than Dürer, employing a more brilliant and decorative style that was particularly suited to scenes of pomp and ceremony. He was a truly great painter, and the altarpieces of his maturity, with their earnest intensity, are extremely impressive.

Born in 1473, he was the son of Thoman Burgkmair. His sister was married to Hans Holbein the Elder. He owed his early grounding in art to his father, who painted in the plain severe Late Gothic style, and to Schongauer, for—unlike Dürer—he had the good fortune of being Schongauer's pupil. Burgkmair later painted a posthumous *Portrait of Schongauer* (Pinakothek, Munich). His early works, commissioned in 1490, include portraits of *Bishop Friedrich von Zollern* of Augsburg and of his friend *Johannes Gailer von Kaisersberg* (Staatliche Gemäldegalerie and Städtische Kunstsammlungen, Augsburg). The latter, a popular Strasbourg preacher and educator, was famous for his book *The Pomegranate*, which Burgkmair subsequently illustrated with woodcuts. In Burgkmair's portrait, his fine features are portrayed simply and naturally, though with a certain youthful timidity—this is still Late Gothic painting of the type Burgkmair learnt from his father and from Schongauer. His own personality did not find expression until the beginning of the new century when, from 1501 onwards, he produced a succession of religious paintings alternating with portraits.

For St Catherine's Convent at Augsburg, Burgkmair worked on the cycle of pictures for the jubilee year to which, as we have seen, Holbein also contributed. In 1501, he produced the *Basilica of St Peter*, in which he showed that he was not just a follower of Holbein's, but, at the age of twenty-eight, had already developed his own personal style. The upper part of the picture represents *Christ on the Mount of Olives*, and we are struck by the part played in the composition by the landscape. The lower half shows the seated figure of the saint in front of old St Peter's (the portal on the right is in pure Renaissance style); he is surrounded by the fourteen saints known as the "Holy Helpers." Burgkmair's figures, though narrow and slender like Holbein's Late Gothic ones, follow a new stylistic principle. In the upper scene showing the Mount of Olives, the figures of Christ and the Apostles are confined and foreshortened by the exigencies of space, yet they have great depth. The group of the Fourteen Holy Helpers shows Burgkmair's delight in pomp and ceremony. The slender figures stand close to one another, almost as disembodied as those in some of Holbein's pictures—they remind us of his female figures who seem to glide above the ground. In the case of Burgkmair, however, we are dealing with something different. Holbein harks back to the old Cologne school, to the chiaroscuro of the "soft style" with its idealized beings. Burgkmair's narrow-shouldered, hollow-cheeked figures with their aristocratic delicacy recall certain features of the incipient Mannerism of the Late Gothic period in Holland. Burgkmair was influenced by his young Dutch contemporaries and not—like Holbein—by Rogier van der Weyden and the old Cologne masters up to Lochner. The colour range of his pictures is mellow and translucent. Warm olive and brownish-grey harmonize with bright true gold. The fiery reds and greenish blues turn almost white where the light falls upon them. The *tone* is of more importance than the local colour.

The *Basilica of St John Lateran* (Staatliche Gemäldegalerie, Augsburg) bears the date 1502. The drama and movement of the *Flagellation* in the apex are a departure from the lyricism of the *Basilica of St Peter*. We are reminded of the *Altarpiece of the Passion* in the Dominican Church at Colmar, a work of the school of Schongauer. But Schongauer is not the only influence at work here. In 1502, the young Jörg Breu returned to Augsburg from Austria, and it is possible that his *Altarpiece of the Passion* for the Benedictine Abbey of Melk was in fact executed in his home town (i.e. at Augsburg). Breu combined the dramatic features of the early Danube School with others derived from Dürer's graphic work. Between him and Burgkmair there existed a relationship of mutual give-and-take. What is dark, passionate, and dramatic in Burgkmair's art—features which make their appearance in this panel of the *Basilica of St John Lateran*—derives from Breu, while Burgkmair's influence on Breu is shown in the narrowness, vertical composition, and ecstatic tone of the Melk altarpiece. The colouring of the lower sequence of scenes in the *Basilica of St John Lateran* is more lyrical and subdued. The rich landscape of *St John on Patmos* also suggests Breu's influence—that in particular of Breu's *Zwettl Altarpiece*. But where Breu is crude and vigorous, Burgkmair is elegant, subtle, and mannered. Evident in the scene of *Drusiana restored to Life* is the influence of the Late Gothic painters of Cologne—the Master of the Legend of St Ursula and the Master of St Severinus, the artists who represented Dutch tendencies in the city.

The *Basilica of Santa Croce* (1504) was—like Holbein's contemporary *Basilica of St Paul*—a donation by the Prioress Veronika Welser. A hasty glance at the whole picture with its flamboyant structure might lead one to dismiss Burgkmair as an artist who was never able to free himself from the Gothic tradition—this, after all, was the year of Dürer's *Adoration of the Magi*. If we examine the details more closely, however, we can see that this painting too was a completely modern work. The side parts depict the *Voyage of St Ursula and the Eleven Thousand Virgins*. The profusion of narrow, serried personages, the flickering lines and undulating contours, the bizarre quality of the fantastic figures and costumes, the decorative features—so oddly archaic, and yet so original and modern—show Burgkmair's connection with Cornelis Engelbrechtsen and the Mannerist trend in Dutch Late Gothic painting that produced the young Lucas van Leyden. Recognizable features of Cologne prove that Burgkmair had a firsthand knowledge of the city and had travelled down the Lower Rhine, probably as far as the Netherlands. At the same time we are reminded of the archaic trend in Venetian painting by the heavy, almost mosaic-like sumptuousness and the abundant use of gilding which echo Crivelli. The gestures of the lamenting angels as they fly above the Crucifix are derived from a *Crucifixion* by Giotto or his followers. Burgkmair's colour range is here fully developed: there are no light colours, only a twilight harmony of deep black and brown, softly glowing gold, tawny red, and brownish moss-green, together with a great deal of grey (in the flesh tints and the hair). Schongauer's pupil had studied Dutch and Italian painting at the source. He had more experience than Dürer, and things came to him more easily. At the same time he could adapt himself to a specific task, making such use of the Gothic tradition as was needed. He could blend various influences into a highly individual whole with emphasis on the elegantly representative and decorative. Unlike Dürer, he was untroubled by the problem of representing figures and space in a rational scientific way. For this reason he was more open to outside influences than Dürer, but they had a less vital bearing on his art.

As early as 1505 Burgkmair made use of an Italianate style as a matter of course when working on an altarpiece that did not have to be adapted to a Late Gothic ensemble. The *Triptych of Sts Sigismund and Sebastian* (Germanisches Nationalmuseum, Nuremberg), dated 1505, was painted for the Elector Frederick the Wise. Here Burgkmair effortlessly produced a highly developed work of the Venice-Augsburg Renaissance, with classical architecture and a classically composed nude, showing an easy command of the new language of forms that Dürer had to strive so hard to learn. What was for Dürer the result of great effort, of searching study into the methods of the Italians, was child's play for Burgkmair, the fruit of greater ability, unerring taste, and a highly developed sense of colour and form. Painting was an indigenous art in the Augsburg of Holbein the Elder, but not in Wolgemut's Nuremberg. Dürer had to seek enlightenment on the Upper Rhine. Nevertheless, the aristocratic art of these Augsburg masters lacked much of Dürer's inner strength and power.

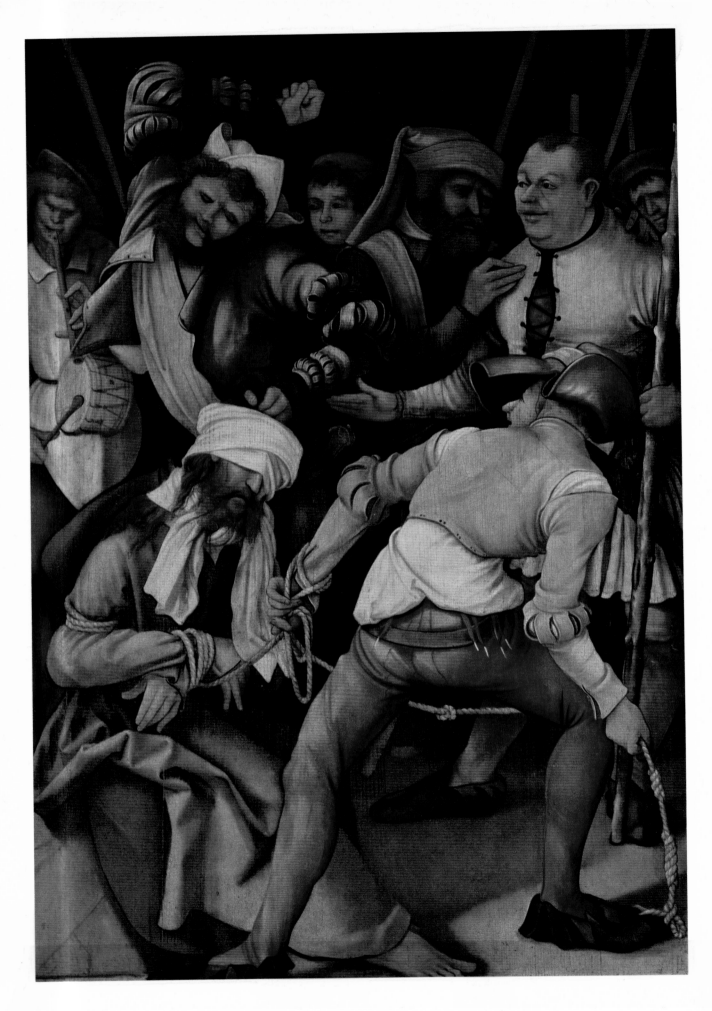

Mathis Gothardt-Neithardt (c. 1475-1528), called Matthias Grünewald.
The Mocking of Christ, c. 1503. (42⅞×29″) Alte Pinakothek, Munich.

Augsburg, with its long tradition of painting, produced many of the greatest works of old German art. Its leading painter in the later fifteenth century was Holbein the Elder, and we have already spoken of the potentialities inherent in one of his outstanding works, the great altarpiece he executed in 1500-1501 for the Dominican church in Frankfurt. On this altarpiece, as modern research has shown, the young Grünewald probably collaborated. Grünewald is one of the most mysterious figures in the history of art. Melanchthon mentioned master "Mathias" as one of the foremost painters of the day along with Dürer and Cranach. A few decades later, when the Emperor Rudolf II (1576-1612), the great collector, wanted to acquire the *Isenheim Altarpiece*, the name of its author could no longer be ascertained. The name Grünewald first appears in Sandrart's *Teutsche Academie* (1675), but it was K. W. Zülch's recent research into documentary sources that finally yielded the painter's correct name, Mathis Gothardt-Neithardt, thus solving the riddle of the monogram on the Frankfurt panel of *St Lawrence*. A wealth of documentary information has now been gleaned from the archives of Frankfurt, Mainz, and Aschaffenburg.

Mathis Gothardt-Neithardt is first recorded in 1505 as active in Aschaffenburg, and his presence in the town is documented up to 1526. In the records, he is described as court painter to Cardinal Albrecht von Brandenburg, Archbishop of Mainz. The Cardinal's predecessor was Uriel von Gemmingen, and in his youth Albrecht von Brandenburg had been his coadjutor. These were the two greatest patrons of the arts among the German clergy of the time. The residence of the Archbishop of Mainz was Aschaffenburg Castle, and Mathis was employed there as early as 1511. Thus in contemporary records he is sometimes referred to as "Mathis of Aschaffenburg." His place of birth was presumably Würzburg. From what we know of his life and from the fact that most of his works were produced for places between Mainz and Bayreuth, we may assume that he was a native of the Main valley in Lower Franconia. His art had firm roots there, even though it was considerably influenced by Augsburg. From the date of his earliest known work, which is still immature in style, it may be conjectured that he was born round about 1475. An unsuccessful attempt has been made to ascribe to him the remarkable *Portrait of a Young Artist*, signed MN, in the Art Institute of Chicago, the work of a Swabian or perhaps of an Augsburg painter of the fifteenth century.

His first known work, dated 1503, is the altarpiece made for the parish church at Bindlach, near Bayreuth in Upper Franconia; it is now in the parish church of nearby Lindenhardt. The shrine and inner wings contain sculptures dedicated to the patron saints of Bamberg. This is a modest altarpiece as befits its setting—a village church in the Bamberg region. Master Mathis, as the records call him, depicted the Fourteen Holy Helpers on the outside of the wings and a Man of Sorrows on the back of the shrine. These paintings already bear the stamp of his highly individual manner, even if the style is not as yet fully developed.

The Fourteen Holy Helpers were usually depicted as a row of half-length figures on the predella. To compress the groups of saints into two narrow wings was a difficult task for the painter. He therefore placed them on a continuous platform so that the onlooker could see them as a whole. This had already been done by an earlier painter in the entourage of the Housebook Master, Nicolaus Schit of Seligenstadt, when he depicted the Fourteen Holy Helpers in the central panel of an altarpiece (Städelsches Kunstinstitut, Frankfurt). In the case of Mathis' altarpiece, however, the group had to be divided into two parts and this raised special problems of composition and rhythm. His solution of these problems already shows the master's touch. The tall figures of St George and St Dionysius stand out in the foreground as the main protagonists, the other saints being shown behind them at varying distances and in varying proportions. This creates an incredibly rich ensemble. The composition is crowded, but—thanks to the use of chiaroscuro—it does not have the stifling effect of Dürer's *Christ among the Doctors*. Where light strikes the colours, they gleam out of the darkness, deep reds turning to bluish whites. Burgkmair's work shows similar transformations of tone.

The influence of the Augsburg school alone cannot account for the style of this altarpiece. When these wings were shown in 1928 at the Dürer Exhibition in Nuremberg, together with a number of works from Upper Franconia, both their links with, and their differences from, Dürer and the Upper Franconian masters became clear. The figures of the *Bindlach Altarpiece* have a transparent quality and seem to glow with light from within. The dark contours, drawn in with characteristically vehement strokes of the brush, link the colour surfaces together; this technique, derived from Dürer, was soon taken up and used throughout Franconia. It is found in Dürer's early pupil Schäufelein, but also in older masters such as Veit Stoss. When the latter was branded for forgery in 1503 and fled from Nuremberg to Münnerstadt, he became very active as a painter, producing the wings for Riemenschneider's altarpiece and the *Altarpiece of the Fourteen Holy Helpers* for Füssen (Pinakothek and Private Collection, Munich). The saints in the latter are so close to those in the *Bindlach Altarpiece* that we may assume a direct link between them. Both works have something outlandish and caricatural about them, as though the artists were straining to be as expressive as possible; the same features occur later in early drawings by Dürer's pupil Kulmbach. Mathis must have had some knowledge of Dürer and the Franconian painters—they may even have played a part in his training.

At the same time there is a profound difference, which becomes apparent when we consider the *Mocking of Christ* (Pinakothek, Munich) painted shortly afterwards (after December 23, 1503). While the *Fourteen Holy Helpers*—as the outside of the wings of an altarpiece—was painted thinly and almost without priming on the wooden panel, the *Mocking of Christ* is a carefully prepared composition painted on several layers of gesso and has a corresponding depth of colour. Its unity and dramatic gradation of colour effects, the way in which the colours glow with a fantastic light of their own out of the shadowy background, relate it to the works of Holbein the Elder and the Augsburg masters. While in the *Bindlach Altarpiece* Mathis is still uncertain and groping, here the strange and terrifying world of his imagination is fully realized. A surging throng of devilish figures emerges from the darkness of a kind of no-man's-land. Dürer, too, depicted raging brutality in the *Large Passion*, and the figure pulling on the rope in the foreground is treated with a dynamic emphasis that is reminiscent of his work. But while there is something forceful and virile even about Dürer's torturers, we are confronted here with the vilest brutality and sadism and the figure of the suffering Christ becomes all the more shattering in its helplessness. There are similar dramatic contrasts in Holbein's altarpiece for the Dominican Church in Frankfurt, but they are treated with a Late Gothic awkwardness and inhibition, whereas here, in the flashing curves and vibrant lines, all restraint has gone. The figure with the raised fist is in the throes of a veritable convulsion of violence and surges upwards like a writhing flame in the darkness. The figures have a trancelike quality. This goes beyond Holbein; it points directly to Bosch, of whom we are also reminded by the strange glassy figures of the *Bindlach Altarpiece*.

At the same time, everything is observed with the most scrupulous realism. One of the figures in the background, a young man, seems to have been painted from life—Holbein the Elder, too, introduced portraits at random in his religious pictures. A pale light from the left illuminates the group; according to the Bible the scene took place at night, but this is a light of the underworld that owes nothing to torches, fire, or the moon. In parts of the painting the colours form pale delicate harmonies, and in others they burn with a deep glowing intensity. The colour variations have a rhythm like that of rousing music and emphasize the frenetic impression of the whole. Colours like this had been unknown in German painting since the Bohemian and Rhenish masters of the fourteenth century.

H.A. Schmid assumed that Mathis followed the elder Holbein to Augsburg after work had been completed on the Dominican altarpiece in Frankfurt, and this is extremely likely. For only in Augsburg do we find pictures related, however distantly, to those of Mathis. In Burgkmair's works there is splendour and pomp combined with an inner fire, and in the Melk

Bernhard Strigel (1460-1528). Portrait of Hieronymus Haller, 1503. (18¾×12¾″) Alte Pinakothek, Munich.

The Habsburg Master (North Tyrol, active c. 1490-1510).
The Adoration of the Magi, c. 1500. (37⅜×23¼″) Oesterreichische Galerie, Vienna.

altarpiece by Jörg Breu there is an analogous frenzy of passion—but they seem studied beside the incredible intensity and sensitivity, the mingling of the realistic and the visionary, found in Mathis' pictures, which can be explained only in terms of the creative originality of a uniquely gifted artist.

At this time Maximilian I of Habsburg was the ruler of Germany. The first territory to come under the young archduke's personal rule was the Tyrol. From his predecessor Archduke Sigismund he inherited also the local artists and culture. A patron of the arts, he actively sought out new talent. Relations between Upper Swabia and the Tyrol in the artistic field had always been close. Swabian artists executed altarpieces for Tyrolean churches and monasteries, and their style appealed to the mountain folk. Maximilian accordingly chose Bernhard Strigel, a sensitive artist from the quiet Gothic town of Memmingen in the Swabian pre-Alps, as his court painter. Maximilian himself belonged to the generation of Strigel and the elder Holbein. Strigel's portraits of the Emperor (as he was soon to become) date from 1500 onwards, and copies of them were widely distributed. In some of them the Emperor is shown in ceremonial dress with crown and Imperial sword, but through a window we catch a glimpse of what was closest to his heart—the Tyrolean mountains with the chamois he loved to hunt. In others he appears as a stately patrician in a cloak, wearing the Golden Fleece, as for example in the portrait of 1504 in the Staatliche Museen, Berlin. Strigel's sensitive art completely seized his personality, conveying without embellishment the warm humanity of the great Utopian.

In 1503, Strigel produced the noble *Portrait of Hieronymus Haller* (Alte Pinakothek, Munich), one of the finest German portraits of the age of Dürer. The calm dignity of the Nuremberg merchant is conveyed in a likeness of an almost religious tranquillity. This was the face of the new merchant class that was taking the place of the knights and the feudal nobility. The contrast between the dark tones and the pallor of the face makes the features appear almost translucent. Their quiet thoughtfulness seems to radiate to the glowing blue of the landscape. This is the old Memling type of portrait, with which Strigel was probably familiar from a journey to the Netherlands. The few items of jewellery have a penetrating brilliance. Highly cultivated and meticulously executed, the painting is a typical example of German court art. The quiet urgency of Strigel's art as a portraitist soon met a worthy challenge. Barbara von Rechberg—Frundsberg by marriage—had been a happy wife and mother, but death robbed her of most of her fourteen children, her husband, and her brother. In 1505 she donated a memorial altarpiece to the parish church at Mindelheim, south of Augsburg. It consists of twenty panels showing the various branches of the Holy Kinship, together with members of Barbara's own family; the panels are now divided between the Germanisches Museum at Nuremberg and Donzdorf Castle. There is something touching in the way this lonely woman sought solace in these pictures of heavenly family bliss when her own earthly joy had gone. Strigel produced a series of paintings that are full of warm living humanity. They are real genre scenes affording a glimpse into the family life—centred on work and the reading of pious books—of the German burghers of the Late Gothic period.

Another of Maximilian's court painters was Gilg Sesselschreiber of Munich. In 1508 he settled in Innsbruck since his main job was to design and cast the bronze statues for the Emperor's tomb. We have seen in Strigel's case that a court painter needed colour sense, a meticulous technique, and an effective grasp of portraiture. We may take it that Sesselschreiber possessed these qualities. As he came from Munich, his work must have had features linking it with that of such Bavarian painters as Jan Polack. As he was working for the court from 1502 onwards, he probably also had some contact with the Tyrolean painters who followed Pacher. All these conditions are fulfilled by the anonymous painter known as the Habsburg Master after a painting in the Oesterreichische Galerie in Vienna. In this work, an *Adoration of the Magi*, Maximilian is shown as King Melchior and his father Frederick as a member of his suite. Despite a certain flatness of design, typical of the fifteenth century, which leads the artist to linger over fine brocades, the figures have a metallic glossiness, and surfaces a chiselled, almost cylindrical finish, which suggest the hand of a metal-founder. The treatment of the draperies, which have something of the Baroque profusion of the Bavarian masters, reveals a strong feeling for sculptural qualities. The colouring, with its combination of greenish blue and deep red, is reminiscent of Pacher. The portraits are striking and tremendously alive. It is by no means improbable that the creator of this and related works was also responsible for the masterly bronze portraits on the Emperor's tomb. Like Strigel's panels, this painting shows Netherlandish influences, and we know that Sesselschreiber visited the Low Countries.

Hans Fries (c. 1465-after 1518).
St Francis receiving the Stigmata,
1501. (25¼×14¾″)
Alte Pinakothek, Munich.

The painters of the mountain regions of Switzerland and Austria and those of the neighbouring pre-Alps formed a close-knit school apart; within it, however, there was a lively interchange of ideas. Switzerland produced Hans Fries, who was born at Fribourg (Freiburg im Uechtland) round about 1465. Judging from his style, he studied under the Bernese painter known as the Master of the Carnation. His travels between 1488 and 1499 took him to Austria. He seems to have been attached to the workshop of the Viennese Master of the Holy Martyrs at the same time as Rueland Frueauf the Younger. In 1501 Fries became the official painter of Fribourg. From the same year dates the altarpiece (*St Francis receiving the Stigmata*, Pinakothek, Munich) which he painted for the Cistercian church there. It is a powerful work in that vein of intense self-expression—one might almost say self-confession—which we find in Holbein the Elder, the early Burgkmair, Mathis Gothardt-Neithardt, and the Austrian works of Breu and Cranach. The lean figures are fanatical and vehement. The deep fervour of the chiliastic 1490s had not yet disappeared, but it was giving way to a new attitude exemplified not only in Mathis' works but in the paintings of the Alpine and Danube countries.

It would be wrong to regard Austria as being an outpost of secondary importance on the fringe of the German art world. If Austria—here synonymous with the hereditary family domains of the Habsburgs—had not held a central place in the history of art, leading painters from Franconia, Swabia, Bavaria, and Switzerland would not have flocked to it at the turn of the century. The Austrian painters were great travellers and had acquired a broad outlook;

Rueland Frueauf the Younger
(c. 1470-after 1545).
St Leopold riding out to the Hunt,
1505. (30×15⅜″) Stiftsmuseum,
Klosterneuburg, near Vienna.

the country formed a bridge between south and north, east and west. Austrian art in the fifteenth century was deeply rooted in nature and the soil. Apart from the Viennese and Tyrolean schools, the most important Austrian school of painting was that of Salzburg. Its greatest figure in the second half of the fifteenth century was Rueland Frueauf the Elder, who worked alternately in Salzburg and Passau and had a large following. His most important pupils were the Master of Grossgmain and his own son Rueland Frueauf the Younger who must have been born in or shortly before 1470 and was still living in Passau as late as 1545. Although he was so long lived, his activity as a painter can now be traced over a period of only two decades at the most. One of his earliest works is a *Crucifixion* dated 1496 (Stiftsmuseum, Klosterneuburg) whose style shows the influence of his father and also of Konrad Laib's crowded Crucifixion scenes. Its circular movement also links it closely with the Viennese Master of the Holy Martyrs, in whose studio the artist appears to have worked.

Frueauf the Younger's pictures are panel paintings, for the most part small in size. They are highly finished and subtly modelled, and there is a radiant harmony in their enamelled colours. All his other known works are linked with Klosterneuburg—a town on the Danube just outside Vienna—and its Augustinian abbey. Thus the artist from Passau had travelled down the Danube to produce his finest work in the vicinity of Vienna. Before the end of the fifteenth century, he produced the small altarpiece with the *Passion of Christ* and the *Life of St John the Baptist* (Stiftsmuseum, Klosterneuburg). Here we have the first intimation of what was to become the outstanding feature of his art—his mastery of landscape painting. Although Frueauf continues to pattern his compositions on those of his father, as for example in the scene on the Mount of Olives, his landscapes are something fundamentally new.

Dürer's watercolour landscapes had been audacious pioneer works with no parallel nor any immediate following in German art. They were not well known, since Dürer kept them for himself, but he used the subjects in his graphic work and this had a very wide circulation. Before Dürer, it was the Netherlandish school that had paid most attention to landscape in painting north of the Alps. At the beginning of the sixteenth century, this school took on a new importance in German eyes. As a result of the stimuli which it provided, Austria became the seminal centre of one of the most delightful movements in old German painting: the art of the so-called Danube School. The works of this school sprang from the discovery of landscape as an artistic subject in its own right and the recognition of the close links between man and landscape—in fact the Danube painters sometimes gave greater prominence to the latter. Landscape painting was now no longer an isolated phenomenon, as with Dürer, but a general trend determining the character of a whole new school of painting.

The old German painters did not represent the picture space as seen from a fixed point in terms of a perspective based either on gradations of tone and colour values (as in the case of the Netherlandish masters) or, more scientifically, on a single central vanishing point (as in the case of the Italians). This latter type of perspective makes its first appearance in Germany in Dürer's *Life of the Virgin*, and even after that there were frequent and deliberate deviations from it (in Altdorfer for example). The picture space is of course conceived *optically*, as in all the more recent art known to the German panel painters. But optical vision has to be kept within limits, it has to be tactile and tangible. When it is not, the representation of space becomes eccentric; the angle of vision veers off in all directions, first one way, then another. Hence the irrational representation of space in old German painting: in a single composition the viewpoint of the onlooker is continually changing. Distant views, such as the landscape in the background of Frueauf's picture of *St Leopold riding out to the Hunt*, were painted on the same plane as the foreground, thus creating an impression of flatness. This use of a single picture plane permitted the background to be directly related to the foreground in a way that would not be possible if central or optical perspective were employed. Thus the course of a river or the line of a mountain range could be related to a figure in the foreground. The artist could give free rein to his fantasy, reshaping and distorting near and distant objects at will, in order to establish a relationship between them. In old German painting this relationship was always determined by the exigencies of the narrative, by the spiritual content of the scene and the desire to convey this effectively. Disparate elements in the picture were united into a single whole, offering tremendous possibilities of *expression* that were quite independent of a rational conception of space. Hence the "expressionism" of old German painting, its deep spiritual feeling, intensity, and narrative power.

St Leopold riding out to the Hunt is part of a small altarpiece depicting the events leading to the foundation of the Monastery of Klosterneuburg. While hunting in the meadows along the Danube, the saintly Margrave Leopold von Babenberg found a valued veil his wife had lost in a storm. In gratitude to the Virgin for her miraculous intervention in this matter, he founded the Monastery of Klosterneuburg on the spot where the veil was found. This legend was popular with Austrian artists since it offered them an excuse for painting fine landscapes.

Ulrich Apt the Elder (c. 1455/1460-1532). The Adoration of the Magi, 1510. (49½×28″) Louvre, Paris.

Such landscapes constitute the chief charm of Frueauf's altarpiece, which bears a date difficult to decipher. Some scholars have read it as 1507. Recently, however, an infra-red photograph has revealed it to be 1505. The style of the altarpiece follows on directly from that of the *Altarpiece of the Passion and St John*, painted in the 1490s.

Frueauf had undoubtedly been to the Netherlands. He must have known the work of Justus of Ghent, whose landscapes in the *Triptych of the Crucifixion* (Church of St Bavo, Ghent)—especially those on the wings—show striking similarities with Frueauf's panels. He was probably also acquainted with the painters of Haarlem and Delft. The Viennese Master of the Holy Martyrs had painted an earlier, smaller altarpiece on the legend of St Leopold for the Abbey of Klosterneuburg. With the experience he had gained in the Netherlands, Frueauf far surpassed it, thanks mainly to the atmospheric use of colour in which he was very adept. Frueauf was a careful observer of nature, and could render with fidelity the glow of evening or a moonlit sky. The hunting scene with St Leopold is an enchanting picture,

Jörg Breu the Elder (c. 1475-1537). St Bernard Praying, 1500. (28×28⅞″)
Monastery of Zwettl, Lower Austria.

filled with a fairylike charm. We might almost say that—like Altdorfer's works at a later date —it is a pure landscape painting, embellished by the religious legend. The narrative is, however, fundamental to the picture and its poetic content is enhanced by its setting. The narrowness of the panel makes it seem like a fragment of an idyllic landscape whose peace is momentarily disturbed by the passing hunt. Despite the stylized abstraction, the picture shows a deep feeling for nature that transcends mere imitation and expresses an inner vision. Gothic painting in Austria—whatever other factors may have contributed to it—is essentially derived from Frueauf the Younger. Not only did he originate the "Danube style," which was to find its greatest exponents in Altdorfer and Huber, but from his art stemmed some of the most characteristic features of German Renaissance landscape painting, notably its expressive feeling for nature and its spellbound atmosphere. The younger Frueauf exerted a momentous influence on his entourage. The earliest evidence we have of the Danube School is directly connected with him, and thanks to the impetus he gave it the Danube style developed rapidly.

Jörg Breu the Elder was born in Augsburg about 1475. In 1483, he was apprenticed to Ulrich Apt the Elder, who was already an independent master painter. In Apt we have the paradoxical example of an artist who was older than Holbein the Elder, having presumably been born in the 1450s, but of whose output only the later pictures, dating from the sixteenth century, are known. There are two works signed "APT": a *Portrait of a Man* in the collection of the Prince of Liechtenstein, and the *Rehlingen Altarpiece* of 1517 (Staatliche Gemäldegalerie, Augsburg). There is a third work, the *Altarpiece of the Virgin*, which was commissioned by the Weavers' Guild in 1510 for the Church of the Holy Cross in Augsburg, and of which two panels have so far come to light (Louvre and Karlsruhe); but the signature is no longer decipherable. As Apt the Elder had three sons who were also painters, it is not certain whether the last-named work should be ascribed to him or to one of his sons. The panels of the *Altarpiece of the Virgin* are paintings of high quality and remarkably modern for an elderly man whose career began at the peak of the Late Gothic period. They contain a wealth of colourful detail, enhanced by a number of portraits from life among the Magi and their attendants. The influence of the Netherlands (the Master of Frankfurt, the Dutch) is clearly apparent. The teaching of this notable master, together with what he may have learnt from Holbein the Elder and Thoman Burgkmair, presumably shaped the course of Breu the Elder's art, though its beginnings are still unknown to us.

The earliest surviving examples of Breu's work date from his journeyman years, which he spent in Austria—not in or near Vienna like Frueauf and Cranach, but in the Lower Austrian town of Krems, on the Danube. There he painted several altarpieces for the monasteries of the Danube valley and the Waldviertel: the Cistercian Monastery of Zwettl (1500), the Charterhouse of Aggsbach (1501), and the Benedictine Abbey of Melk (1502). These works have fortunately been preserved—the first in its original setting—and are full of youthful ardour. The Augsburg background alone cannot explain the volcanic eruptiveness of Breu's art. The strongest influence on him was that of Dürer's early graphic work, the *Apocalypse* and the *Large Passion*, copies and single sheets of which are known to have circulated in artists' workshops. Tidings of this new art must have spread like wildfire among the younger generation, and its influence can be seen in the audacity and vigour of Breu's and Cranach's early Austrian works. A third influence must be added, that of Austrian art and the experience of the Austrian landscape. The *Altarpiece of St Bernard* in the Monastery of Zwettl is dated 1500. With Frueauf's *Altarpiece of St Leopold*, this work contains the most astonishing landscapes to be found in German painting at the beginning of the century. St Bernard is shown praying as he prepares to help his brethren cut the corn. He and his brethren form a loose, spacious, triangular group, his own dark figure being likewise enclosed in a triangle. The figures are forcefully outlined, but they form only a part of the composition, the landscape being predominant. It is a meticulous study of the Austrian pre-Alps. The golden cornfield hugs the hillside; the cowls of the Cistercian monks stand out against the windswept ears of

Master MS (early 16th century). The Visitation, 1506. (55⅛×37¼″) Panel from the Altarpiece of the Virgin. Museum of Fine Arts, Budapest.

corn. The road on the hilltop borders on empty space; a wayside crucifix and a tree split by lightning are silhouetted on the skyline. The onlooker feels almost as though he could enter the picture and stroll through the countryside. This is painting born of the spirit of the landscape.

A unique dramatic peak was reached with the large altarpiece of 1501, with the *Life of the Virgin* on the inside and the *Passion of Christ* on the outside of the wings, which Breu painted for the Charterhouse of Aggsbach (now in the Stiftssammlung, Herzogenburg, and the Germanisches Nationalmuseum, Nuremberg). These are spacious diagonal compositions with sweeping lines and contours and darkly glowing colours. The forms are eccentric, lumpy, and richly expressive. The painter was not afraid to use caricature, and this gives a demoniacal quality to the scenes showing the martyrdom of Christ, in which everything is fraught with menace. The third altarpiece, made in 1502 for the Abbey of Melk (but probably painted in Augsburg), has been discussed in connection with Mathis Gothardt-Neithardt.

More cheerful and festive in spirit, in contrast to these darkly passionate works, are the two wings of an *Altarpiece of the Virgin* executed for St Catherine's Church in the old mining town of Schemnitz (Banska Stiavnica) in Upper Hungary (now in Slovakia). The splendid altar carvings of *St Catherine* and *St Barbara* are now in the local museum, the *Nativity* in Svaty Anton, the *Visitation* in Budapest Museum, and the *Adoration* in Lille Museum. Buchner attributed the paintings to Breu, but he overlooked the fact that there was a *Passion of Christ* (Palace of the Primate, Esztergom) belonging to the same or to a parallel altarpiece, by the same painter, signed with a monogram which, beyond all reasonable doubt, must be read as MS, and bearing the date 1506. Hungarian and Slovakian scholars are unanimous in designating this artist as Master MS. He must have had very close links with Breu.

The importance of the Netherlands for German painting, even in the new century, cannot be overestimated. We have already emphasized this influence in discussing Burgkmair and Frueauf. It was obvious in the fifteenth century, and even in the sixteenth, when fruitful

Marx Reichlich (c. 1465-after 1520).
The Visitation, c. 1500. (26⅛×30¼″) Panel from the Altarpiece of the Virgin. Oesterreichische Galerie, Vienna.

contacts were established with Italy, wave after wave of Netherlandish influence continued to flow into Germany. Whereas in the fifteenth century the impact of the Netherlandish masters was felt mainly in the field of composition, in the sixteenth their principal contribution was in the field of colour. This seems hardly surprising when we consider the part played by the Netherlands in another sphere—that of music.

At that time the music of the Netherlands held at least as much significance for the culture of Northern Europe as their painting—perhaps even more. In the sacred compositions of Josquin des Prés, for example, Flemish music attained the same majesty of form and depth of expression as Dürer's art. The Netherlandish composer Heinrich Isaac, who had earlier been employed by Duke Sigismund, was recalled by Maximilian in 1492 from the service of Lorenzo the Magnificent and was thenceforth attached to the court at Innsbruck, Augsburg, and Vienna. His religious compositions, with their rich polyphony, were the equivalent in music of the colour effects achieved in Netherlandish painting. As artists are always conditioned by their surroundings, Isaac absorbed a great deal from his Austrian and South German environment, especially in his secular compositions which have something of the warmth and simplicity of the local folk music. Paul Hofhaimer, an Austrian composer whose portrait was drawn by Dürer, was also employed at Maximilian's court. Both he and Isaac took an interest in popular as well as classical music, and this tradition was continued by their pupils Senfl and Stoltzer. In the same way, a new kind of painting grew out of the soil and landscape —the painting of the Danube School, to which not only the Danube valley but all the Alpine regions of Austria contributed. In Innsbruck, the workshop of the court painter Jörg Kölderer became a centre for the younger painters of this school, which—like the music just discussed —raised local and popular traditions to the level of great art. We shall see to what a large extent the most solid achievements of Austrian art and those that held the richest promise for the future were based on what we might call folk art, for what is apparently rustic, backward, or provincial may acquire quite a different significance in the light of history.

The art of Michael Pacher had a great influence in the Alpine lands. Even artists who were far removed from his school were influenced by his use of colour, his conception of space, and the plasticity of his modelling. His followers included the best of the traditional folk artists. His most important disciple was the Tyrolean painter Marx Reichlich, who makes his appearance as early as 1489 with a dated *Adoration of the Magi*, painted for the Abbey of Wilten near Innsbruck. In 1494 Reichlich became a citizen of Salzburg, where he helped his master install the high altar in the parish church. Thereafter he was active both in the North and the South Tyrol. This dual orientation was important—as in the case of Frueauf the Elder's work in Passau and Salzburg—for it consolidated the tendencies coming to the fore in the Austrian region and linked them up with the main current of German art.

The most outstanding artists in Maximilian's circle took part in the decoration of the Waldauf Chapel at Hall in the Tyrol, commissioned by Florian Waldauf, the Emperor's Councillor. Michael Pacher made the sculptures for the altarpiece, Reichlich painted the wings, Burgkmair made woodcut illustrations of the relics treasured in the chapel, and Dürer illustrated a German edition of the *Revelations* of St Bridget of Sweden whom Waldauf specially venerated and who was portrayed by Reichlich on the wings of the altarpiece.

Pacher's greatest achievement was his scientific and accurate handling of Italian-type central perspective and the way in which he integrated it with figure composition in the northern style, employing colour in the service of light, space, and form in a highly sophisticated way. Reichlich, who continued where his teacher Pacher left off, was also a great master of colour, as all his works testify, though he, too, came from a simple Tyrolean peasant background. Like Pacher, he had been to Italy and was familiar with the works of such Venetian painters as Carpaccio, Bastiani, and Mansueti. Among his finest achievements are the panels

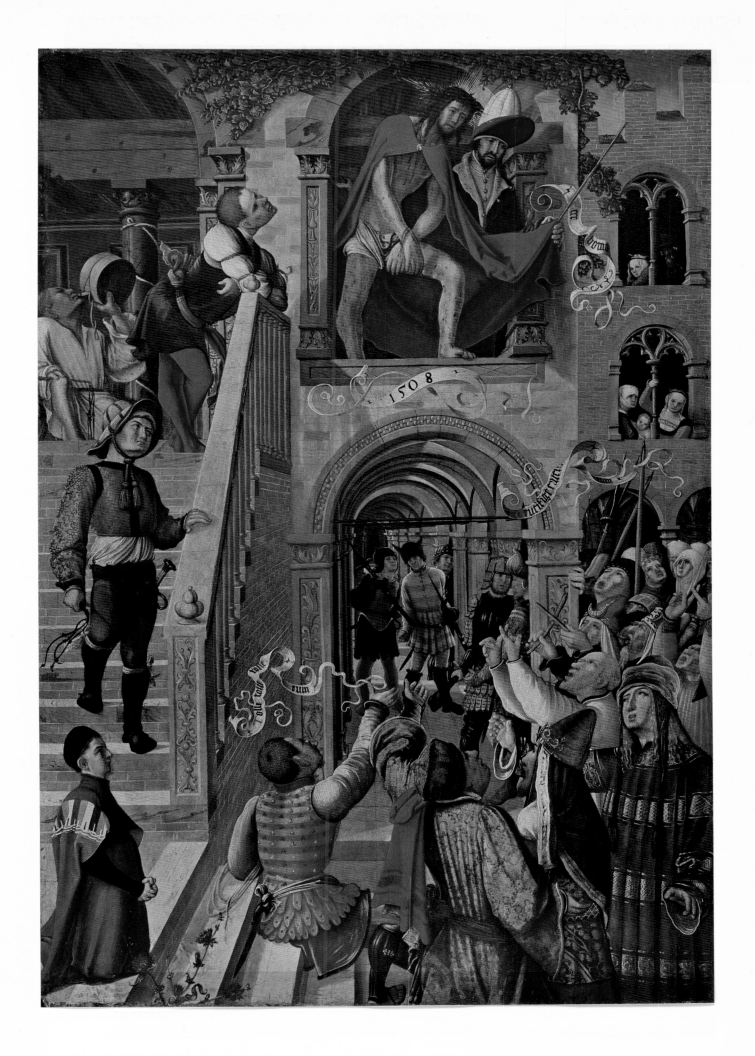

Urban Görtschacher (Villach, traceable 1508, 1524). Ecce Homo, 1508. (33⅝×23″) Oesterreichische Galerie, Vienna.

Lucas Cranach the Elder (1472-1553).
The Crucifixion, 1503. (54⅜×39″) Alte Pinakothek, Munich.

Lucas Cranach the Elder (1472-1553).

The Rest on the Flight into Egypt, 1504. (27⅛×20⅛″) Staatliche Museen, Berlin-Dahlem.

for an *Altarpiece of the Virgin* (Oesterreichische Galerie and Private Collection, Vienna), which must have been executed round the turn of the century, presumably also for Hall since they contain views of the town. The most surprising panel is the *Visitation*. The traditional setting for this theme is mountain scenery. Here, however, it takes place in a square in the old town of Hall—the idea being, no doubt, to bring home the Bible story to the onlooker by representing it in the familiar setting of his own town. This device had been used in Holland, but Austrian artists carried it even further. The vanishing point is set far back in the picture, so that the figures take on a monumental quality. Though they are handled with a peasant awkwardness, the general effect is extremely powerful, largely because of the contrast between the dark, heavy tones in which they are painted and the golden light on the house fronts. It is a remarkably truthful picture of a small Tyrolean town. In the background the mountains rise up almost to the edge of the panel so that only a small patch of the deep blue of the summer sky is visible. We can almost feel the breeze stirring in the streets and leafy alleys—an atmospheric effect of a type normally found only in Venetian pictures. It is almost like an open-air painting. Executed with the greatest care, Reichlich's pictures are brought to life by the use of delicately overlapping colours. The practice of brushed-in contours—usually a feature of the work of South German painters—is rarely resorted to. By his remarkable colour sense, this gifted painter of the turn of the century—his work includes altarpieces dated 1506 and 1511—imbued his figures with an inner cohesion and a new reality that came to its full fruition in the works of the Danube School.

Pacher had a profound influence on the art of the Alpine and Danube lands and thanks to an artist of Reichlich's calibre its effects were felt well into the new century. We can recognize Pacher's handling of space in the works of Urban Görtschacher, a painter of Villach who was also a city magistrate. For an *Ecce Homo* painted in 1508 (Oesterreichische Galerie, Vienna) he provided an artfully contrived spatial setting with foreshortened steps, galleries, and deep leafy alleys, the architecture being in the purest North Italian Renaissance style as practised in Venetia and Friuli. The postures and movements of the clear-cut figures with their typical foreshortened faces show the influence of the Mantegnesque painters and copperplate engravers of North Italy. In the cheerful colours and fluttering scrolls, there is still a remnant of the Late Gothic style of the North. A *Sacra Conversazione* at Gemona, in Friuli (dated 1505), has been attributed to Görtschacher. The proximity of Villach makes this attribution a plausible one. The hand of the Gemona master may also be seen in two splendid half-length portraits of a young couple (Germanisches Museum, Nuremberg) which have been attributed by Buchner to the Middle Rhenish master who painted the magnificent portraits of the Stalburg couple (1504, Städelsches Institut, Frankfurt), and by others to Hans Maler. Görtschacher was a highly skilful and painstaking painter, with a keen sense of form, who translated the best qualities of Late Gothic painting into the idiom of the new age.

By his encouragement of humanism, Maximilian I made the University of Vienna one of the best in Europe. To Vienna he invited scholars from Swabia and Franconia, including Conrad Celtes, who founded a Collegium Poetarum et Mathematicorum and laid down a syllabus based on the classical languages, embracing history, poetry, mathematics, natural science and the new geography. Celtes was in touch with the leading German artists; both Dürer and Burgkmair did woodcuts for him. At his behest, the young philologist and historian Johannes Cuspinian, whose chief work was a history of the Roman emperors up to Maximilian I and Charles V, came to Vienna as a university teacher. Cuspinian was a friend of the painter Lucas (born in 1472) from Cronach in Upper Franconia, who chose Cranach as his pseudonym. According to the artist's own testimony and that of his friends, Cranach spent his early years in Vienna, and this is confirmed by his surviving works. He may have come to Vienna at Cuspinian's instigation or perhaps as the result of a recommendation to Celtes from Dürer. Cranach's Austrian period started about 1499 or 1500 and seems to have continued until he settled at Wittenberg in 1505. Thus when he appeared in Austria, he was already a mature artist who had left his youthful work—of which nothing is known—behind him. From his father, who was also a painter, he seems to have learnt only the rudiments of his art. The years he spent travelling and working in the studios of others remain open to surmise. It is quite possible that he was employed for a time by Dürer, to whose art he owed a great deal; he may have co-operated with him on the paintings for the Schlosskirche at Wittenberg. A remarkable *Portrait of a Man as St Sebastian* in the Accademia Carrara at Bergamo may be in part by Cranach, but has not yet been definitively attributed. In general, the style is like that of Dürer's Tucher portraits, but the colouring, the modelling, and the handling of the features are at variance with Dürer's practice. The date of the picture remains uncertain.

Cranach's Austrian works have, however, been identified by the points of similarity which they show with the woodcuts he issued in Vienna. The earliest work that can be assigned to him with certainty is a *Crucifixion* from the Schottenkloster (Kunsthistorisches Museum, Vienna). Its powerful expressiveness is derived from the early Dürer and, though the panel is small in size, it is great in spirit. However, Dürer's influence is not the only one at work in this picture. The Austrian environment and the impressions received by the artist during his travels made as great a contribution: the wild, baroque upsurge of the terminal phase of Late Gothic as exemplified by Jan Polack, Mair of Landshut in Bavaria, and the Master of the Holy Martyrs in Vienna; the deep, resonant colour technique of Reichlich in Salzburg; and the new feeling for nature revealed in Frueauf's and Breu's altarpieces in the Danube monasteries. There is a strange similarity between Cranach's Viennese paintings and Breu's works of 1500 and 1501: the composition is dense and crowded, and the figures seem to be born of the wild, unkempt landscape with its rough rocks and shaggy trees. The picture space seems to heave and sway in the grip of some titanic natural force. As in Breu's Danubian altarpieces, the figures are gnarled and knotted. Their bodies are twisted under the folds of their garments like the roots of fir trees beneath the sparse soil. Everything is growing, striving, decaying, rotting. This is the beginning of that analogy between human figures and plants which was to become so characteristic of the Danube School. In a manner differing from Dürer's, yet with a related tension, Cranach endows his paintings with an epic, sweeping quality. The very trees and clouds are shaken by suffering and evil, as if caught up in the drama of the Passion. These qualities are given grandiose expression in the *Crucifixion*, dated 1503, in the Munich Pinakothek. Here Cranach's art reached its peak. The composition is unusually daring. As in the works of Reichlich and the painters of the Danube region, the landscape is fundamental to the picture. The viewpoint is that of a solitary onlooker moving across the hill of Golgotha: the crowd, frightened by the impending storm, has fled from the scene, leaving only the lonely distraught figures of Mary and St John. The onlooker enters from the side so that the half-hidden body of the thief on the left looms up before him, gigantic and menacing. Christ's loincloth is billowing in the first gust of the approaching storm. The sky with its swollen grey-black clouds—lit by a yellow flash as of lightning—echoes the dignity of his incredible suffering. Reichlich's colouring reappears, but concentrated and heightened. The deep blood-red of John's cloak, worn over a yellow tunic with reddish shadows, harmonizes with the deep green-blue of the Virgin's mantle. The crucified figures are almost the same colour as the wooden crosses. A similar use of closely approximating tones is found in the altar wings with *St Valentine* and *St Francis* (1501, Akademie der Bildenden Künste, Vienna).

The sense of *Sturm und Drang* introduced into German painting by the young Dürer was transmitted to all the members of the younger generation, particularly in the Danube regions of Austria where it was combined with a pantheistic feeling for nature. The result was a heightened tension and poignancy in their works. In Cranach's Munich *Crucifixion*, the solitary man and woman standing among the dead on Golgotha express such unutterable human sorrow that, beside it, the sacramental meaning of the Crucifixion takes a secondary place. There is no halo, no aureole. We are faced with a human tragedy of such dimensions that nature itself is stirred and shaken in sympathy.

Lucas Cranach the Elder (1472-1553).

Portrait of Dr Johannes Cuspinian, c. 1502. (23¼×17¾″) Dr Oskar Reinhart Collection, Winterthur, Switzerland.

Cranach's wedding portraits of Cuspinian and his young wife (Oskar Reinhart Collection, Winterthur) date from about 1502. They show tremendous vigour and are justly considered as the finest examples of portraiture in old German painting. The boundless optimism of a young and ambitious age is expressed in the bold, yet gentle face—alive to all the beauty and poetry of the world—of the twenty-nine year old scholar. Dürer's portraits and half-length figures were precisely drawn character studies. Cranach's figures seem to grow out of the landscape and to merge with nature. Here, man is no longer surrounded by walls, with the view from a window as the only link with the outside world. Seated on a grassy bank under a pine tree, Cuspinian is closing the book on his knees and surrendering to the spell of nature. For the landscape setting of these portraits, Cranach used thick, bright layers of resinous varnish so that the tones run into each other as though the elements were merging. The landscape—at once realistic and mysterious—is far from being a static backcloth, but pulses with restless life. It plays a symbolic role, and every detail has a hidden meaning. Here landscape painting acquires an underlying significance of a new kind, not religious as in Frueauf's work, but secular—a magical significance. The figures and animals portrayed are more than mere accessories. The owl pursued by magpies is the bird corresponding to the astrological sign of the scholar. At the time of the Renaissance, astrology was a potent force and the stars were believed to exert an influence, good or bad, on man, beast, and plant. In the sixteenth century astrology was linked with the scientific study of astronomy which was particularly cultivated in Austria by Johann von Gmunden, Georg Purbach, and Purbach's pupil Regiomontanus. In the Emperor's humanist circle, astrology was zealously practised. Even serious mathematicians and scientists sought to solve the enigma of the stars and turn their unquestioned influence on human affairs to good account. The planet in the ascendant at a man's birth was thought to determine his temperament. It was well known that the children of Saturn were gifted for creative work; at the same time, Saturn was feared as a malevolent planet.

Hand in hand with this mysticism based on nature went the study of ancient mystical theories in religion and philosophy. Johann Reuchlin's research into occult lore was a serious historical and philosophical study with a mystical motive and background. In his *Philosophia Occulta*, Agrippa von Nettesheim describes a close-knit system of constellations, spirits, angels and demons, supernatural and earthly forces that, in its organized unity, resembles Cranach's compositions in painting. The panpsychism of the Northern Renaissance dominated the artistic scene. Scepticism towards science was expressed in Agrippa's *De incertitudine et vanitate scientiarum*. Faith, unbelief, and superstition sometimes co-existed in the same person. It is against this spiritual background that we must consider Cranach's portraits. In the portrait of Cuspinian's wife, the glowing forms combine with the restless forces of nature to ignite a real fire whose flesh-coloured flames and black smoke soar into the sky. On a gnarled tree of the type known as "saturnine," an astrological bird—a red-tailed parrot—sits like a fiery spark. Further astrological animals are encountered in the small devotional picture of the *Penance of St Jerome* (Kunsthistorisches Museum, Vienna), which dates from 1502 and was probably a wedding present from the painter to the young couple. As in Frueauf's work, the landscape plays a prominent part—here we have a wood of birches, firs, and pines. We can identify the botanical characteristics of each tree—yet, taken as a whole, this is a rich, full composition in which the penance of the saint and the natural background are equally important. Through Cuspinian, Cranach obtained further commissions from the University circle at Vienna. In 1503, he painted the portraits of Dr Stephan Reuss, the jurist (Germanisches Nationalmuseum, Nuremberg), and of his wife (Staatliche Museen, Berlin).

Cranach's first phase ends with the more cheerful Berlin painting of 1504, *The Rest on the Flight into Egypt*. This clearly heralds the idyllic manner of the later Danube School, as exemplified by a number of Altdorfer's early works. The Holy Family is resting beside a small rocky fountain in a flowery meadow. The summer landscape seems to sparkle with a thousand dewdrops, and the scene makes us think of a peaceful outing rather than a hasty flight. Small naked cherubs bring flowers, birds, and water to the child. Three slightly older angels in golden yellow, wine red, and blue are playing recorders. Ice-grey mosses drip from the dark green firs, and a delicate light-coloured birch tree stands out against the rich blue of the sky. The whole picture is a kind of apotheosis of Cranach's experience of the landscape and art of Austria. His Austrian years form a self-contained episode that is among the finest and most significant in old German painting.

Dürer's work in the 1490s had a profound influence on the younger generation. However, the course of art in Augsburg and the beginnings of the Danube School illustrate how soon the direction taken by Dürer after his second journey to Venice (1505-1507) deviated from theirs and how quickly the German art of his time branched off on different—sometimes opposite—paths. This, however, only serves to demonstrate the richness of the period.

After finishing the *Feast of the Rose Garlands* (1506), Dürer again turned his attention to the theory of art and notably to the problems of perspective and human proportions. He pursued the studies that had led to the copperplate engraving of *Adam and Eve* in 1504, as is shown by a series of drawings in which the subject is treated with greater movement and more slender proportions are employed. The drawings were not based on the study of individual models, but on abstract calculated construction. They paved the way for the panel paintings of *Adam* and *Eve* in the Prado (1507). These are a far cry from the expressive naturalism of Cranach's Viennese paintings. The life-size figures—which must have been a self-appointed task—stand against a black background. This made it possible for the artist to emphasize the silhouette—a technique that was later taken up by Cranach, Baldung, and a succession of Mannerist painters. As in Gothic painting, the outline is more forceful than the actual modelling of the bodies. It has also been pointed out that in these pictures the northern Gothic element outweighs the classical element that predominated in the copperplate engraving of 1504 on the same subject. This is not quite true, for the supple inner modelling has nothing in common with the hard contrasts of the Gothic—in fact, what we have here, in the two Prado panels, is a foretaste of Mannerism. Both figures are slender and much more youthful than the ponderous couple of the 1504 engraving; the two nudes stand balanced on tiptoe in a momentary dancing posture. The majestic calm of the couple in the engraving gives place to a certain sensuality and erotic appeal. The strong light coming from the side moulds the bodies in a new way. In *Eve* we have a new ideal of feminine beauty with long, slender thighs, a high bosom, and sloping shoulders. At the same time Dürer was planning a large single nude, *Lucretia* (Pinakothek, Munich). A chiaroscuro sketch in the Albertina (1508) foreshadows it, but the painting was not actually executed for another ten years, since Dürer was busy with other things.

In 1508 the Elector Frederick the Wise commissioned from Dürer the painting representing the *Martyrdom of the Ten Thousand* (Kunsthistorisches Museum, Vienna). Frederick was a diligent collector of sacred relics, and a picture of such a theme—the martyrdom, at the hands of King Shapur of Persia, of ten thousand knights recently converted to Christianity—would have been well suited to figure in a reliquary chamber. This commission may have been prompted by a woodcut on the same subject that Dürer had done a decade earlier, at the time of the *Apocalypse*. The crowded scene is set in a rich wooded landscape. Wölfflin has called this a specifically Northern and Germanic type of composition, but no such crowds appeared in the works of Dürer's Late Gothic predecessors. They are more typical of the historical paintings of the Venetian school, for example, those of Gentile Bellini, Mansueti, and Carpaccio. The tiny figures, many of them nudes portrayed in varying postures, are—like the full-size *Adam* and *Eve* in Madrid—the fruit of Dürer's study of the human form. This is a veritable collector's piece, delicate and painstaking in execution. Such mastery of the human form was felt by Dürer to be no mean achievement: that is why he depicted himself beside Celtes in the middle of the picture, holding a banner inscribed "Dürer alemanus."

Hans Leonhard Schäufelein (c. 1480-1539/1540).

Christ on the Cross between King David and John the Baptist, 1508. (40¼ × 20″) Germanisches Nationalmuseum, Nuremberg.

Dürer's style developed into something systematic and consistent that showed him clearly how much could be learnt and taught; it was thus inevitable that he should take pupils. We must not, however, think of Dürer's workshop as a large-scale concern, like those presided over in Italy by Raphael and Titian. It was too small to accommodate more than a few workers at a time. Unlike his teacher Wolgemut, Dürer was not constantly engaged on large-scale commissions; they did not interest him, as he was an artist in the modern sense who preferred to concentrate on individual panels in the style of a Venetian *pala*, and such works had gone out of fashion in the first decade of the sixteenth century. When Dürer accepted commissions for folding altarpieces such as those executed for the Paumgartner family and Frederick the Wise, he confined himself to works in which he would have an exclusive say. Of the great *Altarpiece of the Passion* commissioned by Frederick the Wise in 1505, Dürer himself prepared only the careful chiaroscuro drawings for the wings, leaving the execution to his assistant Hans Leonhard Schäufelein who added a central panel of his own—the weakest part artistically.

Schäufelein was born about 1480 in Nuremberg, the son of a merchant from Nördlingen, in Swabia. In 1515, he settled at Nördlingen, where he lived and worked as town painter until about 1540. His earliest paintings date from 1503-1504. Schäufelein was the earliest of Dürer's pupils—at least, the earliest one historically known. The *Altarpiece of the Passion* (now in the Diocesan Museum, Vienna) reveals the tragedy of a type of discipleship in which the pupil is unable to attain the stature of the master, yet is so inhibited by the latter's teachings that his own original qualities are repressed. The woodcut illustrations for religious books which Schäufelein produced at about the same time show that he did possess some individuality. His talent as an illustrator was later made use of by the Emperor. His woodcuts have a refreshing folk element of a kind, often very moving in its narrative power, which is distinctive of old German art. The simple, lively faith which they reveal speaks directly to the heart; it is Schäufelein's best quality, and it is found again in subsequent paintings of his in which he managed to free himself from excessive dependence upon Dürer. The *Christ on the Cross between King David and John the Baptist* (1508, Germanisches Nationalmuseum, Nuremberg) is a fine and moving work. The subject is of mystical origin and is taken from the sixth book of the *Revelations* of St Bridget. It recurs a few years later in the *Isenheim Altarpiece*. Although Schäufelein could not match the epic quality of Dürer and Cranach, here he succeeds in conveying a real sense of ecstasy. His art was popular and emotional, but genuine religious art nevertheless.

The next painter definitely known to have been a pupil of Dürer's was Hans Suess von Kulmbach, who was born around 1480 and took his name from his native town of Kulmbach in Upper Franconia. Between 1500 and 1503 he worked as an apprentice under Jacopo de' Barbari, and in 1505 he collaborated with Schäufelein on book illustrations. It was then that he came under the influence of Dürer, who had employed him as early as 1501 and 1502 on woodcut illustrations for the works of Hrosvitha and Celtes, and he became known as a painter of altarpieces. He was also widely employed as a designer of stained-glass windows. His earliest works include the wings of an altarpiece depicting *Sts Cosmas and Damian* (Germanisches Nationalmuseum, Nuremberg) and an *Annunciation* (Kunsthistorisches Museum, Vienna).

Kulmbach was as unable as Schäufelein to achieve Dürer's power, but he had a strong sense of the picturesque and of colour, to which he later added a command of light and landscape. Kulmbach clearly understood the significance of Dürer's achievements during his second visit to Venice, and to some extent he went on where Dürer had left off; Barbari's teaching had already predisposed him to take this path. His figures have a gentleness and an expressive grace which make them very attractive. He was an original draftsman, and later painted some of the finest portraits of his time.

One of the most interesting of these is the portrait of the *Margrave Casimir von Brandenburg-Ansbach* (1511, Pinakothek, Munich). The sitter is splendidly arrayed in bridegroom's costume—the portrait was intended for his fiancée, Susanna of Bavaria—but it fails to camouflage his treacherous character. In fact, the embroidered astrological symbols add to the sinister effect. The colour scheme is a skilful combination of pale golden yellow, silver white, and coral red on a dark background.

By far the most important and most independent of Dürer's pupils was Hans Baldung Grien, who was born in 1484 or 1485 at Weyersheim near Strasbourg. The son of a scholarly family, he was an important member of the humanist circle in Strasbourg and, as one of the new intellectual élite, was in constant touch with the finest minds of this time. He was the chief representative of Upper Rhenish modernism, which was closely linked with the new school of painting in Switzerland. His apprenticeship with Dürer developed into a lifelong friendship. Dürer thought very highly of "Grienhanns," whose fresh, daring character appealed to him, and he took examples of his graphic work with him on his journey to the Netherlands. With his strong personality and intellectual pre-eminence, Baldung embodied in his art all the rational, mystical, and pantheistic tendencies of his age, reflecting not only its brilliance but its darker side as well. In addition to being an important painter, he was outstanding as a draftsman and wood-engraver, far surpassing his fellow-pupils Schäufelein and Kulmbach—with whom he collaborated on book illustrations—in his mastery of form. His earliest authenticated altarpieces come from the church at Halle.

The first of these, the *Altarpiece of St Sebastian,* shows Baldung's predilection for the type of brilliant painterly execution at which Dürer aimed in the *Adoration of the Magi.* Its sparkle and glitter are enhanced by the way the forms are modelled in light, like those of Dürer's *Adam* and *Eve.* In his treatment of the nude, Baldung is again clearly Dürer's follower. He started visually from the model before him; any abstract construction of form was alien to him. The composition still has something youthfully awkward about it, but this is balanced out by the buoyancy of the colouring. Baldung himself, a dashing, long-headed figure in a golden-green jerkin and wine-red hat, is shown holding the clothes of the martyred saint. The brilliant splendour of the landscape indicates that the nature-loving, pantheistic spirit was not confined to the Danube School, but was shared by the artists of the Upper Rhine area. Baldung's second altarpiece for Halle—the *Adoration of the Magi*—shows a progress in composition. The festive, yet ceremonial group have been skilfully adapted to the tall dimensions of the picture, and the individual figures have lost none of their delightful freshness in the process. In maternal warmth, the Virgin rivals Dürer's loveliest Madonnas.

In the spring of 1505, Lucas Cranach appeared in Wittenberg as court painter to Frederick the Wise, perhaps on Dürer's recommendation. The famous university town became one of the main centres of the Reformation. Cranach was in touch with intellectual circles there, and was later friendly with Luther and Melanchthon. He gained esteem and social position, became burgomaster of the town, and served three Saxon princes, Frederick the Wise, John the Steadfast, and John Frederick the Magnanimous, with all of whom he was on intimate terms. Saxony was poor in the arts, and in the sixteenth century was still little more than a colonial outpost. Its leading scholars and artists were imported from other parts. Cranach was completely isolated, and could not maintain the sweep and power of his Viennese pictures. He was asked not only to paint altarpieces and portraits for his patrons, but also to decorate castles and residences with hunting scenes and mythological figures, to design costumes, emblems, and escutcheons. M. J. Friedländer has rightly said: "If Cranach had died in 1505, he would have lived on in memory like one primed with high explosive. But he died in 1553 and so, instead of the expected detonation, we see him simply fizzle out."

Nevertheless the powerful drive and high emotion of the early Viennese pictures were continued in the works produced at the beginning of his Wittenberg period. The *Martyrdom of St Catherine* (Budapest) is a composition in which a multitude of figures form a dramatic, moving vortex. The *Altarpiece of St Catherine* (Dresden) is also imbued with the familiar fervour; it includes a number of portraits, and the background is based on actual landscapes. A novel feature of this painting is the open-air technique used in the modelling of the heads; for this, the painter made special studies of his models in specific lights. The composition of the figures is determined by the landscape with its natural effects of light.

Hans Suess von Kulmbach (c. 1480-1522).
Portrait of the Margrave Casimir von Brandenburg-Ansbach, 1511. (17×12⅜″) Alte Pinakothek, Munich.

Soon after this, Cranach worked on the Torgau *Prince's Altarpiece*, which was completed in 1509; the central panel and the inside of the wings depict the Holy Kinship (Städelsches Kunstinstitut, Frankfurt). In 1508, the artist had visited the Netherlands, and seen the works of the masters painting there. Round about this time Quentin Massys produced the *Altarpiece of the Holy Kinship* for Louvain; this shows a cheerful bustling family in a festive Renaissance hall. Cranach strikes the more pious and simple note of German family life, similar to that depicted in Strigel's *Altarpiece of the Holy Kinship*, with an emphasis on the social value of human virtues. Frederick the Wise and John are portrayed as Biblical patriarchs. The same approach is found in the Dessau *Prince's Altarpiece*, which has a Madonna in the central panel. This has sometimes been linked with Dürer's *Virgin with the Goldfinch*. The powerful portraits of Frederick and John on the wings foreshadow what is best in Cranach's later work. The earliest single portrait of Cranach's Wittenberg period that has been preserved is that of *Dr Christoph Scheurl*, painted in 1509 (Collection of Freiherr von Scheurl, Nuremberg). It faithfully reproduced the features of the Nuremberg jurist who was summoned to the University of Wittenberg and to whom we are indebted for a wealth of biographical data on Dürer and Cranach. In this picture man is no longer subject to the enigmatic forces of nature, but a moral being whose lucidity and intelligence enable him to command his destiny.

Hans Holbein the Elder (c. 1460/1465-1524).
Portrait of a Woman, after 1510. (13¾×10⅜″) Kunstmuseum, Basel.

The art of Hans Holbein the Elder had its roots in the Late Gothic. We have already considered his great achievements in the form of folding altarpieces and devotional paintings. The *Kaisheim Altarpiece* and the *Basilica of St Paul* were his last great commissions of that type. In the first decade of the sixteenth century he aimed at something different, something that Dürer had achieved in masterly fashion in such paintings as the *Feast of the Rose Garlands* —the single, expressive, organic panel in the style of the Italian altar painting, rather than the "story-book" series of pictures of the folding altarpiece. Such altarpieces had become outmoded; they might still be commissioned by donors of the older generation such as Frederick the Wise, but they were not much in favour with the younger artists. It was not until all the possibilities of the single altar painting had been developed—largely thanks to Dürer—that the old folding altarpiece acquired renewed significance. This was not yet the case in 1505—not, in fact, until after 1510. Holbein's art lost favour for a time; commissions fell off and the situation became so critical that he had to give up his Augsburg home. Nevertheless his altar paintings contained the seeds of a new type of art that was wholly in the spirit of the century of the Renaissance. We have seen that Holbein made portrait studies in silverpoint for the figures in his religious paintings. He delighted in these studies for their own sake and did not care whether the model was the Emperor or a beggar, a burgher or an adventurer, Fugger the Rich or one of the monks of St Ulrich with whom the painter sometimes dined. These studies were increasingly used as a starting-point for individual portraits, which provided a fresh outlet for the artist's creative energies despite the shortage of large-scale commissions. In the field of portraiture, Holbein the Elder paved the way for his famous son. The very fine *Portrait of a Woman* in the Kunstmuseum at Basel was probably executed shortly after 1510, and there are also silverpoint drawings of the same model. The subject of the painting—her age is given as thirty-four years in an inscription on the frame—is an intelligent-looking woman whose searching, slightly sceptical look reveals an inner peace and equilibrium that made her a perfect model for the painter. Such simple convincing portrayals of the human character gave Holbein the Elder an added claim to fame as he moved into the new century.

The individual portrait was one of the greatest achievements of Augsburg painting in the early sixteenth century. Both the artists of the older generation such as Apt and Holbein and the younger ones like Burgkmair and Breu began to accomplish outstanding things in this field. The *Portraits of Hans and Barbara Schellenberger* (1505 and 1507) in the Wallraf-Richartz Museum in Cologne show the intensity and concentration that Burgkmair brought to the art of portraiture. It seems as though this painter had been predestined to portray the greatest intellectual personalities of his age. The splendid *Portrait of Sebastian Brant* (1508, Staatliche Kunsthalle, Karlsruhe) shows the poet in pure profile, the effect being that of an Italian Renaissance medallion. Burgkmair was more expressive in his outlines than Dürer, but could not match him in the modelling of features, which is why he deliberately chose this pose. The luminosity of the clear intellectual profile is enhanced by the dark background. Such pictures reveal all the spiritual nobility of German humanism.

Burgkmair was an artist who was deeply imbued with the spirit of the Renaissance. Nevertheless, the *Altarpiece of the Rosary* painted in 1507 (Staatliche Gemäldegalerie, Augsburg) has Gothic decorative features in the framework. This, however, is Gothic that has lost its structural meaning and is used as a purely decorative feature, rather as it was used at the beginning of the century by the Netherlandish masters, who had a great influence on Burgkmair. Gothic and Renaissance forms are combined in a richly decorative whole, and form a noble setting for the almost hieratic splendour of the sacred figures. This is no longer the Late Gothic of Schongauer, but a creation of the early Renaissance and its eager striving after new modes of expression—a Late Gothic in the style of Mathis Gothardt-Neithardt and of Cornelis Engelbrechtsen, Jan de Cock, and Jan de Beer in the Netherlands. In fact, it is no longer Gothic but an approximation to flamboyant Mannerism.

This style was continued and developed by Burgkmair, though he also produced such purely Renaissance works as the *Virgin* of 1509 (Germanisches Nationalmuseum, Nuremberg). Like Dürer in the *Virgin with the Goldfinch*, Burgkmair pays homage in this painting to the Venetian *pala*, the single panel in which the new knowledge and style could be most brilliantly concentrated. The Gothic rose bower has been transformed into a sumptuous setting of Venetian architecture, but the northern feeling for nature has survived in the charm of the vegetation and landscape so that the work seems to be a forerunner of the Stuppach *Madonna* of Mathis Gothardt-Neithardt, which it predates by a decade.

During the Middle Ages, research into nature formed part of the great speculative systems based on theology. With the growth of empiricism, this research increasingly freed itself of theological limitations and merged with the philosophical movement of humanism. Both trends of thought, the theological as well as the scientific and philosophical, were anchored in the central idea of a divine creator. As scientific thought endeavoured to interpret the universe as an embodiment of the Deity, with whom it was interwoven down to the smallest atom, the term "pantheism" is used in connection with Renaissance philosophy and science.

Hans Burgkmair the Elder (1473-1531).

Portrait of Sebastian Brant, 1508. (14¾×12⅜″) Staatliche Kunsthalle, Karlsruhe.

At the beginning of this era, what would later become the sciences of biology, physiology, and chemistry were closely linked with medical science. Rational science in the modern sense was as yet unknown north of the Alps. Magical and mystical ideas—some of medieval, some of late classical origin—were often interwoven with scientific discoveries. Abstract calculation starting from an axiom and verified by an experiment had not yet replaced the intuitive understanding of the universal and the empirical investigation of the particular. It was believed that numbers had magical properties. Philosophy endeavoured to fathom the deeper causes and motive forces behind all natural processes. Medicine strove to master the secret powers of nature and enlist them in its service. The way in which such great physicians as Paracelsus and Cardano tried to approach nature was as intuitive and all-embracing in its relationship to the cosmic whole as it was experimental and empirical in detail. In the early phase medicine covered a variety of fields, and this led naturally to a philosophical synthesis. Paracelsus, the most famous physician of his time and one of its most representative intellects, made it his business to study the secret forces of nature, the organic development and decline of all things. As a scientist he attempted to formulate intellectually the knowledge that was expressed in visual terms by the discoverers of nature and landscape in painting. It is amazing how often Paracelsus' definitions seem to be a literary interpretation of the new concepts of nature which the pioneering painters had embodied in their art. This is yet another example of an important intellectual trend that found expression in the fine arts before it could actually be worked into a scientific, philosophical, or moral system by the thinkers.

The new tendencies in painting that were linked with the discovery of nature found their chief expression in the Danube School. The name of Albrecht Altdorfer is associated more closely with this school than that of any other painter. The founders of the Danube style —Frueauf the Younger, Cranach, and Breu—belong only partially to this attractive chapter in the history of German art. Wolf Huber, a younger contemporary of Altdorfer's, gives a free rein to his feeling for landscape only in the intimate world of his drawings. Such feeling, the most precious achievement of the Danube School, is the keynote of all Altdorfer's work —his paintings, as well as his drawings and engravings. Even his large-figure compositions are dominated by problems of space in landscape, of light and colour and atmosphere. He was the first to make landscape an independent genre, thus providing an inexhaustible source of strength and refreshment for modern man in the absence of the certainties of medieval faith.

The origins of Altdorfer's art used to be one of the most puzzling problems facing the art historian; today we have a clearer view than our predecessors of a few decades ago, although many aspects of his background remain obscure and much that we should like to know still eludes us. As he was enrolled as a burgher of Regensburg in 1505, Altdorfer must have been born shortly before 1480. He came of an old Bavarian family. His father was a painter, and from him he presumably received his early training. There is no mention of his apprenticeship and journeyman years in the written records, so that in trying to trace his antecedents we are wholly dependent on the internal evidence of his paintings and engravings. Of these, the earliest known are the so-called *Mondsee Seals*, primitive woodcuts of saints which Altdorfer executed for the Monastery of Mondsee in the Salzkammergut. Like his landscape drawing of scenery in the Salzach Valley, they prove that he was living in Austria. The Monastery of Mondsee was a centre for the painters of Michael Pacher's school and for a traditional school of wood engravers. Altdorfer's earliest known painting is a *Martyrdom of St Catherine* (Kunsthistorisches Museum, Vienna) from the Abbey of Wilten near Innsbruck. It shows links with the works of Marx Reichlich, as his copperplate engravings of 1506 do with pictures by Pacher. However, they contain no trace of the hardness and angularity of the Late Gothic. The garments billow like sails in the wind and are arranged in deep parallel folds. The dynamic quality of Altdorfer's drawing is already evident in the wreaths, curls, and sweeping curves and the play of dovetailing forms. The abstract ornament of the Late Gothic is replaced by plants, natural forms, and living creatures.

A basic feature of Altdorfer's art is already apparent in these early works—the indivisible union of nature and human events. Nature is in a state of upheaval: fire and hail rain down from heaven, and in the stormwind the tops of the trees are bowed low. Although the sense of nature was still contained within the framework of Christian legend, the way was being prepared for the cosmic pantheistic thought of the new age.

Altdorfer's development as a draftsman can be observed in works produced at the same time as his early paintings and engravings. His chiaroscuro drawings on tinted paper are not mere sketches, but works of art in their own right, intended for the pleasure of connoisseurs and collectors. They are a particularly clear illustration of his decorative technique, in which curving, soaring parallel lines and charming curly spirals are employed. It dominates both landscapes and figures and enhances their unity. Human figures and fantastic imaginary ones seem to grow out of the soil like trees or plants, to be condensed out of the elements.

The diptych of *St Francis and St Jerome* (Staatliche Museen, Berlin) dates from 1507; it shows the two saints absorbed in their devotions and in the dreamlike charm of the landscape that surrounds them. The figure of St Francis is derived from a woodcut by Dürer, that of St Jerome from Cranach's *Penance of St Jerome* of 1502. Everything is unified by the landscape with its golden evening tones. For the first time the domination of local colour in old German painting seems to have been completely overcome.

Altdorfer's pictures are usually small in size, and each is conceived as a microcosm of a growing and breathing natural whole. The world of Antiquity, from which Dürer was for ever trying to wrest the laws governing human proportions, ran riot in Altdorfer's hands, the figures of classical mythology becoming assimilated to the gnomes of northern folklore. In a gem-like sparkling picture of 1507 (Staatliche Museen, Berlin), he shows a *Wild Man's Family* emerging from a wilderness of bluebells, lilies-of-the-valley, and wild orchids.

Christian myths, too, were interpreted in a new spirit of closeness to nature. The *Nativity* (Kunsthalle, Bremen), set amidst ruins like Dürer's copperplate engraving of 1504, also dates from 1507. Dürer's scene creates the impression of a well-ordered home compared with Altdorfer's weird vista of ruins. The decay and dilapidation of the walls emphasize the ephemeral quality of human achievements and their subjection to the ineluctable processes of nature. Like the crumbling walls, everything is in transition—daylight giving way to dusk, and the hard frost to a warm, thawing wind. At a later date, Paracelsus' book *Meteorum* expressed this idea of the transitional and changing nature of the elements in terms of empirical science. In this natural setting, enhanced by magical lighting effects—the fireworks of the morning sky, cool moonlight, lanterns and torches—the cherubs disport themselves like the gnomes in fairy-tales.

Altdorfer's technique has been compared with that of the miniaturist; he himself in fact had undoubtedly practised the craft of miniature painting. The picture on vellum of *The Forest with St George* (1510, Pinakothek, Munich) can be explained in terms both of highly developed draftsmanship and of schooling in miniature work. The treatment is extremely original: a section of the dense virgin forest fills the picture to the very edge; in the mind it can be continued to infinity. Here we stand on the threshold of modern landscape painting, for the encounter of St George with the dragon is treated as a mere episode in the quiet course of nature, as an incidental, an accessory. While the light in the *Wild Man's Family* is still shown as a precious ornament set against the green of the forest background, here every pattern and feature of the foliage has been conquered by it, every tree and plant has been conceived and painted in terms of light. Only in his watercolours did Dürer come so close to nature. Nature here nevertheless has a narrative tension, is filled with the spirit of the legend—which seems, in turn, to be born of the landscape. In this, Altdorfer had been anticipated by Frueauf.

Leonhard Beck (c. 1480-1542). St George and the Dragon (detail), c. 1515. Kunsthistorisches Museum, Vienna.

The Age of the Great Altarpieces

THE folding altarpiece, a polyptych consisting of several hinged panels painted on both sides, and enriched with sculpture in relief, had a set range of iconographic themes, though inventive artists rang the changes on them. Essentially a creation of the Late Gothic period, it was not superseded until the first decade of the sixteenth century. As artists began to concentrate on single paintings—aiming at a new perfection of form like the painters of the South, or at a microcosm based on new concepts of nature and human character—the large altarpiece fell out of fashion. Secular subjects, in the form of portraits, landscapes, and mythological scenes, became proportionately more frequent.

Once this development had been perfected and the new gains consolidated, there was a surprising revival of altar-painting on the grand scale, but with certain differences. There was no longer a balanced combination of painting and carving. The emphasis was now on pure painting, and even if sculpture was used it was secondary to the work of the painter. The decade between Dürer's *Heller Altarpiece* and Wolf Huber's *Feldkirch Altarpiece* was the age of the great altarpieces, which combined the new grandeur of form and knowledge of nature with genuine religious fervour. During this decade, too, the Emperor Maximilian's patronage brought a new brilliance to official art.

For years negotiations had been going on between Jakob Heller—a rich burgher of Frankfurt and a great patron of the arts—and Dürer concerning the painting of a folding altarpiece, with a central panel showing the *Assumption and Coronation of the Virgin Mary,* for the Dominican Church which already contained Holbein's *Altarpiece of the Passion.* In 1508, after finishing his work for the Elector Frederick the Wise, Dürer started on this commission, and its progress is revealingly documented in his correspondence with the donor. The completed altarpiece was sent to Frankfurt at the end of August 1509. A century later, the Dominicans sold Dürer's altarpiece to the Elector Maximilian of Bavaria, whose collector's zeal was surpassed only by that of the Emperor Rudolf II. The central panel was unfortunately destroyed in a fire at the Elector's Munich residence. Only from a seventeenth-century copy and from Dürer's magnificent preliminary sketches can we gain an idea of this outstanding work, for which its author predicted a lifespan of more than five centuries. Only the wings, whose inner sides were painted by Hans Dürer, have survived (Historisches Museum, Frankfurt). It is probable that Albrecht collaborated on the donor portraits.

The lower half of the central panel of the *Heller Altarpiece* consisted of a rich landscape in which the Apostles were assembled round the open tomb of the Virgin. Similar compositions, conditioned by the subject, are found in certain Late Gothic paintings of the Nuremberg school depicting the Apostles as worshippers kneeling in church. Dürer's work, however, belonged to the new age. It portrayed the Apostles as a group of dignified scholarly men of zealous faith, engaged in discussion of the astonishing event—the Virgin's miraculous ascent into heaven. Here we see the influence of the Italians and their mastery of composition; Dürer was still drawing on the knowledge he had gained in the South. The Apostles are not—as in Titian's *Assumption*—shaken by pious fervour and amazement, but are engaged in a sober conversation as in Raphael's *Disputa*. They form a semicircle round the open tomb, the foreground figures large and powerful, the more distant ones presented on a diminishing scale. This is reminiscent of the grading of the figures in the *Martyrdom of the Ten Thousand*. They form a sort of wedge in the picture plane, and a portrait of the painter is placed where it opens into the landscape. This V-shaped wedge echoes the triangular composition of the upper part of the picture, and at its point St John is shown bending over the open grave.

The picture is divided into two parts, an earthly one and a heavenly one. The upper part shows the Virgin Mary being crowned by Christ and God the Father. The whole group creates the impression of the keystone of an arch that has been lifted out of its context and is miraculously suspended in mid-air. A similar composition is found in Dürer's woodcut on the same subject in the *Life of the Virgin* (1510). The magnificent portraits of the Apostles can now be studied only in the preliminary sketches (Albertina, Vienna; Kupferstichkabinett, Berlin; and other collections).

Some parts of the correspondence with Heller tell us a great deal about Dürer's ideas on perfection in painting. He denies Heller's assertion that he had promised to complete the work with "the utmost diligence" because, he said, it would take more than a lifetime to complete it satisfactorily; he admits only to having promised "a particular diligence." In this he reveals his awareness of the danger of "painting himself out" that sometimes threatened him when he was engaged on such commissions. In such cases a return to copperplate engraving became a therapeutic necessity, and he wrote to Heller: "But this finicking work doesn't advance things. So I'll attend to my engraving."

Artistically the most valuable sections of the grisailles on the weekday side of the altarpiece are the supporting wings painted by Mathis Gothardt-Neithardt. These did not form part of Dürer's original plan, but were decided on independently by the donor, who thus brought the two greatest geniuses of German art together in the execution of a single work. Mathis probably began them shortly after Dürer had finished his part of the commission and had sent it to Frankfurt (end of August 1509). The upper wings show *St Lawrence* and *St Cyriac* (Historisches Museum, Frankfurt), the lower *St Elizabeth* and *St Lucy (?)* (Fürstenberg Collections, Donaueschingen). They are in the "stone colour" prescribed in the contract for the outer side of the altar panels, but were painted by an artist who could develop the full range of natural colour in any given tone with incredible skill and beside whom Dürer, for all his great qualities, appears gaudy and glassy. The magic of nature, the secret life of the plant world, has invaded the stone niches that frame the two women saints—one of whom has a cloistral repose, the other a smile that could be called either provocative or enraptured. The figures are modelled by unmistakable daylight, and at the same time by a supernatural lustre, so that they seem to glow from within. This is a new form of organic Gothic, influenced by Paracelsus—not "terminal Gothic," as German Late Gothic has been called, but "initial Gothic"! The two male saints have the dancing quality of the Baroque forms that stemmed from Late Gothic; this is also found in Leinberger and in the Master of the Breisach Altar. All the healing power of the physician is concentrated in the brutal grasp of St Cyriac's right hand as he gives "shock treatment" to Artemia, the King's epileptic daughter. We feel the spasm of pain in the horribly twisted fingers of the possessed woman. This is the idiom of a psychologist, a neurologist, a soul-searching painter very different from Dürer, but no less profound and shattering. The coming together of these two artists at the end of this great opening decade of the century of the Renaissance was like a fiery symbol for the future.

Max Dvořák has pointed out that the visions of heaven on the central panel of the *Heller Altarpiece* and on Dürer's *Adoration of the Trinity* are typical of the period and illustrate the trend away from naturalism towards a new idealism. The turning-point in this direction came in Italy with Fra Bartolommeo's *Last Judgement* fresco (begun in 1499), and in the North with Dürer's *Apocalypse* woodcuts (1498). Then, Dvořák suggests, there was a ten-year interval, after which Raphael's *Stanze*, the *Heller Altarpiece*, the *Adoration of the Trinity*, the *Isenheim Altarpiece*, Raphael's *Sistine Madonna* and *Transfiguration*, and Titian's *Assumption* followed in quick succession. These were the peak achievements of the new idealism, in the development of which Dürer's altarpieces played an important role.

This analysis by an eminent scholar clearly indicates the part played by the great altar-pieces of the German masters in the second decade of the sixteenth century and shows the gulf that separated them from the Late Gothic painters, despite the lingering traces in their work of the Late Gothic conception of form. The Late Gothic altarpieces are painted picture-books conforming to a traditional liturgical viewpoint, whatever individual touches the painter might bring to them. Notwithstanding their connection with the traditional treasury of Christian iconography, the altarpieces of the second decade of the century express both the desire for ideal form and a completely personal vision. Where they were linked with older things, these were things that had been forgotten for centuries and were now revived. Where literary sources were used, these were not imposed on the artist, but chosen freely by him because they fired his imagination. All this illustrates the stupendous creative power of the new age, in which freedom of expression took the place of conformity to accepted values.

As an act of piety towards the Apostles, a wealthy brass-founder of Nuremberg named Matthias Landauer endowed a home, called the Zwölfbruderhaus, for twelve old men. The foundation included a chapel dedicated to All Saints. Designed by Hans Behaim the Elder, it was a small masterpiece and Dürer was entrusted with its most precious adornment—an altar painting which, when placed in position, glowed in the light of the stained-glass windows. This work, dating to 1511 and now in the Kunsthistorisches Museum, Vienna, was not the old type of shuttered altarpiece, but a *pala* on the Italian model, like the *Feast of the Rose Garlands*; the frame was designed by Dürer himself. Taking its name from the chapel, it became known as the "All Saints Altarpiece," but its real title is the *Adoration of the Holy Trinity*. Its dominant feature is the Throne of Mercy, which was also the subject of a large woodcut executed by the artist in the same year. The upper part of the painting shows God the Father with his crucified son in his lap; the two figures form an inverted triangle. God is enthroned on a rainbow, as in the fourth revelation of the Apocalypse, and surrounded by the hosts of the Elect. Four superimposed circles of figures hover round the Throne of Mercy. The uppermost is formed of cherubim and seraphim and the Dove of the Holy Ghost. A little below them, larger angels hold the instruments of the Passion and the cloak of the Almighty. Then follows a circle consisting of the interceders for the human race: on the right, headed by John the Baptist, are the precursors of the Saviour, with the patriarchs and prophets of the Old Covenant; on the left, headed by the Virgin Mary, are the female saints and virgins. These circles are not complete, for it would not then have been possible to leave a free view of the great central tableau. The lowest circle is closed: it contains the earthly representatives of the Church and men and women of every class and rank. On the left is the ecclesiastical group, headed by the Pope, with cardinals, bishops, monks, and nuns; on the right, the secular group led by the Emperor and King, with Doges, oriental princes, nobles, knights, burghers, and peasants. This circle, with its mass of figures that the eye cannot take in, stretches out

Albrecht Dürer (1471-1528).
The Adoration of the Trinity, 1511. (56¾×51½″)
Kunsthistorisches Museum, Vienna.

of sight. The figures in the foreground have their backs turned to us, so that we too seem to form part of the circle. In this incredibly lifelike assembly of the faithful united in expectation of their salvation, we meet people from Dürer's own circle. To the left of the picture is the pious donor Matthias Landauer and to the right his son-in-law, a Haller, depicted as a proud knight. There are probably other portraits among the crowd, and it is accordingly wrong to call the painting an "All Saints" picture.

This vast structure of divine and human figures hovering in the clouds is controlled and unified by the simple forms of a grandiose, ideal composition. It has often been compared with Raphael's *Disputa*, but the latter has a tectonic foundation anchored to the earth, while the heavenly idealized part is in the clouds. In Dürer's work, the whole composition is set in the clouds and this, combined with the tremendous realism in the treatment of the figures, creates an impression of something fantastic and visionary. Although Dürer achieved this effect by dint of his own powerful imagination, the picture is nevertheless linked with the iconographic tradition of the Church. Its literary source is St Augustine's *Civitas Dei*, and its prototype is to be found in the numerous representations of the heavenly and earthly City of God in medieval prayer books and books of hours. The subject of the picture is the ultimate state succeeding the end of all temporal things. After the Last Judgement, which is shown in relief on the carved frame, all that is temporal enters cleansed and transfigured into eternal bliss.

Dürer's painting goes far beyond the medieval representations of the subject. The picture as a whole is dominated by the new Copernican concept of circular space, which was to be taken up also by Altdorfer, Tom Ring, Bruegel, Tintoretto, and the masters of the Baroque. The group of the Trinity acts as an axis, as the plummet and pendulum of the various circles hanging freely in space, as the δὸς ποῦ στῶ. The Trinity is the pivot to which everything is anchored, forming a powerful triangle that recalls a symbol well known as a magic anagram in the drawings of alchemists and natural philosophers. The whole is held together by the concision of this form—the others could not remain aloft if they were not subject to the force radiating from it. The figure of the Almighty shines out in gold, moss green, and deep blue. The cherubim and seraphim above him gleam fiery red and yellow. The sky in the background is built up of delicate clouds that are suffused with a pink glow as though touched by the morning sun. The colour scheme of the painting is based chiefly on a harmony of red and gold, and this gives it a festive radiance.

But the most powerful thing in the picture is probably the circle of the Blest, and it is to this that it owes its extraordinary resonance. Here the profound experience of portraying human beings that Dürer had gained in his work on the *Heller Altarpiece* stood him in good stead. The throng of people is not a disorganized mass as in Late Gothic compositions, but has a rhythmic structure of the kind introduced by the Italians. But, while in the *Disputa* we have idealized types, here we are confronted by characters, conscious representatives of their respective classes, morally aware of their social responsibilities. They represent their station in life honourably and positively, the peasant as much as the knight, the craftsman as much as the Emperor, the simple monk as much as the Pope. This was something new, both in relation to Gothic and to the Italian Renaissance, something that began timidly in the *Apocalypse* but is here—on the eve of the Reformation—clearly and distinctly formulated: the ethos of Man as an individual and the bearer of a social duty. Thus all men come together, in spiritual equality, to worship God Almighty. They kneel on light pillars of cloud as on firm ground, or hover freely in the air. They are so close to us that we seem to touch their garments and yet those at the back are set above the most distant cumulus clouds stretching far into the depths of the landscape. Here temporal relationships have ended—this is the timeless realm of heaven. No other painter of the period could show this as convincingly as Dürer, who depicts himself as a tiny modest figure in the corner of this mighty picture.

Dürer's work is imbued with the greatness of vision and tremendous inner intensity that were his most individual traits; in Italy, similar qualities were found only in Michelangelo and they earned him his reputation for *terribilità*. But in Dürer they did not take the form of Michelangelo's single-minded and terrifying creative drive that found its expression in a world of naked bodies and naked rock. In Dürer there is a reconciliation of the cosmic diversity of the universe, of the landscape, which he introduced into German art as Leonardo had introduced it into Italian art. He took over the legacy of the northern Middle Ages, fostered in Germany and the Netherlands, and brought it to its peak. Thus everything in Dürer's work —a garment, a tuft of grass—becomes a world in itself, a microcosm filled with an inner greatness and measure. The macrocosm expressed in such complete creations as the *Adoration of the Trinity* is built up of an ordered gradation of such "worlds."

In his biography of the painter in his *Teutsche Academie*, Sandrart describes the wings painted by Mathis Gothardt-Neithardt for the *Heller Altarpiece* and goes on to speak of a *Transfiguration of Christ* by the same master that stood nearby in the same church, the Dominican Church at Frankfurt. The work itself has not survived, but some of the preparatory sketches for it have been preserved (Kupferstichkabinett, Dresden). They show the Apostles falling to the ground, shattered and blinded by the radiance of the supernatural event. These moving, highly expressive studies of the human figure and face give us some idea of the spiritual tension and powerful religious feeling bodied forth in the completed work. It was presumably executed shortly after the wings of the *Heller Altarpiece*.

Only a small number of Mathis' paintings have survived, but his total output was probably not very extensive. Nevertheless each work has an incomparable intensity and concentration. His art resides in the way he gives visual expression to spiritual processes —expression carried to the very limits of the painter's medium. In Mathis lived on something of the spirit of the great religious minds of the medieval past; he voiced the most extreme experiences of the mystics, visionaries, and ecstatics of earlier centuries who had gone to the limits of what was tolerable and possible within the institutional framework of the Church. His wrestling for expression almost burst through the bounds of form, with which he dealt freely and arbitrarily despite his great closeness to nature. His language of form has a sovereign disregard for those considerations of accuracy that preoccupied Dürer. Nevertheless, he treats form with delicacy and care, so as to preserve both the outer colour and breath of life, to show in its structure the inner network of nerves and fibres, the coursing of blood through the veins.

A series of marvellous sketches from living models that Mathis made as preliminary studies for his pictures has been preserved. They are all black chalk drawings, sometimes emphasized with Indian ink and heightenings in white, and are even more lifelike than Dürer's sketches. They not only show tremendous mastery of line and plastic form, as Dürer's do, but also a mastery of light such as no other painter has attained. In Mathis' hands light becomes a magic attribute like colour, and both seem compounded of the same spiritual substance. Neither can exist without the other.

Only two of Mathis' works bear autograph dates, and these form the basis for a chronology of his œuvre as a whole. They are the *Bindlach Altarpiece* (1503) and his magnum opus, the *Isenheim Altarpiece* (1515). It can be assumed that the supporting wings which he painted for the *Heller Altarpiece* were finished in 1509 at the latest. The *Mocking of Christ* and the *Maria Schnee Altarpiece* were dated on the frames. All other dates are conjectural, being based on historical clues and stylistic evidence. There was an interval between the Munich *Mocking of Christ* and the Frankfurt works. To the period before Mathis started work on the *Isenheim Altarpiece* may be assigned two *Crucifixions* (Basel and Washington) which seem to be a sort of prelude to that great masterpiece.

Mathis Gothardt-Neithardt (c. 1475-1528), called Matthias Grünewald.
The Crucifixion, c. 1510-1512. (29½×21⅜″) Kunstmuseum, Basel.

In the *Crucifixion* in the Basel Museum, the painter concentrates on a handful of figures—the Virgin Mary, John, Mary Magdalene, Salome, and the pious captain. Their profound emotion becomes a moving lamentation. Mathis was not at all concerned with that correct rendering of proportions aimed at by Dürer after his second Italian journey (there had been no sign of it yet in the *Apocalypse* woodcuts!). The kneeling figures of the two Marys are dwarflike. Their bodies are outlined in oddly soft, amorphous curves reminiscent of the works of Giotto's followers and the northern "soft style." "Correct" form meant nothing to Mathis; he sacrificed it readily in order to achieve the expressive effects he was aiming at. The figures seem adrift in infinite sorrow. That of John blazes forth in a mantle of rusty red with brilliant areas of lighter colour. Like the draperies in paintings of the fourteenth and early fifteenth centuries, it falls into folds—magnificently painted folds—that have nothing to do with the natural weight of the material. Mary, on the other hand, is a powerful figure muffled in a cloak that betrays nothing of the body beneath it, for this did not interest Mathis. All expression is centred in the face and hands. This, too, is a century-old formal tradition. The crucified Christ towers above the group, standing out pale against the darkening sky.

A more mature and even more expressive work is the *Small Crucifixion* (now in the National Gallery, Washington), which used to belong to the collection of the art-loving Elector William V of Bavaria. Here Mary and John are joined in their mourning only by Mary Magdalene. The form of the cross is different: the crosspiece is bent, drawn like a bow, so that the body is agonizingly stretched upwards instead of hanging down as it does in the Basel picture. This was a characteristic of the so-called mystic's crosses, made of rough untrimmed branches, that appear in fourteenth-century paintings of the Crucifixion. The face of the crucified Christ seems to contain a last flicker of life, but the body is already beginning to be suffused by the green of decay (the modelling of the flesh is reminiscent of the Sienese school of the fourteenth century). The body glows phosphorescently against the night sky with its darkened sun and twinkling stars, so that the pointed, Gothic-type outline is emphasized—but this is no longer Late Gothic, but that Trecento Gothic to which the master increasingly harked back. It was characteristic of the exciting new art of the Renaissance that it breathed fresh life into the forms of earlier centuries. Mary has the haggard features of the mourning women in Crucifixions of the later fourteenth century. The colour of her mantle is akin to that of the night sky. This enhances the brilliant colouring of the figure of John, which seems to form a single glowing flame. Mathis handled his changes and breaks in colour with incredible subtlety. Like Dürer, he anticipated the colouring of the Late Renaissance, but in a less dogmatic, more sensitive and intuitive—and accordingly more natural—fashion.

It might be thought that intensity of expression had here reached its limits, yet Mathis went even farther in his greatest masterpiece, the altarpiece for the Antonite Monastery of Isenheim in Alsace. The Antonites were Augustinian canons whose order went back to St Anthony, the hermit of the Thebaid. They were cultured and scholarly men who devoted themselves to the care of the sick and to surgery. Among the preceptors of the monastery, who were mostly Frenchmen or Italians, the principal figures at that time were Johannes de Orliac of Ferrara and Guido Guersi of Sicily. Orliac, who had already donated the old High Altar by Schongauer, presented the sculptured shrine for the new one. We know Guersi's magnificent head from a drawing by Mathis that shows him in old age. It is a strange historical phenomenon that two Italians should have been the donors of altarpieces that count among the classic achievements of German art, the second one being the most powerful German painting of the century of the Renaissance.

Work on the Isenheim altar seems to have started at an early date under Orliac, who resigned his post as precentor in 1490; it was he who commissioned the carvings of the altar shrine. This was a late work by Niclas Hagnower from Strasbourg, who died in 1506—which is why the structure and the figure sculptures of the shrine are still Late Gothic. Mathis thus had the task of furnishing an existing shrine—on which work had been stopped for almost a decade—with a series of paintings. His problem was how to fit his tremendously daring, advanced paintings into the fantastic glittering ensemble of the altar, giving his own, modern reinterpretation of Late Gothic. This was an incredibly difficult commission. It is doubtful whether someone like Dürer, who was accustomed to designing his own Renaissance altar-frames, would have accepted it. Yet this resplendent work conveys an impression of complete unity, despite its juxtaposition of two great ages of artistic and intellectual history.

Mary Magdalene's ointment jar in the *Crucifixion* bears the date 1515. As Mathis was occupied as master builder on the Aschaffenburg Residence in 1511, and in 1516 entered the service of Cardinal Albrecht von Brandenburg, the date must mark the end of the work.

The altarpiece is a folding polyptych with two pairs of wings which were opened or closed according to the requirements of the church year. In altarpieces of this type it is impossible to determine how the work proceeded, which parts were done first, and which later. The fact that the date of completion is inscribed on the outer panel suggests that this was the part on which Mathis worked last. On the other hand, the handling of the outer panel links up with that of the *Small Crucifixion*. We shall discuss the altarpiece in the order in which it appeared to the onlooker as it opened up like a mighty book.

The weekday side was visible most of the year when the altar was closed. The Crucifixion is in the centre, St Sebastian on the right supporting wing, and St Anthony on the left one. The Antonites were an order of hospitallers, and care of the sick their *raison d'être*. As patron saints, St Anthony offered protection against erysipelas, St Sebastian against the plague, and the two St Johns against epilepsy. These four saints are united on the weekday side under the outstretched arms of the crucified Christ as under mighty wings. Patients brought to the monastery hospital were first taken before this side of the altarpiece in the hope that they might be miraculously cured. When this did not happen, medical treatment began. This side thus played an important part in the medical practice of the hospitallers.

If the *Small Crucifixion* in Washington is like the cry of a solitary man suddenly confronted with a vision of the Passion, the impression created by the weekday side of the *Isenheim Altarpiece* is something greater and more universal, while remaining intensely subjective and unique of its kind. The picture is dominated by the body of the dead Saviour, grown to a terrifying height—as if it were still growing and would finally fill the whole world. Dürer's figures of Christ are in correct human proportion to the others; his Christ is the true Son of Man. Here there is none of Dürer's careful measurement and construction. This disproportionate Christ is deliberately intended to hit the onlooker like a blow in the face. John the Baptist, a solid figure firmly rooted to the ground, looks small beside him. Pointing to the Crucified, he is speaking the words from the Gospel of St John (iii. 30): "He must increase, but I must decrease." The gigantic body of Christ is hanging on a cross that has been put together from rough-hewn tree trunks. It is a heavy, almost peasant body, lacking the delicacy of the crucified Christ in earlier pictures. Despite the free and daring emphasis on expression, it clearly shows the painter's remarkable knowledge of anatomy—a knowledge he must have gained by the direct study of dead bodies. Here we have the Christ of a Renaissance artist, treated with all the expressiveness of the late Middle Ages. This expressiveness cannot be explained in terms of the habitual iconography of the Late Gothic. The key to it was found some forty years ago by a German Catholic scholar, Heinrich Feurstein, who identified the *Revelations* of St Bridget of Sweden as the source for Mathis' imagery.

The most popular books in Germany at the beginning of the sixteenth century were the *Apocalypse* and the *Revelations* of St Bridget, both of which were illustrated by Dürer in his period of *Sturm und Drang*. The book of the Swedish visionary, who died in 1373, had a wide circulation. Through it, the ardour and imagination of the late Middle Ages lived again in the troubled period round about 1500. St Bridget's *Revelationes de vita et passione Jesu Christi* was the poetic source from which Mathis drew inspiration for the *Isenheim Altarpiece*. It was not just suggested to him by his patrons—he must already have known the *Revelations* since echoes of the book can be found in some of his other works. Moreover, the cult of St Bridget was held in high esteem in his Franconian homeland. Reporting to the visionary saint on the death of her Son, the Virgin Mary says: "When death drew near and his heart was breaking with the excess of pain, his limbs trembled and his head sank down. His open mouth could be seen and the bleeding tongue. His arms and hands opened and spread out." No artist could have depicted these visions more starkly and shatteringly than Mathis.

The sign language of hands plays an important part in Mathis' work. Mary Magdalene's figure is like a great wave of lamentation beating against the crucified Christ. Most eloquent of all are her hands which are not folded devoutly in prayer but shaken in mindless, inconsolable anguish, as though refusing to accept the reality of the calamity. The painter deliberately portrays her as a dwarflike figure, so that the vastness of her grief can break forth all the more forcefully. Above her stands the group of Mary and John the Evangelist, in which the painter embodied Bridget's words: " . . . his sorrowing mother . . . was held up . . . as if dead." In the background is a primitive landscape, enshrouded in the gloom of night, belonging to a world that has been alienated by the death of Christ. A closer scrutiny of the outer panels of the altarpiece reveals the emphasis given to the *drawn line* as employed by Dürer and the whole Franconian school of painting. The forms have dark contours drawn with the brush. In every respect the technique is linked with that of the Nuremberg school.

The figure of the crucified Christ, stretching right to the upper edge of the painting, is modelled with such tremendous vigour that it seems almost like a sculpture standing out from the rest of the picture. To look into his face, Mary Magdalene has to bend away from the picture rather than into it. This harks back to the older tradition of altar painting that we already noted in the *Heller Altarpiece*—the treatment of the pictures on the weekday side as painted sculptures executed in grisaille. The figure of Christ dominates the painting, in which the overall effect of grey tinged with blue or green is relieved only by the burning red of the subsidiary figures. There is nothing comparable in German sculpture or painting during this period, though a similar intensity of feeling is found in certain fourteenth century sculptures which Mathis must have known.

The figures of St Anthony and St Sebastian on the supporting wings, on either side of the *Crucifixion*, are placed on pedestals like sculptures. While the four saints painted in grisaille on the *Heller Altarpiece* were brought to life by the wonderful effects of light and shade, here real colour fulfils the same function. Each saint stands on a stone pedestal which is constructed like the polygonal pulpit-supports favoured by the old craftsmen. The Gothic decorative motif of foliage is present, not in the grey of carved stone, but in the fresh green of wild vines and hops twining round the base of the pedestals. The towering figures are emphasized by a Renaissance pillar (behind Anthony) and column (behind Sebastian). St Anthony, as the patron saint of the Order to which the altar was dedicated, is depicted as a head taller than St Sebastian; here the influence of Hagnower's sculptures on the shrine is apparent. Sebastian, with his bare torso, is a splendid figure, painted from life, virile and mature, modelled in the warm sunlight that streams in through the open window. This is a figure that Dürer might well have admired. It has been thought, not without reason, that it is a self-portrait of the painter. Sebastian's scarlet mantle, with its billowing spiral folds, is a particularly sumptuous piece of painting and balances the carmine-violet garment worn by Anthony. Unlike Dürer's colours, which are solid and light-reflecting, those of Mathis are translucent and seem to be woven of tinted light. Both these panels are endowed with a certain restraint by the use of the grey tones considered appropriate for the weekday side.

The predella depicts the *Lamentation of Christ*. One half of the picture is occupied by the dead body, the other by the open tomb. The dark outlines of the hills serve to emphasize the shape of the predella panels. Not only the landscape but the whole scene produces a desolate, washed-out effect, as if overswept by a tidal wave or deluge. Here we have none of the formal density, the inner fire of the *Crucifixion*—the picture expresses complete exhaustion, utter emptiness.

When the outer pair of wings was opened and folded back, the onlooker was confronted with a feast of colour unrivalled in sixteenth-century painting. The Glorification of the Virgin Mary is the main subject, and it displays all the painter's skill in the treatment of light and colour. The whole of this side of the altar is a great hymn of praise to the Virgin, ranging from the Annunciation through the Glorification to the joyful day of Christ's resurrection. Here again the influence of St Bridget's writings is apparent.

The advent of the angel in the *Annunciation* panel is portrayed as a moment of fear, of physical shock, for the Virgin, who seems to recoil and turn away. No other painter, apart from Rembrandt, conceived the scene in this way. The sudden appearance of the magnificent towering figure of the angel alarms the Virgin so much that she averts her face, half closing her eyes, while her hands—which were folded in prayer—fall apart. She is depicted as a child-like figure with something of the peasant-girl about her, and her face has a naive visionary quality. Shock and shame have driven the blood into her cheeks, bringing a glow to her face, which is framed in flowing ash-blond hair. The angel's clothes are billowing as if he were just alighting from the air. The Late Gothic chapel which forms the setting has been greatly admired as a masterpiece of colour composition. It is closed at the back by a small, bright choir in which the halo of the Holy Ghost shimmers like a sunbeam.

The central panel consists of a composition in two parts, divided by the joint of the inner wings which is masked by a greenish-black curtain. On the left is a fantastic chapel-like structure containing music-making angels, while on the right the figure of the Virgin Mary, oblivious to all the rejoicing, is absorbed in the joys of motherhood. Here again there is a literary source in a work by St Bridget, the *Sermo angelicus de excellentia Beatae Mariae Virginis*, which, she claimed, had been dictated to her by an angel to provide her with subjects for prayer and meditation for each day of the week.

The rejoicing and worship of the angels on the left side are focused on the visionary figure of a woman in the front opening of the chapel. The Sunday lesson was based on the "idea" of the holy Virgin as part of the pre-ordained plan of creation, and the Monday lesson on the rejoicing of the angels over this plan of creation; it is their jubilation which is conveyed in the glowing aura of this visionary figure. Mathis could not have expressed an "idea" in terms of painting more vividly than in this radiant apparition kneeling in the portal of the chapel. The figure has no clearly defined zones of colour, but each hue flows into the other as in the free play of the elements; above the deep green and greenish-blue of her robe there is a glow of violet, turning to fiery red, light yellow, and radiant white with a purple core. "Like a blazing flame she immediately began to burn with love of God," St Bridget wrote. The chapel is an open building with a portal—a symbol of the Mother of God, according to the word of the Prophets. No real model existed for this architecture—it is a dream structure in gold and brightly glowing colour, and each of its parts has a secret life like that of plants left to grow wild. The sculptures adorning it—figures of the Prophets—are gesticulating and talking. The music of the adoring angels, led by a large angel with a bass viola, is echoed by the rich harmony of colour. The angel with a tenor viola is covered with bird feathers, and flowers are sprouting from his head. This is an expressive, visionary world that does not stop at the strange and surrealist. Supernatural beings glowing with all the colours of the rainbow shine from the dark depths of the building.

Mathis Gothardt-Neithardt (c. 1475-1528), called Matthias Grünewald. The Annunciation, 1515. (105⅞×55⅞")
Left Wing of the Second Stage of the Isenheim Altarpiece. Musée d'Unterlinden, Colmar.

Out of the iridescent dream world of the left side of this panel we step into the broad daylight of the right, where Mary sits with the Babe in a radiant landscape. This is the old theme of the Virgin seated on a grassy bank, with which we are familiar from Schongauer and the Housebook Master. There is no Biblical source for this symbolic conception, which is based on mystical writings; Dürer used the same theme in his *Virgin with Many Animals*. What is new here is the way in which Mary has taken all the nursery furniture into the open air with her on this fine day. Genre-type details of this kind are found in the interiors depicted in prints such as those of the E S Master, but their use here in a solemn altarpiece intended for religious worship is something entirely new. This is in fact a modern touch. Its purpose is to humanize the Saviour, to suggest the wants and needs that attach to existence in this world. We shall see that other painters with similar extremist views even emphasized the proletarian poverty of Christ's earthly existence. But here the poverty is transmuted into wealth by the unrivalled splendour of the colour.

The Sunday side of the altarpiece is dominated by the figure of the Virgin Mary, which is accordingly enlarged out of all proportion, like the crucified Christ on the weekday side. The triangle formed by Mary and the Child shows that Mathis knew the principles of composition of the classical High Renaissance. The intimacy of their spiritual relationship is, however, specifically German. The carmine of Mary's dress floats and ripples in the light like smoke or water. The landscape behind her is one of the most splendid in old German painting. The steep blue walls of the high mountains shimmer in crystalline translucency. An ultramarine bank of cloud settles over the mountains as though breaking in a shower on their slopes. We are instinctively reminded of Leonardo's drawing of a thunderstorm over the Alps. The cloud is dark below, violet above, and merges with a sea of transparent yellow and red light in the midst of which are angels bearing religious banners, crosses, and canopies. On the peak stands the visionary figure of God the Father.

The right wing shows the *Resurrection*. The figure of Christ, soaring upwards, is pure spirit, a rainbow-coloured flame. Nothing could better express his incorporeal state than the gesture with which he points to the stigmata. Here the colours have an intense inner radiance. Objects continually change colour in the upsurge of the elements. The linen of the whitish-blue shroud streams upwards out of the coffin, takes on a violet glow, flames into red on Christ's body, and ends in a yellow radiance. Christ's body is moulded in pure light.

On feast days, when the inner pair of wings was opened, Hagnower's powerful sculptures could be seen. When St Anthony founded his monastery in the desert of the Thebaid, he yielded to vain pride and was rebuked for this by an angel. He thereupon went for instruction to St Paul the Hermit. After St Paul's death, he buried him and retired to his hut where he was tormented and tempted by devils. This legend is depicted on the inner wings.

The *Legenda Aurea* describes how St Anthony was held in the air by the angels of the Lord, and how the demons saw this as an opportunity to attack. Schongauer made this story the subject of a famous copperplate engraving and Cranach of a woodcut in which the scene of horror is set above a peaceful landscape. Mathis transferred it to a wilderness in a rocky hollow of the mountains, where the prostrate saint is exposed to the torments of the devil, far from all human help. The figures form a horrifying tangle in which the strongest colour contrasts are used to distinguish the chief actors in the drama. Anthony is shown as a very old man whose dignity is being mercilessly assaulted by the demons. These are frightful hybrid creatures, some of them covered with revolting boils like the lepers and syphilitic patients admitted to the hospital of the Isenheim monastery. Mathis must somehow have been acquainted with Bosch's demons. His imaginary creatures have one thing in common with those depicted by Leonardo and Bosch—they are completely viable and biologically possible, though based on premises that are perversions of nature.

Mathis Gothardt-Neithardt (c. 1475-1528), called Matthias Grü
(104⅜×119⅝″) Central Panel of the Second Stage of the

ewald. Virgin and Child with Concert of Angels, 1515.
enheim Altarpiece. Musée d'Unterlinden, Colmar.

Mathis Gothardt-Neithardt (c. 1475-1528), called Matthias Grünewald. The Resurrection of Christ, 1515. (105⅞×56¼″) Right Wing of the Second Stage of the Isenheim Altarpiece. Musée d'Unterlinden, Colmar.

The left wing depicts the meeting of the saintly hermits Paul and Anthony. Their edifying conversation is interrupted by the raven bringing them bread for their nourishment. H. A. Schmid wrote about this painting: "It is the loveliest celebration of the peace that dwells in secluded mountain valleys to be produced by a period that was decisive for landscape painting." The subject provided the pretext for the landscape. In a woodcut that Mathis must have known, Dürer placed the two saints on the edge of an Alpine forest. Mathis depicts Paul's retreat as a high Alpine valley with a bubbling spring and the palm-tree that provided the hermit with food and drink. It is a wild solitary tract of country in which the palm-tree grows side by side with the trees of the German forests. The farther back it recedes in space, the more delicately and thinly is the colour laid on, until the steep pinnacles of the Dolomites finally seem to melt in the yellowish-pink light of evening. St Anthony is wearing the habit of his order and his features are those of the donor, whose coat-of-arms lies against a rock at his feet. Paul's haggard limbs are wrapped in a garment of palm-leaves. The doe, the saint's guide, is portrayed with the same realism as the still life of flowers, which consists of plants similar to those in Dürer's *Great Piece of Turf*. Each work presents us with a microcosm full of enchanting life. In the period that followed Leonardo's penetrating pioneer work in this domain, such intimate observation of nature was found only in German art. Notwithstanding a certain similarity of basic ideas in Dürer and Mathis, they differ enormously in interpretation, in their artistic view of the world. Dürer pursued the detail with incisive energy, Mathis the rhythm of the whole—Dürer the line, Mathis the flow of colour and the vibration of light. In the paintings of Mathis the elemental forces of nature are made visible, just as they are both in the older works of the Danube School and in those of Mathis' own time. He could scarcely have been ignorant of the achievements of this school of landscape painting. But other features, such as the rendering of the high-lights on the trees, are reminiscent of the early works of Baldung. Much of this must be attributed to the fact that certain ideas and problems were in the air and occurred quite independently to artists working in different places. The *Isenheim Altarpiece* had great and far-reaching effects on the art of its time. Its influence was apparent in the work of all the artists of the Upper Rhine, and as far away as Swabia, Switzerland, Bavaria and the Danube countries. This altarpiece must have acted like a beacon for the artists of the period.

After completing the *Heller Altarpiece* and the *Adoration of the Trinity*, Dürer relinquished his place among the great altar-painters, contenting himself with sketching the outlines for altarpieces to be completed by his pupils. He no longer took the trouble to execute them himself, but devoted all his time to smaller pictures. His whole creative energy was channelled into graphic work, as if the complaint he had made in his letter to Heller had now become true. To these years belong the two sets of the *Little Passion* (one on wood, one on copper) and the major engravings. From 1512 on, he was increasingly tied by his commissions from the Emperor Maximilian. His small-scale paintings were modelled and chiselled like gems. In the Vienna *Virgin and Child* of 1512, the chief artistic problem was that of the disposition of the two figures. The Virgin is holding the Child in a horizontal position, and there is not the usual close contact between them. It looks as if the child were lying down rather than resting in his mother's arms. *Putti* in similar positions are found in Verrocchio and Leonardo. Dürer's treatment of the Child demonstrates his mastery of the nude. The highly enamelled finish gives the picture an artificial quality that is new in Dürer and anticipates Mannerism. A second, similarly "artificial" Virgin is the *Virgin with the Carnation* (1516, Alte Pinakothek, Munich), a work intended for a private collection and painted on vellum. The faces of both Mother and Child are empty and cold, with an icon-like stiffness. Ludwig Justi has pointed out that the face of the Virgin is constructed geometrically. Did Dürer have the idea that divine perfection was to be achieved by following mathematical rules? Was he searching for something that had impressed him in the Virgins of the thirteenth century? Few artists had anticipated Mannerism as Dürer did in these two pictures. The *Virgin and Child* of 1516 in the Metropolitan Museum places more emphasis on simple humanity.

Mathis Gothardt-Neithardt (c. 1475-1528), called Matthias Grünewald. The Meeting of St Anthony and St Paul the Hermit, 1515. (104⅜×55½″) Left Wing of the Third Stage of the Isenheim Altarpiece. Musée d'Unterlinden, Colmar.

Mathis Gothardt-Neithardt (c. 1475-1528). The Temptation of St Anthony, 1515. (104⅜×54¾″)
Right Wing of the Third Stage of the Isenheim Altarpiece. Musée d'Unterlinden, Colmar.

The other occasional paintings executed by Dürer in the same year are the two *Heads of Apostles* in the Uffizi. Here the interest is no longer focused on the strongly marked type as it was in *Christ among the Doctors* of 1506, but on character, on the morally oriented human being. These Apostles are simple, plain men made spiritually great by faith. By far the most interesting work painted by Dürer in this period is his *Portrait of Michael Wolgemut* (1516, Germanisches Nationalmuseum, Nuremberg). It depicts his teacher—the author of so many Late Gothic altarpieces and head of a large workshop—in his eighty-second year. Time has passed over him. His haggard, bony face, like a fossil that has survived into the new century, has a Late Gothic harshness, but still glows with intellectual energy. The portrait is a token of the reverence in which his old pupil still held him.

While Dürer was beginning to devote himself increasingly to meticulous graphic work, his pupils were turning to the tempting and lucrative field of altar-painting that he had forsaken. There were plenty of commissions to be had, since the painted shuttered altarpiece had come back into fashion. Churches and donors were on the look-out for good artists for their many commissions. There was a growing taste for more elaborate and more brightly coloured decoration in churches. The new age and the new style permitted gayer and more exuberant outpourings of colour, and a deeper appreciation of nature and the things of this world, than had been possible in Late Gothic which, notwithstanding its wealth of form, was wedded to the medieval eschatology. The leading personalities among Dürer's followers—of whom mention has already been made—increasingly developed their artistic individuality, and new disciples emerged.

Wolf Traut, who was born in 1486, painted the *Artelshofen Altarpiece* for the Drapers' Chapel of the church of St Lawrence in Nuremberg (Bayerisches Nationalmuseum, Munich); this is a lively work in which the Holy Family forms a joyous bouquet of colour, set in a friendly landscape against a pale sky and not against the usual background of gold. The influence not only of Dürer but also of the Master of Frankfurt is present in this work, whose author must have seen Dürer's *Heller Altarpiece* in the Dominican Church at Frankfurt. Traut's Heilsbronn *Altarpiece of St John* with the *Baptism of Christ* (1516-1518, Germanisches Nationalmuseum, Nuremberg) is so like Dürer in style that when it was presented to Rudolf II, he accepted it as a presumed work by the master.

One of the most interesting Franconian members of the Dürer school was the Master of the Ansbach Winepress Painting. This was a memorial picture for Prior Mathias von Gulpen of the church of St Gumbert at Ansbach, and Dürer prepared a rough sketch for it. The subject is drawn from an old mystical fantasy which had already been depicted in broadsheets: Christ as the grape in the winepress, his blood being squeezed out for the redemption of mankind. Because of its wealth of glittering detail, it was once attributed to Baldung.

The fame of the sensitive colourist Hans von Kulmbach as a painter of altarpieces extended beyond Nuremberg and led to several commissions from Cracow. In 1511 he completed an *Altarpiece of the Virgin Mary* for the church of the Monastery of St Paul in the Skalka district of Cracow; its central panel, the *Adoration of the Magi*, is now in the Berlin Museum. The setting is an elaborately conceived ruin in which sumptuously apparelled courtiers ceremoniously approach the Mother of God. The elongated figures with their uncertain gliding gestures and the light, soft, harmonious colours are typical of this lyrical artist.

In the same year, 1511, Kulmbach was commissioned by the Tucher family to paint a panel in memory of Prior Lorenz Tucher. Dürer himself drew the preliminary sketch for this painting, which was installed in the church of St Sebald in Nuremberg. It was divided into three fixed sections, so that it was midway between a *pala* and a shuttered altarpiece. Kulmbach's completed work (1513) goes significantly beyond Dürer's preliminary design.

Hans Suess von Kulmbach (c. 1480-1522). The Altarpiece of St Catherine: St Catherine converted by a Picture of the Virgin and Child shown her by a Hermit, 1514-1515. (47¼×25⅛″) Church of St Mary, Cracow.

Hans Baldung Grien (1484/1485-1545).

The Three Ages of Woman and Death, c. 1510. (18⅞×12¾″) Kunsthistorisches Museum, Vienna.

The airy Renaissance spaciousness of the scene is further emphasized. The Virgin is enthroned in the centre in a southern-type aedicule between St Barbara and St Catherine, and the side sections show St Peter and St Lawrence with the Prior, John the Baptist, and St Jerome in a panoramic landscape. There is no trace of the Late Gothic in this great and spacious work.

The peaks of Kulmbach's achievement were the *Altarpiece of St Catherine* (1514-1515) and the *Altarpiece of St John* (1516), both for the family chapel of Mayor Jan Boner in the church of St Mary at Cracow, where the artist undoubtedly stayed for a time in order to paint them. The conversion of St Catherine by means of a picture of the Virgin and Child shown her by a hermit in the forest is depicted in a landscape full of deep poetry and magical colour. The saint's dress of muted strawberry red stands out against the moss-greens and browns of the thicket. Altdorfer's influence is unmistakable in the merging tones employed for the forest gloom and for the horseman engulfed in it. The predella of the *Altarpiece of St John* shows the saint going down to the tomb after his last Mass. The setting—the dusk-like semi-darkness of a cathedral—is a wonderful example of the suggestion of space by means of light.

Shortly before these two altarpieces, Kulmbach executed the dramatic *Altarpiece of Peter and Paul* (Uffizi, Florence). It was probably also intended for Cracow, and is linked with the Danube School through its landscape setting and *mise en scène*. The change to deep-toned effects of light and colour in Kulmbach's later Cracow works suggests that he passed through Austria on his way to Poland.

The anonymous master who painted the fine *St Quirinus*—a pensive figure in armour with a flag—in the Germanisches Nationalmuseum in Nuremberg has been erroneously identified with Hans von Kulmbach. The hand of this master can be recognized in a large altar-wing (Busch-Reisinger Museum, Harvard University) depicting St George, St Michael, and John the Baptist.

As a result of Schäufelein's move to Nördlingen, Dürer's style spread to Swabia. The art of the Master of Messkirch (so called because of his high altar for the town church at Messkirch), who worked in the region of Lake Constance, continued Schäufelein's style, but with a tendency to baroque decoration indicating contacts with the Augsburg and Danube schools.

Meanwhile Hans Baldung, the greatest and most daring of Dürer's pupils, went on to new heights of achievement. On reaching maturity, this fiery spirit forged ahead and produced one masterpiece after another. The altarpieces for Freiburg Cathedral marked the peak of his work, but the same artistic and intellectual tension is to be found in his secular paintings, whose poetic or allegorical subjects were designed to appeal to the aesthetic interests of a new class of society educated in the humanistic spirit.

Since Dürer's *Promenade*, allegories of the beauty and transience of existence had become a favourite subject with the German Renaissance masters. Baldung took it up with youthful verve and turned it into a celebration of the beauty of the female nude imbued with an almost pagan spirit—even though the sense of a dark and threatening fate that pervaded this age of universal agitation and deep social and intellectual upheaval was ever present. "It is a joy to be alive!" wrote Ulrich von Hutten, and yet death was constantly in the thoughts of this short-lived generation which burnt itself out so quickly. *The Three Ages of Woman and Death* (c. 1510, Kunsthistorisches Museum, Vienna) shows death in the shape of a half-decayed corpse carrying an hourglass and advancing on a fresh young girl who is combing her golden hair. In vain an old crone tries to dissuade him—but the victim's hour has struck. The old notion of *Vanitas* is here combined with nature symbolism by means of the magical forest setting with its message of growth and decay. Notwithstanding its grim subject, the painting radiates optimism. Things may pass away, but nature renews itself in ever-fresh beauty of form and colour. Here the pantheistic view of life prevails.

One of Baldung's favourite themes—treated more frequently in his drawings and wood-cuts than in his paintings—was that of witchcraft. Like religious hysteria, this form of psycho-logical disorder was considerably on the increase in the sixteenth century, being fostered by war and social unrest as well as the growing pantheistic feeling for nature. With the discovery of the enchantment of wood and mountain, there was a revival of interest in the spirits and gods of pagan times. The superstitions of the common people became the poetic fables of the educated. The German painter could now join with the Italians in portraying not only sensuous young women, but old hags based on Mantegna's shrivelled spectral creatures. In Baldung's portrayals of witches there is often an erotic element. This is a characteristic feature of secular German art up to the bathroom scenes of the Late Renaissance—the expression of a wild and boundless lust for life.

Baldung's religious pictures have something of the exuberance and forcefulness of his secular ones. In *The Dead Christ held by God the Father, the Virgin Mary, and St John* (1512, National Gallery, London), the figure of Christ is a powerful painting from an actual model, full of manly beauty even in death and quite different from Mathis Gothardt-Neithardt's flayed and broken image of grief and horror. Baldung's rather worldly tone and *éclat* is as far removed from Dürer's brooding, melancholy ethos as it is from the mystical rapture of Mathis. Even such tragic pictures as the *Lamentation of Christ* (Ferdinandeum, Innsbruck; prelimin-ary sketch dated 1513 in Basel) are filled with rich painterly effects and a sense of the presence of nature. As in Cranach's Munich *Crucifixion* of 1503, the strongly sectional composition brings the scene closer to the onlooker and enhances the sense of drama. The deep blue Alpine land-scape is enclosed on the horizon by the snow-covered Swiss mountains.

In 1512 Baldung moved his studio to the Black Forest town of Freiburg-im-Breisgau in order to paint the high altarpiece for the Cathedral. His brother was a professor at the Uni-versity there and, as hitherto in Strasbourg, the painter moved mainly in intellectual circles. Through the study of living models, he became increasingly familiar with the form and struc-ture of the human body. Work on the altarpiece continued until 1516. During this time he produced numerous small paintings as well as designing some magnificent stained-glass win-dows for the Cathedral and the Freiburg Charterhouse. For the chapel of Ritter Johannes Schnewlin in the choir of the Cathedral, Baldung added two wings, with the *Baptism in the Jordan* and *St John on Patmos*, to a splendid little altarpiece with a central shrine carved some years before by Hans Wydyz. These two paintings show a strong feeling for nature and landscape that in this case owes nothing to the Danube School but is closely linked with Switzerland. The cool greys with which Baldung sets off the glow of the other colours are exquisite—he was fond of these tones for clouds. The young Evangelist is shown sitting under a fine old willow tree and gazing raptly at the miraculous apparition of the Virgin.

Whereas the *Schnewlin Altarpiece* is intimate and poetic, the main altarpiece in Freiburg Cathedral is full of majesty and power. In this great mobile polyptych, with its two pairs of wings, Baldung's art attained its zenith. The central panel is taken up with a *Coronation of the Virgin*. The chief figures are impressively portrayed, with imposing draperies and free, daring gestures. The deep glowing blue and gold of the Virgin's mantle are set off by the sonor-ous reds of the robes worn by Christ and God the Father. The way in which these two figures—the triumphant youth representing Christ and the dignified old man representing God the Father—reach forward to bestow the crown on the Virgin is extremely touching. Dürer strove for depth and spatial recession, but Baldung condensed plastic relief into flat surface patterns. We might almost speak of a *horror vacui*; the intermediate spaces are filled with dense clusters and ribbons of grey or blue cloud, whose coolness acts as a foil to the fiery centre. Above and between them are whirls of angels—both naked and clothed—with musical instruments; these are continued in the wood carvings on the frame. Here again we can see Baldung's tendency to depict nudes in light tones that shine out against a dark background.

Hans Baldung Grien (1484/1485-1545). The Coronation of the Virgin, finished in 1516.
(110¼×94¼″) Central Panel of the Main Altarpiece in the Cathedral of Freiburg-im-Breisgau.

The colour contrasts on the wings are dramatic. Clad in white garments, the Apostles with their burning sulphur-yellow haloes are set against the dark blue-black of a thundery sky. They are strong characters, not types but individual personalities standing up for their faith with almost knightly determination. The altar flares like summer lightning from the solemn centre to the dramatic wings, reminding us of Mathis' great altarpiece for nearby Isenheim. The influence of the latter can be seen in Baldung's bold and expressive treatment both of the wings and the dramatic *Crucifixion* on the reverse. Mathis pioneered in the representation of light, and Baldung went a step further. When the inner shrine of the altarpiece is closed, the four panels of the *Life of the Virgin* appear on the Sunday side. In the *Nativity*, the Christ Child is transformed into a miracle of light radiating to the Virgin and the attendant angels.

From Baldung's Freiburg period dates the portrait of *Margrave Christoph I of Baden* (1515, Alte Pinakothek, Munich). The splendid head of the Margrave with its hoary sailor's beard reminds us of the Apostles in the Freiburg altarpiece. At the time of the portrait, the Margrave was already a tired old man, broken by illness, who had ceased to govern and had divided his lands between his three sons. His weary resignation is eloquently expressed in this marvellous character study. All the freshness of youth, on the other hand, is to be found in the portrait of the fourteen-year-old *Count Palatine Philip the Bellicose* (1517, Alte Pinakothek, Munich) who was then studying at Freiburg University. Baldung's portraits are splendid character studies, depicting aristocratic and intellectual self-consciousness in masterly fashion. They are among the most profound human documents of the German Renaissance.

In 1517 Baldung returned to Strasbourg. With growing maturity, the radiance, sumptuousness and optimism that characterized the period of the great altarpieces disappeared from his work. The gloomy, tragic mood of the later Renaissance gained the upper hand and he lost his earlier warmth. The decorative glitter and exuberance of the Vienna *Vanitas* gave way to the solemnity of the Basel *Death and the Maiden*. The terrible lover uncovers the soft ripe body which no longer offers any resistance but is peeled out of the cloth like the pale centre of a plant. The girl is aware of the kiss of Death and her impending end, and tears are running down her cheeks. The colour range of this thoughtful work is muted and gloomy.

In Augsburg Hans Holbein the Elder, a product of the Late Gothic world, could no longer evade the demands of the new age. To his inner change of style an external one was added at the beginning of the second decade of the century: the adoption of the architectural and decorative forms of the Renaissance. In 1512 he executed for the Convent of St Catherine—which already possessed a number of his works—an altarpiece dedicated to its patron saint (Staatliche Gemäldegalerie, Augsburg). Here the Gothic framework has been replaced by exuberant Renaissance grotesques. The figures are heavy, even ponderous, as compared with those in his earlier works. The absence of the old ease and inventiveness, and a certain joylessness that seems to pervade these pictures, might be regarded as a deterioration in quality. But this was not the case with Holbein. It can be explained by the fact that this was not his natural idiom but rather a way of working through to the new manner of the Renaissance—an unavoidable necessity for an artist making his living in Augsburg.

In Holbein's last works the ice has been broken completely and the artist is wholly at home in the new manner, while retaining all the old elegance, mastery, and self-possession. In 1516 he executed the *Altarpiece of St Sebastian* (Alte Pinakothek, Munich), again for the Convent of St Catherine in Augsburg. The outside of the wings depicts the *Annunciation* in monochrome tones. The architectural features are in the purest Augsburg Renaissance style. The scene of the action is revealed through two openings in an arcade and is closed off at the back by Tuscan columns. The forms derive from the early Lombard Renaissance rather than the Late Renaissance. They are slender, delicate, and in perfect harmony with the figures. The dress worn by the majestic Virgin has a long train that spreads across both wings.

Hans Baldung Grien (1484/1485-1545).
Portrait of the Margrave Christoph I of Baden, 1515. (18½×14⅛″) Alte Pinakothek, Munich.

The inner side of this altarpiece has a *Martyrdom of St Sebastian* in the centre. The subject was a favourite one with early German painters, who liked to show their skill in painting nude figures from life and reproducing the strenuous gestures involved in drawing and shooting the crossbow. In this respect Holbein was equal to all the difficulties, but this was not his main concern. While Dürer and his pupils were chiefly interested in dynamic emphasis, Holbein was more preoccupied with achieving a noble equilibrium, a harmonious balance of the whole. The figure of Sebastian demonstrates his concern for beauty of line.

Artistically the finest parts of the altarpiece are the inner sides of the wings, which depict *St Barbara* and *St Elizabeth*. Each of the saints stands in a setting of classical Lombard architecture; the horizontal entablatures are decorated with friezes of sphinxes and grotesques derived from the ornamental engravings of Northern Italy. The figures have a fine nobility of demeanour and great purity of form, enhanced by a disciplined use of colour. Here we have the essence of the German Renaissance—the northern feeling for atmosphere combined with the tranquil nobility of the South.

Sigmund Holbein (active 1501-1540). The Entry of the Virgin into the Temple, c. 1515.
(65½×40¾″) Alte Pinakothek, Munich (on loan from the Georg Schäfer Collection, Schweinfurt).

The greatness of Hans Holbein the Elder is strikingly demonstrated by the fact that so many of his son's achievements are already to be found in embryo in his work. The classical German manner of his son's first mature period in Basel is foreshadowed here, in the Munich *Altarpiece of St Sebastian*. Because of this, it has been wrongly assumed by some scholars that Holbein the Younger co-operated in this work, which is in fact entirely by his father's hand. The face looking up devoutly at St Elizabeth from behind the lepers, on one of the wings, is that of the artist himself.

Despite the high quality of his achievements, Holbein the Elder no longer seems to have been the leading master in Augsburg as he was at the turn of the century, but rather a figure from the past. Perhaps he found it difficult to hold his own in competition with young artists like Burgkmair who had fully mastered the Renaissance style. In any case, he moved to Isenheim in 1516. His last surviving work is the *Fountain of Life* (1519, National Museum, Lisbon). This was an old theme in Netherlandish painting, and is here combined with a representation of the *Virgo inter Virgines* and the Holy Kinship (in this case, the Virgin Mary's parents). The figures are set in a rich Renaissance hall derived from a relief by Hans Daucher. This is a showpiece in itself, containing a host of music-making angels arranged in three separate choirs. The large palm-tree beside it may be derived from the *Isenheim Altarpiece*, in the shadow of which the master spent his last years. In the background are curious ruins reminiscent of the first Roman features introduced into Netherlandish painting (by Jan Gossaert). The assembly of holy women also suggests the influence of the Netherlands. The symmetry of the composition befits the ceremonial style, but it is relieved in the most pleasant way by the wealth of precious fabrics and jewels, flowers and animals. It is extraordinary for a German painting of the time to show such a command of the whole range of European art from Italy to the Netherlands. This particular painting, however, was produced in isolation and was in effect the personal affirmation of a great ageing master who died in obscurity five years later.

Sigmund, the younger brother of Hans Holbein the Elder and his collaborator on the altarpiece for the Dominican church in Frankfurt, had shown himself to be a crude follower of his brother's in his early paintings of martyred Apostles. In his later years Sigmund Holbein moved to Berne. That he unreservedly accepted the new art, as represented by Burgkmair and Breu in particular, is shown by the wing of an Altarpiece of the Virgin attributed to him by Ernst Buchner. In the *Entry of the Virgin into the Temple*, we see a church vestibule in Lombard Renaissance style with a stream of worshippers going up flights of steps to the service. The young Virgin Mary has broken away from the hand of her mother Anne—who lingers behind in astonishment—and is running towards the high priest. The interruption of the calm progress of the worshippers by this incident is presented in a most human and lifelike way. The *Presentation in the Temple*, with its rich contrast of light and shade in the Renaissance pillars, is reminiscent of Jörg Breu's panel on the breastwork of the organ in the church of St Anne at Augsburg. The slender figures with their elongated faces might have stepped out of a painting by Burgkmair.

Another artist who outgrew the Late Gothic tradition and was in his early work a follower of the elder Holbein's was Martin Schaffner of Ulm, born about 1477 or 1478. His numerous altarpieces reveal him as a pleasant rather than a powerful or independent artist, and show that he was receptive to the most diverse influences. But throughout his long life Schaffner followed the general line of development of the Augsburg school and thus in a mature work—the second altarpiece for the Augustinian Monastery of Wettenhausen (1523-1524, Alte Pinakothek, Munich)—he unreservedly accepts the rich Renaissance style that had set its mark on both life and art in Augsburg. The bright and colourful temple hall in which the Christ Child is being presented to the high priest, is resplendent with marble columns and decorated pilasters.

In the meantime Holbein's brother-in-law, Hans Burgkmair the Elder, had become the leading figure among the Augsburg painters of the new era. He managed the transition from the old Late Gothic manner to the new idiom with supreme ease and elegance, maintaining the highest standards of form and colour and developing an aristocratic manner that did not exclude emotion or pantheistic feeling. The new experience of nature and landscape had a place in his works, which in the second decade of the sixteenth century well illustrate the rich, pulsating ferment of this tremendous period of German painting. They were as receptive to the decorative beauty of colour as to the sap and power of life, of which men were just beginning to be fully aware.

As an artist Burgkmair was instinctively drawn towards the rich and sumptuous. He was the ideal person for official commissions, and became the principal wood-engraver and book-illustrator in the service of the Emperor Maximilian. His woodcuts occupied him for most of the decade, but towards 1520 he began to make up, with all the vigour of his genius, for the time he had taken off from altar-painting. The altarpieces of *St John* and of the *Crucifixion* (both in the Alte Pinakothek, Munich) are the greatest achievements of Augsburg painting during the decade.

In the *Altarpiece of St John*, dated 1518, Burgkmair radically revised the old Late Gothic lay-out of the shuttered altarpiece by extending the landscape of the central panel through to the wings on either side. St John is shown on Patmos in a tropical setting with palms and dragon-trees; as the citizen of a prosperous trading city with overseas connections, such as Augsburg then was, the painter was familiar with such exotic vegetation. As the glowing vision of the Virgin appears in the sky, the trees are shaken by a mighty wind, which breaks off a palm-branch, carrying it over to the right-hand wing. Looking up from his writing, the saint turns his rapt face towards the apparition. His posture corresponds exactly to that of the figure in a retouched drawing by Mathis (University Library, Erlangen), which was identified from a later inscription as a self-portrait but was actually a portrayal of the Evangelist. The faithful rendering of the exotic plants also shows a link with Mathis. The vegetation, in which these plants are combined with the brushwood of a German forest, has a richness equalled only in Altdorfer's work. The enchanting natural setting is enlivened by brightly coloured birds and reptiles. It is as though Burgkmair was striving to catch up with those distinctive features of the Danube School that Dürer had long since foreshadowed in his *Virgin with Many Animals*. The atmosphere is pervaded by a thundery light that recalls the dramatic pathos and emotional tension of the *Isenheim Altarpiece*. Burgkmair far surpassed all his contemporaries in the unification of atmosphere and landscape on the grand scale. A single breath informs the three parts of the *Altarpiece of St John*, drawing men and nature into a unity that is as strong on the visual as on the spiritual level.

The same visual and spiritual intensity is to be found in the *Altarpiece of the Crucifixion* (1519), commissioned by the Peutinger family. The unity of the picture space is complete to the last detail. We seem to be looking through three windows into the melancholy charm of a single eastern landscape with a sky overcast by sorrow at the Saviour's death.

Another artist greatly favoured with commissions from the Emperor was Leonhard Beck, whose *St George and the Dragon* (Kunsthistorisches Museum, Vienna) reflects the chivalrous spirit of Maximilian's circle. It is the peak of Beck's achievement as a painter, as rich in landscape and natural forms as in exquisite figures. The wooded landscape is like a splendid tapestry with those layers of vegetation that are so typical of this painter. The most refreshing and impressive feature of all these German paintings is the way in which they combine narrative and drama with a profound understanding of nature. The Germans were aware of the underlying forces of growth in nature, whereas the Netherlandish masters showed only what was visible to the naked eye.

Hans Holbein the Elder (c. 1460/1465-1524). St Barbara (right) and St Elizabeth of Hungary with Three Beggars (left),
1516. Inner Side of the Wings of the Altarpiece of St Sebastian. (Each panel 59⅛×18½″) Alte Pinakothek, Munich.

Hans Burgkmair the Elder (1473-1531). The Altarpiece of St John, 1518. (Le

"; central panel 60⅜×49⅛"; right wing 57⅜×19¼") Alte Pinakothek, Munich.

Martin Schaffner (1477/1478-1547/1549). The Presentation in the Temple, 1524.
(118¼×62¼″) Inner Left Wing of the Wettenhausen Altarpiece. Alte Pinakothek, Munich.

The spirit of nature and landscape that found such forceful expression in the work of the Danube School also pervaded the art of Mathis Gothardt-Neithardt at this period. As we have seen, the *Isenheim Altarpiece* already contained several very fine landscapes which showed a strong feeling for nature. This feeling culminated in Mathis' work on the altarpiece commissioned by canons Kaspar Schantz and Heinrich Reitzmann for the Maria Schnee (Our Lady of the Snows) Chapel in the collegiate church of Aschaffenburg. In the church itself there now remains only the original frame of the altar, bearing the date 1519, the monogram of the painter, and an inscription with the names of the two donors. The altarpiece having been dismembered, the central panel found its way to the village of Stuppach near Mergentheim (Württemberg), and one of the wings is now in the Augustinian Museum at Freiburg-im-Breisgau. The subject of the central panel is the Virgin Mary, who is shown with the Christ Child in a radiant landscape on a summer morning. This *Madonna in the Garden* is surely the loveliest portrayal of the Virgin that exists in German painting. Again its literary source is to

Leonhard Beck (c. 1480-1542).
St George and the Dragon, c. 1515. (53×45¾″) Kunsthistorisches Museum, Vienna.

Mathis Gothardt-Neithardt (c. 1475-1528). Madonna in the Garden, 1519. (72⅞×59″) Central Panel of the Altarpiece of Our Lady of the Snows (Maria Schnee Altar). Parish Church of Stuppach, near Mergentheim (Württemberg).

be found in the *Revelations* of St Bridget of Sweden. The Virgin is drawing attention to the decaying condition of the Church; hence the cathedral in the background. A rainbow curves away from the apse of the cathedral like a flying buttress and plays round the head of the Virgin, who is saying: "When through the bow I understand myself, when I bend over the dwellers on the earth . . ." The Virgin is surrounded by a garden containing a variety of plants and flowers and also some beehives; these are all Marian symbols in Christian iconography, and the individual vision of the painter endows them with poetic intensity. The majestic figure of the Virgin, triangular in form, is modelled in colour—the deep blue of the mantle and the carmine of the rich brocade dress which gleams pink in the light. Her face glows transparently like an aureole in the light of the morning sun rising behind her, and her eyes have a dreamy look. The sense of rapture is heightened by the seeming imprecision of the handling.

Here the painter forsook the tangible three-dimensional modelling and the brushed-in contours in the manner of Dürer that still played an important part in the *Isenheim Altarpiece*. Everything is expressed by means of a flat colour surface with atmospheric depth. This surface was applied in layers, with the thinner upper layer not always quite covering the lower one, but alternately advancing and receding. The result is a miraculous play of light that sets the figure of the Virgin even more firmly in the surrounding atmosphere. In its spiritual quality and closeness to nature, this painting surpasses even the *Isenheim Altarpiece*.

The surviving wing of the *Maria Schnee Altarpiece* depicts the legend of the foundation of Santa Maria Maggiore in Rome—the miraculous fall of snow sent down by Our Lady to indicate the spot on the Esquiline hill where the basilica should be built. The Pope in full regalia is marking the spot with a hoe, accompanied by a great crowd of clergy and layfolk; a dreamlike vision of Rome rises in the background. This visionary view of the city is not the work of a Late Gothic artist but of a Renaissance master standing in the forefront of his time. Rome is conceived in classical terms, with the Romanesque architectural forms that were a feature of the Renaissance style. Mathis must have used foreign prototypes—perhaps he also obtained information from the donor of this panel, Canon Heinrich Reitzmann, who had been to Rome —in order to create this elaborate architectural setting which reminds us of similar things in the painting of the Augsburg, Bavarian, and Danube schools. In the background everything is indistinct and wavering, expressing the bustle of the great religious festival of Santa Maria Maggiore that fills the painting with its resplendent reds and whites.

The inscription on the original frame of the *Maria Schnee Altarpiece—"Maria Mater Graciae . . . Tu nos ab hoste protege"*—seems to be a prayer from the pious donors and the painter. This was the year (1519) of Luther's disputation in Leipzig. Confusion in the sphere of Church and religion was mounting dangerously. This situation lent added significance to the ecstatic confessions of St Bridget, her admonitions, and her faith in the help of the Mother of God. The altarpiece must therefore be seen as a heartfelt appeal from the painter, who was himself to be drawn into the spiritual upheaval of the years that followed. Faced with the threat of fanatical religious movements, social revolution, and general lawlessness, the leading minds of the time hankered after the stability of a supreme law conceived in terms of a divine necessity, a moral imperative, or a deep inner conviction. In this sense both Dürer and Mathis were seekers of the law, and in the coming decade they were to become more representative of their age than ever.

In 1520 Mathis executed three altarpieces for Mainz Cathedral. They too may have been expressions of his religious hopes and fears, but they were destroyed by war and only a few magnificent drawings remain to give an idea of what they were like.

Albrecht Altdorfer (c. 1480-1538).
Forest with St George and the Dragon, 1510. (11⅛×8⅞″) Alte Pinakothek, Munich.

The Spell of Nature

"... And though you may know the four principal
colours which belong to the four elements and are associated
with them—blue for the earth, green for water, yellow for
air, red for fire—there are still many other incidental colours
that it is almost impossible to identify with certainty."

PARACELSUS, *Liber de imaginibus*

IN the works of the Danube School—which culminated in the paintings of Albrecht Altdorfer
—we find a new awareness of nature and her vital forces that is intuitive and poetic rather
than scientific and rational. Altdorfer's earliest pictures have affinities with those of
contemporary artists, both native and foreign, who were working in Austria; and even later
it seems as though his occasional contacts with that country always spurred him on to fresh
achievements. During a visit to Austria in 1510-1511, he produced a landscape drawing of
Sarmingstein on the Danube (Museum of Fine Arts, Budapest) which is a reflection of cosmic
forces rather than a mere view. The paintings he did round about the same time convey a
similar impression.

One of Altdorfer's greatest achievements was the altar panel of *St John the Baptist and
St John the Evangelist*, which used to be in the abbey church of St Emmeram at Regensburg
(Alte Pinakothek, Munich, on loan from the Katharinenspital, Regensburg-Stadtamhof).
Never before had the creative vigour of the new type of art been so convincingly demonstrated
in one painting. The two saints are shown as apostles of the wasteland: the "voice crying in
the wilderness" and the visionary who withdrew to a desert island. Altdorfer used his brother
Erhard as the model for the Evangelist, while the Baptist resembles the painter's self-portrait
in the *Washing of Hands* in the St Florian altarpiece. They are sitting at the edge of a virgin
forest; a view of mountain slopes and the seashore can be glimpsed through a clearing made
by stormy winds. Where the life-giving sun breaks through to the forest floor, there is an
exuberant growth of wild flowers, grasses, and medicinal herbs. The seascape in the background is like a vision of the creation of the world: mist rises from the sea, changing to smoke
higher up, then crystallizing into mountains and snow fields that in turn are transformed into
drifting banks of cloud. Each form is distilled from and sublimated in another. The elements
shift and alter in the flux of space; a subtle alchemy is at work. The idea of depicting the
artist as a sacred figure, the demiurge of the world he has created with brush and palette,
is a typically Renaissance one.

In the Kassel *Crucifixion* Altdorfer's art achieves tragic grandeur and power. Though
he started out as a master of the small-scale painting, he had by now adapted himself with
ease to the requirements of the altarpiece. The towering, solitary figures are set against a
wide, gleaming landscape. The figure of the crucified Christ is unmistakably modelled on
that in Cranach's Munich *Crucifixion* of 1503. The landscape is very similar to that in the

Rest on the Flight into Egypt (Staatliche Museen, Berlin), dated 1510, which was a votive offering from the artist to the Virgin. Here, in this small picture, the inner strength and integrity of Altdorfer's art enabled him to indulge in a wealth of painstaking detail without obscuring the broader outlines or damping the pulse of life. The background features soar upwards to reveal their full splendour, imbuing the picture with an unreal, dreamlike quality despite their delightful verisimilitude. They are totally unrelated to the unfolding backgrounds of Late Gothic painting, and with the emergence of this new cosmos the laws of perspective and spatial construction cease to play a part. The basin of the fountain even seems to lean towards the Christ Child as he dips his hand in the water. Organic and inorganic matter blend into one another. The playful cherubs seem to have climbed down from the ornamental shaft of the fountain, which is pervaded by the same breath of life. The colouring of the picture is close to that of *St John the Baptist and St John the Evangelist*: the Virgin Mary is wearing the same terracotta red and Joseph the same blue as the saints. The same golden olive and fluorescent blue are found in the landscape. The ruins are partly based on the Romanesque buildings of Regensburg.

The impression made on Altdorfer by Austria is shown by an increased breadth, understanding, and significance in his handling of his subject matter. That he was influenced by Austrian art can be clearly demonstrated. Thus Ludwig Baldass has proved that his graphic work in the years that followed his visit to Austria in 1510-1511 shows the influence of Michael Pacher's composition and treatment of space. Like Pacher, Altdorfer was fond of using perspective in depth, except in works such as the one just discussed where a steeply rising background is chosen to enhance the significance of a particular moment.

At the beginning of the second decade of the sixteenth century, Altdorfer produced an increasing number of drawings and engravings. The technique of chiaroscuro drawing is successfully employed to convey the sparkling brilliance of Christmas in a painting like the Berlin *Nativity*. The setting is a group of dilapidated, frost-covered ruins in a lonely corner of the earth, over which a meteor-like sun is rising—it was Altdorfer who first introduced a feeling for the magic of ruins into paintings. The tufts of grass and flowers are drawn with a fine brush in shimmering threads of silver and gold.

Like the leading masters of Nuremberg and Augsburg, Altdorfer had little time for painting in the earlier and middle years of the decade, since he was kept busy with woodcuts and illustrations commissioned by the Emperor Maximilian. When he came to Austria in 1510-1511, Kölderer's workshop at Innsbruck was engaged on the extensive series of miniatures that were used as models for the cycle of woodcuts depicting the Emperor's *Triumphal Procession*. The young artists concerned adopted Altdorfer's up-to-date style so unreservedly that we must assume that the master himself was present in the workshop and perhaps even took part in the work. In fact, the blocks of a number of the woodcuts suggest that he actually designed them.

As a result of these activities, the great altarpieces with which Altdorfer had been commissioned earlier progressed but slowly and were not completed until the second half of the decade. The *Corpus Christi Altarpiece* from the Minorite Church in Regensburg (Museum, Regensburg) bears the date 1517. Its central section, the *Nativity*, may have been sketched out as early as 1512 or 1513. The cool sharp air of the heights pervades this Christmas scene in which Bethlehem is shown in the guise of a small town in the Bavarian mountains. The vaulted room in which the *Last Supper* is represented is at once spacious and intimate. A window in the background shows a view of a Tyrolean church and churchyard set amid friendly houses whose flat shingle roofs are weighed down by stones. Shades of dusk are beginning to invade the lofty room. Here the great master of light and atmosphere skilfully conveys the spirit of the Last Supper.

Albrecht Altdorfer (c. 1480-1538).
The Rest on the Flight into Egypt, 1510. (22⅜×15″) Staatliche Museen, Berlin-Dahlem.

Albrecht Altdorfer (c. 1480-1538). The Resurrection of Christ, 1518. (27½×14½″)
Right Predella Panel from the St Florian Altarpiece. Kunsthistorisches Museum, Vienna.

In 1518 Altdorfer completed work on the altarpiece donated by Prior Peter Maurer to the collegiate church of St Florian, near Linz, in Upper Austria. This is his masterpiece. Simply from the point of view of painting, it is—next to the *Isenheim Altarpiece*—probably the greatest German altarpiece of the sixteenth century. The contract for it may have been concluded as early as 1511, when Altdorfer went to Austria. Work on this stupendous painting must have gone on at intervals through the years when the artist was occupied on woodcuts and illustrations. With the exception of the *Isenheim Altarpiece*, the magical glow and opulent colour of the *St Florian Altarpiece* have no parallel in German painting. This opulent colour was not, however, an end in itself, but was used to deepen and intensify the drama of the Passion. The ruby reds, emerald greens, and blues glow as if they were underlaid by gold and other precious metals. They go beyond the usual concept of "colour," representing the living essence that the alchemists sought to distil from nature. Not only do they conjure up the awesome drama of nature suffering and triumphing with the Saviour but they heighten the shattering quality, the spiritual tension of the narrative. All that Altdorfer had attempted in his earlier works and during his stay in Austria in 1511 in the way of significant emphasis, daring transformation, and even the distortion of figures and space for the sake of greater expressiveness is here endowed with the force and finality of maturity. This altarpiece, which was entirely his own work, was painted in a carefree rapturous spirit. Passages of intense concentration alternate with sudden captivating flights of inspired improvisation, and the painter's outstanding narrative gift is amply demonstrated. But Altdorfer was more than a good story-teller. In works such as this, the apocalyptic, visionary, and elemental side of his nature breaks through.

The *St Florian Altarpiece* was a folding polyptych with two pairs of wings. The weekday side showed the *Martyrdom of St Sebastian*, the Sunday side the *Passion*. The feastday side had carvings, now lost, on the shrine and wings. It was a tradition in Late Gothic altarpieces to employ gold backgrounds as a distinguishing feature of the Sunday side. Altdorfer harks back to this practice, but his use of gold always has a purpose—to convey the glow of a sunset, the reflection of torches on a coffered ceiling by night, or the light of noon gilding the tracery of a rose-window. The scenes are rarely set in a restful light. Nature usually provides a dramatic effect such as a menacing sunset, a magical night, a blazing noon, a splendid dawn. In the scene on the Mount of Olives, daylight bleeds away in a glory of purple and scarlet in the clear, deep, sultry air. In the *Arrest of Christ*, there is a veritable fireworks display. Storm lanterns, braziers, and torches rouse the wood from its slumber with their flickering brightness; the branches are lit from below by a multitude of lights. *Christ before Caiaphas* is a night-piece far in advance of its time—not until Tintoretto and Elsheimer was anything like it attempted again. The architectural settings are modelled on Bramante and Burgkmair. In the wings of the predella (Kunsthistorisches Museum, Vienna) the drama of the Son of Man is played out in a natural setting of epic dimensions. The *Resurrection* is a dawn breaking with a thousand voices in heaven and on earth, whose message reaches the plant and spirit world, while slothful humans are still fast asleep. Not only does Altdorfer express the miracle of the Resurrection in colour and light, he also voices the secret life of the plant world, the soughing of the fir trees and their first stirring in the morning light. Altdorfer also produced a grandly conceived single painting in the style of the *St Florian Altarpiece—Christ Taking Leave of Mary* (Sir Harold Wernher Collection, Luton Hoo, Bedfordshire)—in which the influence of Mantegna can be discerned.

From the *St Florian Altarpiece* onwards, Altdorfer concentrated on strong, pure colour effects, whose force and depth gave his works an even greater atmospheric subtlety than before. In the early 1520s, he produced a second altarpiece for the monastery of St Florian— the *Legend of the Patron Saints* (Florence, Nuremberg, Prague). It has a simpler, more factual, and more realistic narrative quality, and treats the lives of the saints in a popular style, so that it corresponds more closely to Paracelsus' idea that an altarpiece should be a picture-book for the illiterate. Certain features of the clear and unpretentious compositions it contains recall folk art. The landscapes are treated from the subjective viewpoint of an individual participant. There are views of the landscape in which the legend of St Florian was set and of the town of Enns and the Marktkirche of St Florian (still standing today) with its miraculous fountain from which pilgrims drew water—a most charming genre picture. The astonishing indoor scenes anticipate the Dutch architectural paintings of the seventeenth century.

Wolf Huber (c. 1485/1490-1553). The Nativity, finished in 1521. (28¾×18¾") Panel from the St Anna Altarpiece in Feldkirch. Kunsthistorisches Museum, Vienna (on loan from the Bührle Collection, Zurich).

However, Altdorfer's finest architectural painting was the *Birth of the Virgin Mary in a Church* (Munich, Alte Pinakothek). St Anne's childbed is set up in a spacious church choir through which angels fly in joyful circles. The astonishingly strong sense of space reminds us that Altdorfer was also employed as city architect in his home town of Regensburg. A preliminary sketch of this picture (Kupferstichkabinett, Berlin) shows an attempt to clarify the lay-out by applying architectural principles. But in the actual painting such considerations are thrown to the winds and the artist is interested only in the magical chiaroscuro of the church interior.

The most important representative of the Danube School, apart from Altdorfer, was Wolf Huber. Born round about 1485-1490 at Feldkirch, in Vorarlberg, Huber was employed as official painter to the Bishop of Passau until his death in 1553. In 1510 or 1511 he was presumably in Innsbruck working in Költerer's workshop on the miniatures for the *Triumphal Procession* commissioned by the Emperor. Round about the same time he travelled through the Austrian and Bavarian Alps and the Danube regions, and began to depict them in realistic pen drawings. These were advanced for their time and anticipated principles of landscape composition that have remained valid from the seventeenth century until the present day. Huber and Altdorfer worked in neighbouring Danube towns (Regensburg and Passau are less than seventy miles apart); they knew each other, and each was influenced by the other.

Erhard Altdorfer (c. 1485-1561). St Leopold finding the Veil, c. 1510-1511. (45×39″)
Panel from an Altarpiece of St Leopold. Stiftsmuseum, Klosterneuburg, near Vienna.

Master of the Historia Friderici et Maximiliani (active c. 1508-c. 1525).
The Nativity, 1511-1512. (47×29¼″) Courtesy of The Art Institute of Chicago. W. L. Mead Fund.

The portrait of a bearded architect by Wolf Huber in the Strasbourg Museum has been identified by Ernst Buchner, not without reason, as a portrait of Altdorfer. Huber's new intimate conception of landscape and nature—similar to that of Altdorfer's later phase—pervades the *Christ Taking Leave of the Virgin* (1519, Kunsthistorisches Museum, Vienna). It has some affinities with Dürer's woodcut on the same subject in his *Life of the Virgin*, but it impresses not so much by grandeur of conception as by its poetic handling of light and atmosphere. The onlooker gazes across a pleasant pre-Alpine landscape to the distant

Master of Mondsee (Upper Austria, early 16th century). St Benedict absorbed in his Devotions outside the Cave of Subiaco, c. 1515. (31⅛×17″) Oesterreichische Galerie, Vienna.

Hans Wertinger, called Schwabmaler (before 1470-1533).
The Month of February, 1525-1530. (9×15¾″) Germanisches Nationalmuseum, Nuremberg.

peaks. Instead of rising steeply, the horizon is set far back, and this conveys a sense of space. The sun is hidden behind thin clouds so that the scene is suffused with a calm, sober light. While Altdorfer was a master of colour and light, Huber's colour is not very varied. There is always the same harmony of green, brick-red, orange, gold-ochre, and turquoise. But Huber was unique in his observation of light, the natural light of day, of morning, evening, and night. His art is one of inner translucency, and of gently varied transitions. His simple, almost primitive range of colour is allied to the greatest subtlety of light. Unlike Altdorfer, he dispenses with spectacular effects. Everything is natural and poetically redolent of the eternal rhythm, the infinite tranquillity, the peace of nature.

Huber was not, like his predecessors, a monumental painter in the grand manner. His altarpieces are relatively modest in size, but are nevertheless just as significant as those produced elsewhere in the second decade of the century. His principal work is the *St Anna Altarpiece* in the parish church of Feldkirch (Vorarlberg), undertaken in 1515 and completed in 1521. The reverse of the carved shrine shows the *Lamentation of Christ*, the wings (Bührle Collection, Zurich), the *Life of the Virgin*. The figures in the *Nativity* are bathed in the light radiating from the Child, and seem to glow from within. With infinite mildness, the natural light from a moon hidden in haze blends the radiance from below with the unearthly radiance from above. We are not—as so often in Altdorfer's work—confronted with a violent opposition of sources of light so that the figures are shown in menacing contrast, but with a gentle blending of the different lights, a uniform shimmering chiaroscuro against which the overgrown ruin is silhouetted. Here we have a deeper co-existence with nature, a more tranquil and obvious surrender to it than we find in the works that the more emphatic Altdorfer was painting round about the same time. Altdorfer adopted this style only when he undertook the *Legend of the Patron Saints* for the monastery of St Florian, with its strong folk element —in this he was probably influenced by the achievements of his friend Huber.

Albrecht Altdorfer's first pupil and follower was his brother Erhard, whose earliest works were small engravings and pen drawings in the style of Altdorfer's prints of the years 1506-1508. In 1512 Erhard Altdorfer became official painter to the ducal court at Schwerin, in Mecklenburg. His activities in the intervening years are obscure, but a surviving drawing —a preliminary sketch— has established that he painted three of the wings of one of the altarpieces dedicated to St John in the Monastery of Lambach in Upper Austria. His hand can also be recognized in a splendid *St Leopold Finding the Veil* (Stiftsmuseum, Klosterneuburg) which formed part of an altarpiece dedicated to the patron saint of Lower Austria.

Between his early days in Regensburg and his move to North Germany, Erhard Altdorfer worked for a time in Austria, more particularly at Klosterneuburg where Rueland Frueauf the Younger had also worked. His altarpieces are notable for their landscapes and their wealth of lush woodland vegetation. A series of splendid pen and brush sketches and landscape studies by his hand have been preserved. In Austria he met an anonymous painter, presumably of the Viennese school, who is known as the Master of the Historia Friderici et Maximiliani after a story of the Emperor Maximilian's youth (now in the Vienna State Archives) which he illustrated with exquisite pen drawings. Like Erhard, he followed the style established by Albrecht Altdorfer in his pen drawings and paintings of the first decade of the century, subsequently developing it in independent and imaginative fashion. The paths taken by Erhard Altdorfer and the Master of the Historia were parallel in many respects including the handling of figures and the treatment of landscape. The figures of the Master of the Historia are irregular, organic forms issuing like mandrakes or goblins from the undergrowth of the forest. In his more spacious altarpieces, such as the *Nativity* in the Art Institute of Chicago, they gain in amplitude, attaining truly Austrian, Viennese proportions. The drawing is the principal element in the structure of his pictures. His colour-range has a folk-like simplicity, and light held no problems for him. His luscious, sweeping line, pregnant with natural life, is typical of the Danube School. His predilection for parallel folds is one that is also found in sculptors of the period. As time went on, his flowing lines became luxuriant and baroque—a tendency that reached its peak in the high altar (1520) of the Church of the Holy Blood at Pulkau, Lower Austria.

Altdorfer was a Bavarian and his art must have been based just as much, if not more, on the traditions of Bavarian art. His chiaroscuro drawings link up with those of Mair of Landshut. One of the pioneers of landscape painting in Bavaria was Hans Wertinger, known

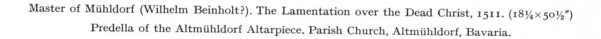

Master of Mühldorf (Wilhelm Beinholt?). The Lamentation over the Dead Christ, 1511. (18¼×50½″)
Predella of the Altmühldorf Altarpiece. Parish Church, Altmühldorf, Bavaria.

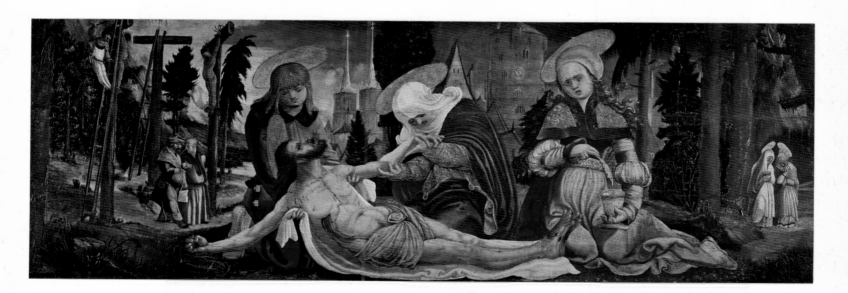

as Schwabmaler ("the Swabian painter"), who was born in Landshut round about 1470, or perhaps even earlier, and died in 1533. He was a prolific portrait-painter, and his sitters included members of the Bavarian ducal house. In a sequence showing the months of the year he transformed the Netherlandish calendar picture into a delightful series of independent landscapes that anticipated Bruegel's great series of the Months of the Year. This was a surprising achievement for an artist who was older than Dürer. In the *Month of February* (Germanisches Nationalmuseum, Nuremberg) he depicts with a naive freshness and originality a snow-covered wood, woodcutters and hunters, sleigh-riders and people having fun on the ice.

One of the most original and striking of the anonymous artists of the Bavarian Danube school was the Master of Mühldorf, who was responsible for the folding altarpiece, dated 1511, in the parish church of Altmühldorf on the Inn (Upper Bavaria); he is probably to be identified with the local painter Wilhelm Beinholt. His work shows clear links with Altdorfer's Kassel *Crucifixion*, though it is not certain which painter influenced the other. The central panel of the Altmühldorf triptych consisted of a carving, which has not survived. The wings depict the *Passion of Christ*, a work full of peasant strength and wildness. The forms are either lumpish and heavy or wilfully distorted, elongated, and twisted. The body of the dead Christ, as depicted on the predella, is still stretched in the attitude it held on the Cross. The kneeling group of mourners stands out like a frieze against an Upper Bavarian landscape in which weather-beaten fir trees alternate with the buildings of a picturesque old town. Most of the horizon is set far back, and this gives expressive emphasis to the silhouettes of the foreground figures. The Master of Mühldorf is one of the most original products of the Bavarian Danube school, which stylistically has many points of contact with the sculptures of Hans Leinberger.

The Danube School, whether Bavarian or Austrian, had many links with the Augsburg school. One of these was provided by the anonymous master who painted the Oberaltaich *Man of Sorrows* (Alte Pinakothek, Munich). This artist worked in the Lower Bavarian Danube region, perhaps at Straubing, and has been identified by Buchner as the author of two other panels: the *Apostle James the Lesser Driving Out Demons* (Germanisches Nationalmuseum, Nuremberg) and the *Martyrdom of the Apostle James* (Staatsgalerie, Stuttgart), which were part of a larger altarpiece. He was probably also the author of the extremely fascinating *Altarpiece of St John* at Gutenstetten (Central Franconia), dated 1511; it once bore the signature "Hans Jehen." An artist of passionate temperament, he maintained the dignified tone of a lofty classicism in all his pictures. His connections with Augsburg artists (such as the etcher known as the C. B. Master) and Erhard Altdorfer remain to be investigated. Another artist of great originality was the anonymous master who collaborated with the Oberaltaich master on the *Altarpiece of the Apostles* dated 1518. He has been given various appellations: the Master of the Legend of St Philip, the Master of Mary Magdalene, and the Master of St Christopher with the Devil. He was the painter of the exquisite small *St Christopher* in the Munich Pinakothek. The panels of the little altarpiece dedicated to St Mary the Egyptian and St Christopher, to which this painting belongs, come from Austria, which was probably the master's homeland.

The artists of the Austrian Danube school had a gentler, softer temperament than the Bavarians. They were lyrical rather than dramatic, and were chiefly concerned with atmospheric effects of colour and light. The Austrian Danube school at its best is represented by a picture of *St Benedict outside the Cave of Subiaco* (Oesterreichische Galerie, Vienna) painted about 1515 by the Master of Mondsee. The saint is shown devoutly absorbed in his breviary, sheltered by the trees of the wood. Dusk is falling over the wilderness; the evening sky is tinted in reds and blues. This poetic rendering of nature is a work of enchanting sincerity.

The feeling for nature and landscape, the sense of atmosphere, of the soil and the plant world, that first made its appearance in the Danube painters of Austria and Bavaria, quickly spread and became an important feature of German painting in the age of Dürer. Not only

Niklaus Manuel Deutsch (1484-1530).
The Beheading of John the Baptist, c. 1520. (12¾×10¼″) Kunstmuseum, Basel.

Hans Leu the Younger (c. 1490-1531).
Orpheus and the Animals, 1519. (22¾×20″) Kunstmuseum, Basel.

did it sweep through the whole of South Germany, but related developments—for which the foundations had been laid in the fifteenth century—occurred in Switzerland, where the younger generation was able to make a complete breakthrough.

Niklaus Manuel Deutsch, who was born in Berne in 1484, was not only a painter, but also a politician, a soldier, a poet, and a pioneer of the Reformation. His works show a delight in local colour and folk traditions with a strong emphasis on landscape. His interpretations of antiquity in Swiss terms (*The Judgement of Paris*, Basel) are gay and colourful, handled with poetic freedom and decorative skill. Like Baldung, he tended to stress poetry and fantasy. The *Beheading of John the Baptist* (Kunstmuseum, Basel) is a work of overwhelming fervour. Although it was not produced until about 1520, it has all the apocalyptic rapture that marked South German painting at the beginning of the century—here, however, the rapture is poetic rather than religious. The scene of martyrdom is transformed into an atmospheric landscape, a thrilling natural event. No sooner has the executioner severed the saint's head from his torso than the henchmen rush off anxiously through the dark gateway with the headless corpse.

The daring sectional composition of this picture is as astonishing as the fantastic setting. All nature erupts in revulsion at the crime. Sinister flashes of light shoot up like lances from behind the trunk of a fir tree. A rainbow spans the wood, which surges in the tempest like an angry sea. A yellowish light flashes through the lowering storm clouds in a star-shaped explosion. That it is an electrical discharge is shown by the fiery red lining of the clouds. Rarely before had natural phenomena been observed in such a novel manner and mastered so well in painting. Such a picture reveals a new depth of poetic awareness, a new feeling for the cosmic.

Hans Leu the Younger, another Swiss artist, was born about 1490 and killed in 1531 in the battle on the Gubel. The leading painter in Zurich, he studied under Dürer and Baldung. His *Orpheus* (1519, Kunstmuseum, Basel) depicts a peaceful animal paradise in which the beasts of the wilderness are lying down to listen to a bearded minstrel playing his lyre in a Swiss mountain landscape. The deep peace and meditative calm of this evening scene are in the spirit of Wolf Huber.

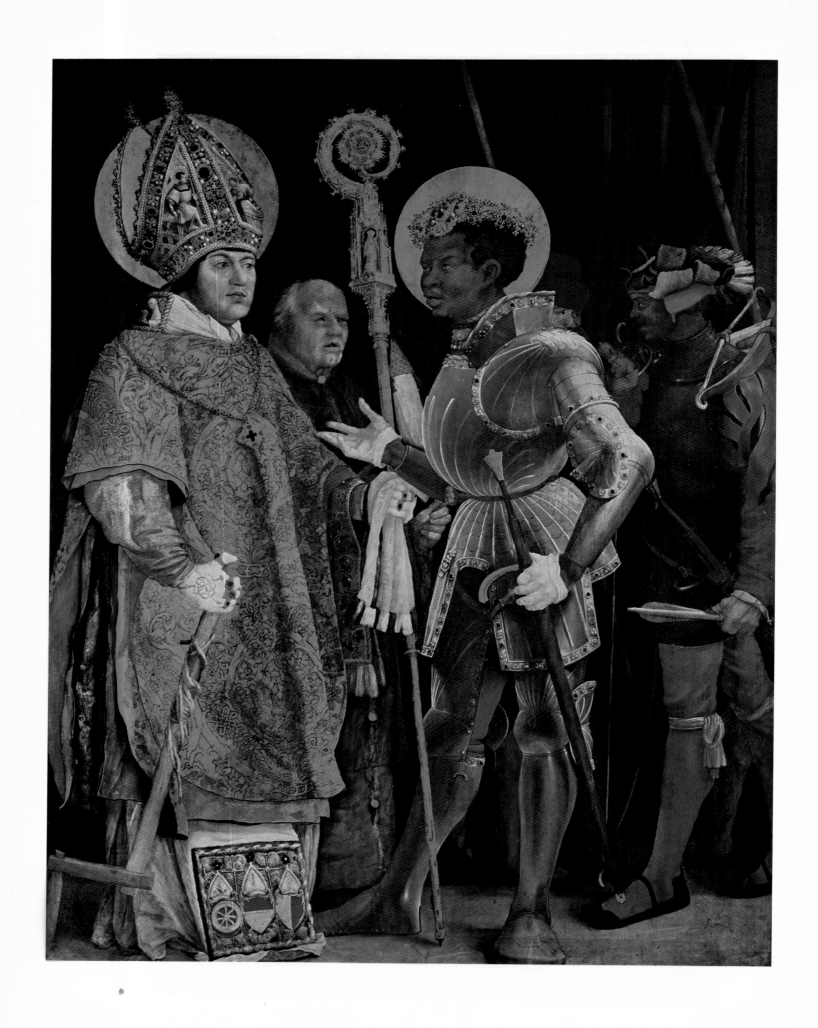

Mathis Gothardt-Neithardt (c. 1475-1528), called Matthias Grünewald.
The Meeting of St Maurice and St Erasmus, 1521-1523. (89×69¼″) Alte Pinakothek, Munich.

Doctrine

And the same revelations and miracles concern you and me equally as if they had occurred specially for your eyes or mine.

MELANCHTHON, *Reason why the community and churches of Christ... hold fast and adhere to the Bible—that is, the pure word of God.*

IN the last decade of his life, Dürer was increasingly preoccupied with the preparation and compilation of his theoretical writings. In our time it has been regretted that—as in the case of Leonardo—this concern with theory kept him from the actual work of painting and engraving. But for both these masters, the Italian as much as the German, the establishment of intellectual foundations and theoretical justifications was so much a part of their creative and artistic achievement that they could not have conceived their art without it. Dürer's later style, which became increasingly powerful and monumental, synthesizing all his strivings in ever more simple and telling terms, was not the result of his theoretical views but ran parallel with them. His art gained new ease and mastery; no longer was there any trace of the labour with which he had striven to free it from Late Gothic "falseness in painting." His industrious search for formal values, his investigation of the microcosm, his experience of Italy—these gave him the supreme freedom and mastery of form and composition that are apparent not only in his altarpieces but also in his richly decorative works for the Emperor, the woodcuts of the *Triumphal Arch* and the *Triumphal Car* as well as the drawings of the *Prayer Book*. Now the time had come to draw conclusions, to sum up the principles underlying his work. In the last ten years of his life, Dürer became essentially a *teacher* in everything he drew, painted, and engraved, in all he said and thought, in the example set by his art. In this he was not alone in his age. There were others, too, who in the 1520s were summing up their ideas and experience: Erasmus and Zwingli, Luther and Melanchthon. There was a feeling that, by means of *doctrine* with a religious, moral, and generally human foundation, the contemporary world could be freed from its doubts and uncertainties. This situation could not be achieved without struggle—in the outside world, the scene was more disturbed than ever, for the Peasants' War and the depredations of the iconoclasts were threatening to turn the cultural world of Central Europe into a wilderness. Fanatics and visionaries were no longer content to confine themselves to words, but were actively attempting to reverse the whole state of things. It was no longer possible for the intellectual elite—which included the great artists— to remain aloof. They had to take position, for their word had weight. This word took the form of a creed, a *doctrine*, not only in the mouth of the theologian but in everything the artist said and did. This was especially true in Germany.

In Dürer's final period, his artistic work decreased in volume. He was no longer able to carry out his ideas for paintings on the same scale as before. His output of copperplate engravings and woodcuts also declined, though at their best—as in the splendid portraits and the figures of the Apostles—they carried greater authority than ever. This is also true of the few paintings he did towards the end of his career. He still had many ideas and plans, which we know only from brilliant sketches. He continued to draw on the old scale, but here too the main subject of his later art—Man—sprang from the microcosmic and macrocosmic preoccupations of the past. In fact, as form and character, Man filled his thoughts more than ever.

With manifest devotion and commitment, Dürer also employed his complete mastery of form and brilliant jewel-like colours—the embodiment of perfection—in the service of religious ideas. The *Virgin at Prayer* (1518, Staatliche Museen, Berlin) may have been part of a diptych, with the other (missing) panel depicting Christ—a combination frequently found in Netherlandish painting. The painter paid meticulous attention to the modelling of the hands, which look almost chiselled, but even so they do not succeed in diverting attention from the expression of faith on the Virgin's face. This picture is perhaps more resplendent in colour than anything Dürer ever painted. The colour, however, is not a decorative end in itself, however much its use may seem a foretaste of Mannerism, but is intended to heighten the dignity and solemnity of the expression. The greatest beauty and perfection of external form and colouring are employed to enhance the inward, spiritual content of the painting.

How decisively the works of Dürer's final phase must have influenced the Mannerist painters of the Late Renaissance can be seen from the painting of the *Virgin and Child with St Anne* ("*Anna Selbdritt*") of 1519 (Metropolitan Museum, New York). Mother, daughter, and grandchild are grouped together in a solemn pyramidal composition. Dürer seems to have striven for a canon of colour, as well as one of form, and here we find a calculation that is far removed from the impulsive delight in colour that marked his more youthful work. It runs like a cold breath through the colour-scheme of the picture, giving it an abstract, almost lifeless quality. St Anne was based on a monumental sketch from life (Albertina) drawn with the brush. In the picture she lays her hand on the shoulder of the lovely young Virgin —a typical Nuremberg girl—as though to console her. The mother is worshipping the child with a pensive expression on her face, as though she foresaw the Passion. Greenish shades play round the child's cheeks and lips. Is this style an anticipation of Mannerism? This is one of the questions that come to mind as we contemplate this chilling, oppressive picture.

The work Dürer had carried out for Maximilian over a period of years culminated in a meeting between the Emperor and the artist during the Diet of Augsburg in the summer of 1518. There, on the 28th of June, Dürer executed a lifelike charcoal drawing of the Emperor Maximilian I (Albertina, Vienna). From Augsburg, the Emperor, who was seriously ill, travelled to Austria, dying in 1519 at Wels, near Linz, during his homeward journey. On the basis of the Augsburg drawing Dürer in 1519 painted the portrait—so imposing in its majesty— that is now in the Kunsthistorisches Museum in Vienna. This panel painting, together with another version on canvas (Germanisches Nationalmuseum, Nuremberg) which Dürer made in the same year, is the most lifelike surviving portrait of the Emperor.

With the Emperor's death Dürer was liberated from decorative miniature work, and this accounts for his resumption of painting on a larger scale between 1518 and 1520. The latter year brought an event as decisive and important to the artist as his earlier visits to Venice —his journey to the Netherlands. The reason for it was financial rather than educational: he was trying to obtain confirmation from the new emperor Charles V of the continuation of the income granted him by Maximilian. This journey, of which a detailed account survives in the master's diary and sketchbook, was in the nature of a triumphal progress. Now internationally famous, Dürer was received and honoured like a prince everywhere he went. He took with him a great number of his own and his pupils' works to be offered as presents or exchanged. At the coronation celebrations in Aix-la-Chapelle (Aachen), he met Mathis Gothardt-Neithardt whom he presented with "two florins' worth of art." As well as being a social triumph, the journey was deeply important to Dürer as an artist. After the relative narrowness of Nuremberg, this visit to the great world of the west marked a change of intellectual climate. He felt the same contrast between his new surroundings and his homeland as he had experienced in the South. The attraction of the Netherlands for artists of the fifteenth and sixteenth centuries was as strong as that of Paris for those of the nineteenth and twentieth centuries.

Dürer made the flourishing trading city of Antwerp his headquarters during his visit. He kept his eyes open for works of art, past and present. He was profoundly impressed by the gifts received by the Emperor from Mexico, which gave him his first glimpse of exotic art. His artistic sense was aroused in a way that seems to belong to a later period, reminding us, for example, of the collector's zeal shown by Rembrandt. At the same time he was working ceaselessly. His deep understanding of human character was tremendously furthered by the numerous portraits he did in the Netherlands—these included many drawings of eminent people, as well as painted portraits. The portrait of *Bernaert van Resten* (Gemäldegalerie, Dresden) equals the finest portraits of the Netherlandish masters in the enamelled smoothness of its modelling, and surpasses them in its firm establishment of form in space. For the portrait of the tax-collector *Lorenz Sterck* (1521, Isabella Stewart Gardner Museum, Boston), Dürer chose a picture space as narrow as that of his drawings. This enhances the force of the living personality confined within it. The least feature of the face has its importance in bringing out the psychology of the subject. In this the portrait equals the work of the old Netherlandish masters, but at the same time it has that sense of absolute form that was Dürer's alone.

The most significant work produced by Dürer during his visit to the Netherlands was the *St Jerome* (1521, Museo Nacional, Lisbon) which he painted for his friend Rodrigo d'Almada. His inspiration for this picture was an old man of ninety-three whom he also portrayed in a splendid brush drawing (Albertina, Vienna). St Jerome is shown leaning his head pensively on his hand, raising his eyes to the onlooker and pointing to a skull—a *memento mori*. The colour is deep and sonorous.

In July 1521 Dürer returned home. In the concluding years of his life, his pictures were few and far between, for he was more than ever preoccupied with the literary formulation of his ideas. But the works he produced at this time outweigh all the rest in ethical content. A few portraits and a panel of the Virgin and Child have survived from 1526—the year of the *"Four Apostles."*

While the *Portrait of a Man* of 1524 (Prado, Madrid) and those he produced in the Netherlands still show the hands of the sitter, Dürer now applied the same rule to his painted portraits as to his later engraved ones: a close-fitting aperture, a narrow picture space that barely encloses the chest and shoulders, but emphasizes the powerful modelling of the head. Two of his friends on the Town Council of Nuremberg have been magnificently immortalized in this fashion. *Hieronymus Holzschuher* (Staatliche Museen, Berlin) had already served both as junior and senior burgomaster when Dürer painted his portrait. Experience, strength, and unbending sincerity and integrity of character are revealed in the sharply modelled features; the white hair is set off by a background of shining blue. The eyes are fixed on the onlooker with a penetrating gaze against which no falsehood could prevail. Dürer's joy in decorative form can be seen in the elaborate treatment of the curling hair and beard, his fondness for the microcosmic in the texture of the fur. But these details pale to insignificance before the concise relief of the face, the firm mouth, the strongly modelled nose, the bold treatment of the puckered brows where they meet the eyelids. The surface of the face confronts us like something embossed, and seems to be shaped and wrought by the forces concentrated within it. Thus, despite all the detail, the form is reduced to fundamentals, expressing the moral bedrock of a strong personality. This is the look of the men who made the Reformation.

Albrecht Dürer (1471-1528).

Portrait of Hieronymus Holzschuher, 1526. (18⅞×14⅛″) Staatliche Museen, Berlin-Dahlem.

Barthel Beham (1502-1540).

Portrait of Count Palatine Ottheinrich, 1535. (17×12⅝″) Alte Pinakothek, Munich.

The face of Holzschuher's fellow-Councillor *Jacob Muffel* (Staatliche Museen, Berlin) is no less intelligent and energetic, but it is more reserved and betrays a dogged sense of purpose. While Dürer did not spare or beautify his models, but showed both their attractive and less attractive features, he intensified their spiritual significance. The portrait of Pirckheimer's son-in-law *Hans Kleberger* (Kunsthistorisches Museum, Vienna) is conceived in terms of classical sculpture. The head is set in a moulded circular window as in a medallion—Dürer must have seen portraits of this type in Augsburg and in Italy (Eremitani Chapel, Padua). It might be thought that the "classicizing" of the subject would reduce him to a mere type. But in Dürer's hands the contrast seems to heighten his individuality. The extent to which Dürer now interpreted the sacred in terms of the human is shown in his tender and poetic painting of the *Virgin and Child* in the Uffizi. The model was a girl whom Dürer had sketched in the Netherlands as "the beautiful maiden of Antwerp."

In the closing years of his life Dürer prepared three books for publication. The most important to him personally was the one dealing with the proportions of the human figure, but he felt that he should first publish his work on the representation of space and of objects in space. Thus, in 1525, appeared the *Instructions on Measurement with Compass and Ruler*, a textbook on representational geometry. The Italians had done as much in the fifteenth century, but Dürer's real achievement was that he had caught up in theory and practice with a century of intellectual progress. Although his main aim was the construction of works of art according to rational principles, a by-product of his studies was a contribution to military theory, *Various Instructions for the Fortification of Cities, Castles, and Towns*, which appeared in 1527. The extent to which Dürer's rational theories of spatial representation influenced the artistic work of his contemporaries can be seen from the scientific precision of the settings in the great series of historical paintings commissioned by Duke William IV of Bavaria in the years following Dürer's death from such leading Bavarian, Swabian, and Franconian painters as Altdorfer, Refinger, Schöpfer, Feselen, Breu, Burgkmair, and Dürer's pupil Beham. Artistically the finest results of the Duke's commission were Altdorfer's *Battle of Alexander* and Burgkmair's *Esther in the Presence of Ahasuerus*. In the rest of the paintings, which depict the heroic deeds of men in vertical format and those of women in horizontal format (nearly all in the Alte Pinakothek, Munich), the didactic element smothers any breath of originality. Dürer did not live to see publication of his principal theoretical work, *Four Books on Human Proportions* (1528), but he spent his last days preparing it for the press. It treats the human body architecturally, and the possibilities of variation are shown by means of cross-sections and profiles. Dürer himself was not versed in architecture, but some of his outstanding contemporaries, such as Altdorfer and Huber, were. The artistic building in Altdorfer's *Susannah at her Bath* (1526, Alte Pinakothek, Munich) is the work of a potential architect that has been endowed with a dreamlike, magical quality by the art of a great painter. While it has not been proved that Altdorfer based this building on Upper Italian engravings, he probably knew the splendours of Lombard architecture at first hand. The setting of the *Birth of the Virgin in a Church* is probably derived not only from the Late Gothic choirs of Germany but also from such Bramante-style interiors as the gallery in the Cathedral of Pavia.

The theory of the learnable and teachable nature—of the "rightness"—of art was extremely important for Dürer in clarifying and consolidating his late style. Erasmus wrote of him: "*Observat exacte symmetrias et harmonias.*" In addition, his theoretical works established the language for German scientific writing for centuries to come. Dürer's theories also had a negative effect, however, not only in his immediate circle but throughout the whole of Germany. They exerted a direct influence on his disciples and followers. Their rigidity left no place for the freshness and immediacy of invention that the master had earlier encouraged and fostered in the art of such painters as Baldung, Kulmbach, Schäufelein, and Springinklee. The achievements of the last generation of Dürer's pupils were not on the same level as those of his earlier ones. They simply assimilated the system he taught, but not its deep ethical

Hans Burgkmair the Elder (1473-1531).
Esther in the Presence of Ahasuerus, 1528. (40¾×61½″) Alte Pinakothek, Munich.

meaning. Thus there is a certain stiffness, an inhibition of the natural flow of life in such artists as Barthel and Hans Sebald Beham, Georg Pencz, and even Baldung in his last phase (although he was no longer under the immediate influence of Dürer's art). This led in the case of Pencz and the two Behams to an exclusive preoccupation with formal correctness, especially in their copperplate engravings. Artists took to producing meticulous small-scale engravings, which earned them the title of "little masters," and never went beyond the level of competent craftsmanship.

A similar development can be seen in Cranach, whose official commissions contain numerous studies of the nude that are highly cultivated and carefully chiselled paintings, but contain no trace of his earlier fire. This is also true of his mythological painting *Apollo and Diana* (1530, Staatliche Museen, Berlin). Even Altdorfer, a grandiose painter to the very end, paid tribute to the ideal of Italian-style figure-painting in his latest works, such as *Lot and his Daughters* (1537, Kunsthistorisches Museum, Vienna). This work is of some importance in the history of art since it marks the first phase of Mannerism in German painting. But the old free flow of the imagination, the immediacy of approach, were lost. Barthel Beham was gifted, but his true qualities as a painter emerge only in his portraits, which have affinities with those painted by Dürer towards the end of his life. His portrait of the *Count Palatine Ottheinrich* (1535, Alte Pinakothek, Munich) is a splendid, colourful work. Georg Pencz's portrait of the master of the mint *Jörg Herz* (1545, Staatliche Kunsthalle, Karlsruhe) is also a powerful work which shows that portraiture was the forte of Late Renaissance German painting. In it the influence of the Florentines is added to that of Dürer's teachings.

Lucas Cranach the Elder (1472-1553).

Apollo and Diana in a Wooded Landscape, 1530. (20×14⅛″) Staatliche Museen, Berlin-Dahlem.

Such works are nevertheless far removed from Dürer's lofty conceptions. His theories had an ethical basis. He sought for the law of beauty which he could not fathom, but could only indicate in the changeable canons of form. In the great excursus at the end of the third book of his *Treatise on Human Proportions*, he wrote: "But such things God alone knows; he to whom it has been revealed knows it too. Truth alone holds what should be Man's best proportion and measurement and nothing else." To Dürer artistic perfection, truth, and the knowledge and will of God were identical.

It was in this spirit that, in 1526, Dürer painted his last and perhaps his greatest picture, the *"Four Apostles"* (Alte Pinakothek, Munich). He presented it to the City of Nuremberg as his artistic, intellectual, and moral legacy. It consists of two panels in the shape of altar wings, but no central panel was ever intended. The figures are more than life size, the panels tall and narrow. The same principle is applied as in the later portraits: the picture space encloses the figures as narrowly as possible in order to emphasize their powerful plasticity. They are arranged close together, those in front in profile, those at the back full-face and slightly smaller; on the left are St John and St Peter, on the right St Paul and St Mark. (As the Evangelist Mark was not one of the Apostles, the title is not strictly correct.) Dürer had seen compositions of this kind in Venice, and his memories of the small altarpiece by Giovanni Bellini in the Frari Church may have influenced him here. The saints are not, however, placed in an architectural framework, but set in glowing relief against a background of deepest black. Under each painting is a space containing texts from the writings of the Apostles, selected by Dürer and executed by the calligrapher Johannes Neudörfer.

The saints are imposing figures in draperies, similar to the Apostles Dürer started to engrave in 1523 with the idea of producing a copperplate series. St Paul seems to be derived from the *St Philip*—dated 1526—in that series. The militant Apostle stands like a mighty pillar, firmly planted on both feet, leaning on his sword and supporting a weighty Bible on his horizontal left arm—like an embodiment of the new Protestant Church based only on the pure word of God. Behind him, Mark looks out with flashing eyes. John is a tall, noble figure standing in a relaxed posture. He and his companion Peter are looking at a book that is open at the beginning of the Gospel according to St John. Beneath his horizontal right arm, which corresponds to Paul's left one, his mantle billows in majestic folds.

It has been justly observed that St John, with his high curved forehead, resembles Philipp Melanchthon, of whom Dürer did a copperplate engraving in the same year. Melanchthon—the most humane and perhaps the most noble of the Reformers—endeavoured to combine the religious autonomy of the Reformation with the spirit of humanism. For him, theology was first and foremost a matter of bringing morality into human life. At the time of the painting he was staying in Nuremberg, whose municipal authorities wished to appoint him Rector of St Sebald's College. Although he did not accept the post, he helped to set up the new school and selected the staff. Like all Nuremberg intellectuals, Dürer frequented the circle of the Reformers and his relations with them were very close. The idea of the renewal of Christianity was contained in his artistic message from the very beginning. He greatly respected Erasmus, of whom he made a drawing during his visit to Antwerp, and was a passionate admirer of Luther's. On the occasion of Luther's mock arrest following the Diet of Worms, Dürer expressed his fears for the Reformer's life in a grief-stricken entry in his diary.

The Reformation, however, also liberated revolutionary forces that threatened the new Church as much as the old. These were concentrated in the Baptist and Protestant spiritualist movements. The new dogmatism that menaced the Lutheran Church just as it was being consolidated turned several deeply reflective and religious members of Luther's intimate circle against him. In Nuremberg, an acquaintance of Dürer's, Johannes Denk, Rector of St Sebald's, belonged to the Baptist-minded spiritualists. The Peasants' Revolt was one consequence of this spiritual upheaval. Dürer's block-cutter Hieronymus Andreae sympathized with the insurgent peasants, while some of his pupils—the Beham brothers and Georg Pencz—were accused of atheism. Waging a war on two fronts, Luther fought the new enemy and the old with equal bitterness. The radical spiritualism formulated in a tract by Andreas Karlstadt fostered iconoclastic tendencies, and these touched Dürer to the quick. He had already taken a firm stand against them in his preface to the *Instructions on Measurement*. Now, in the *"Four Apostles,"* he took position against the "false prophets" and in the inscriptions appended to this work he warned those in authority "that they should not mistake human temptation

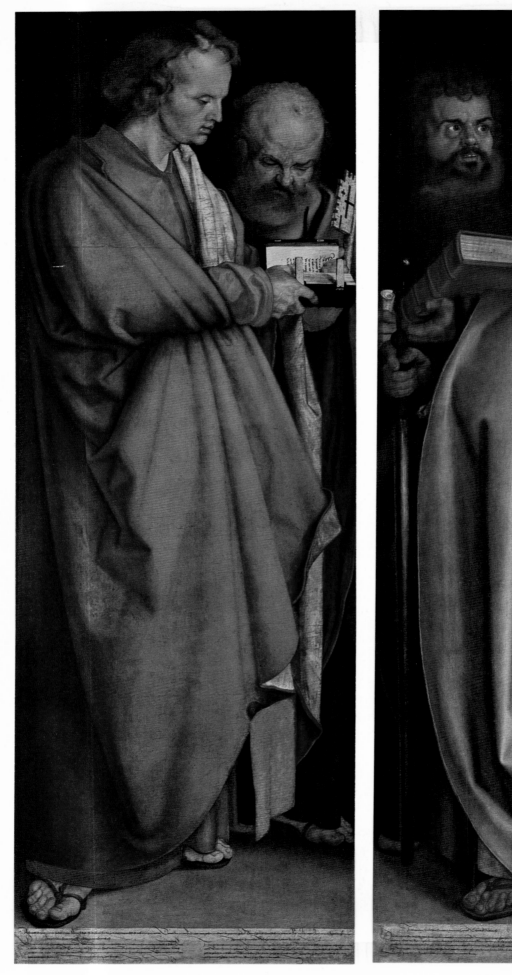

Albrecht Dürer (1471-1528).
The "Four Apostles," 1526. (Left panel 84⅝×29⅞"; right panel 84⅜×29⅞") Alte Pinakothek, Munich.

for the Word of God." This is the essential message of the painting. The assumption that the four saints represent the "four temperaments" of the Renaissance theory of human character rests solely on an unconfirmed statement by Neudörfer.

These two panels are Dürer's artistic testament. He devoted the last two years of his life to his treatise on proportion, and succeeded in completing it. Then, on April 6, 1528, he died with unexpected suddenness. His death—which was due to a lingering ailment he had contracted in the Netherlands—was mourned in Northern Europe with the same grief as Michelangelo's would later be mourned in Italy.

Despite the wide differences between the two great figures of German painting, Dürer and Mathis Gothardt-Neithardt, their art took the same direction in one respect: both of them in their later works were increasingly preoccupied with the human face. Portrait-painting was undoubtedly among Mathis' tasks as court painter to the Bishops of Mainz. Many attempts have been made to ascribe portraits to him, but the evidence is convincing only in the case of the portraits of *Counts Thomas and Hans Rieneck* (Wallraf-Richartz Museum, Cologne). These two portraits have something of the spiritual quality of his religious paintings.

Mathis' art as a portrait-painter reaches its climax in the powerful central panel of the *Altarpiece of St Maurice and St Erasmus* executed in 1521-1523 for the collegiate church of Halle. It depicts the *Meeting of St Maurice and St Erasmus* (Alte Pinakothek, Munich). St Erasmus, one of the Fourteen Holy Helpers, was martyred under the Emperor Diocletian; St Maurice was a captain in the Theban Legion. There is no historical foundation for their meeting, and the scene represented in the picture is really a political and religious allegory made for propaganda purposes. St Maurice was the patron saint of the abbey and town of Halle. St Erasmus became prominent in Halle only through the agency of Albrecht von Brandenburg, the "Great Cardinal" who united the Sees of Mainz, Halberstadt, and Magdeburg. In 1516 he arranged for the bones of St Erasmus to be transferred from the monastery of Oliva, near Danzig, to Halle, in order to make him the patron saint of the university he intended to found there as a bulwark against the pro-Reformation University of Wittenberg. This was done as a tribute to Erasmus of Rotterdam, whom Albrecht hoped to entice to his university. Mathis' altarpiece formed part of the Cardinal's plan. In 1520, a bejewelled silver statue of St Maurice in armour was dedicated to the patron saint of the town and erected in the choir of the collegiate church in front of the high altar. The armour worn by Mathis' St Maurice was inspired by this life-size work. The picture shows St Maurice greeting St Erasmus and welcoming him to Halle. Although the altarpiece was dedicated to St Maurice, the fêted guest in his sumptuous array plays an equally important part in it. The implication was that the great scholar Erasmus would be welcomed to the city with similar ceremony.

But the plan misfired, since Erasmus did not accept the invitation, preferring to remain quietly at Basel, and only the painting remained as a souvenir of the incident. Mathis then —probably by request—gave the features of Cardinal Albrecht, the originator of the plan, to the St Erasmus of the painting. Albrecht was one of the foremost humanists among the German ecclesiastics of the period; in fact, because of his liberal views, he was for a time suspected of sympathy with the Reformation. He gave a number of commissions to the Protestant painter Cranach, who frequently depicted him as St Jerome. Nevertheless, through the sale of indulgences, Cardinal Albrecht directly helped to provoke the outbreak of the Reformation. It is easy to understand his respect and liking for the great Catholic scholar Erasmus, who went to the brink of the Reformation but no farther.

As pure painting, as a portrayal of material splendour, the Halle panel is outstanding among Mathis' works. The combination of gold and red tones in the figure of St Erasmus is worthy of Titian. A contrasting note of coolness is provided by the silver armour worn by

St Maurice. The heads are lightly and loosely painted. As the saints are more than life size, there was no room for a crowd of other figures; the painter accordingly strove to create the impression of a host of followers by means of fragmentation. The picture aimed at expressing greatness in terms of worldly splendour. Mathis succeeded brilliantly in this, but his heart was not in the task, as a comparison with his other works clearly shows.

Erasmus of Rotterdam said that if the Saviour came back to earth he would undoubtedly again be scourged and crucified. Thus the faithful, tormented by conscience, felt the Passion of Christ as something eternally present. It confronts us shatteringly in two further works by Mathis: the *Aschaffenburg Predella* and the *Tauberbischofsheim Altarpiece*. The predella shows nothing except the body of the dead Christ stretched out horizontally. It is not a fragment, but the painter has daringly cut off the figure of the Virgin so that only her hands, the most eloquent witness of her grief, are visible. The dead Christ, bearing the marks of his appalling suffering, lies at rest. The symbols of power, in the form of the escutcheons of Cardinal Albrecht and Archbishop Dieter von Erbach, are reduced to insignificance by the sorrow of the mourning Virgin. Round about the same time, Holbein the Younger was painting his predella of the *Corpse of Christ in the Tomb* (1521, Kunstmuseum, Basel). The two works are similar in conception: all incidentals have been left out, and only the dead Christ remains. There is no transfigured divinity—only a reminder of the enormity of the suffering endured by the Son of Man. Yet what a difference there is between them! How clear, rational, and realistic is Holbein's depiction of the body, based on a model; how shattering is Mathis' painting in its sense of the drama that has taken place, its visionary power.

As we have seen, the tremendous spiritual and religious tension that prevailed in the early years of the century was reflected in the art as well as the thought of the period. It now moved to its catastrophic climax, finally erupting in the Reformation and the upheavals that accompanied it. At the outset, Luther's work was considerably advanced by the forces of chiliasm. The loosening-up of religious thought made it possible for an extreme individualist —verging on the visionary—like Mathis to work within the framework of the Church. But the important events were no longer taking place in the realm of the fine arts. The time had come for action and moral decisions, and even the mystic could no longer remain shut off in his solitude. The old Church seemed to fall in ruins. Luther put a new one in its place in Wittenberg, and Zwingli did the same in Zurich. The revolutionary forces had to be restrained

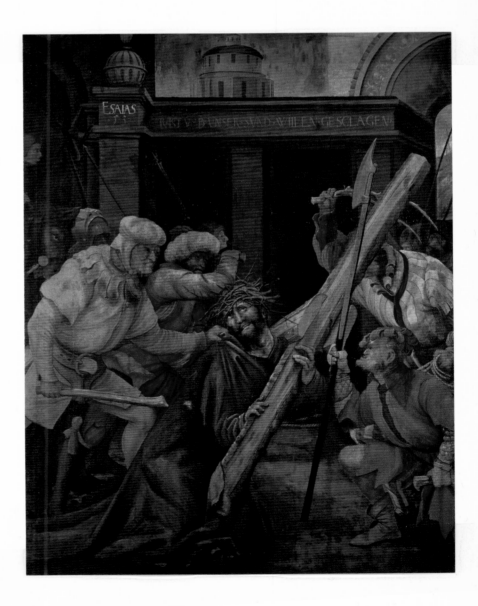

Mathis Gothardt-Neithardt (c. 1475-1528), called Matthias Grünewald. The Bearing of the Cross, c. 1525-1526. (77×60″) Back of the Crucifixion Panel from the Tauberbischofsheim Altarpiece. Staatliche Kunsthalle, Karlsruhe.

by the institution of some form of organized faith, otherwise they would reduce everything to chaos. But this was not possible everywhere. The spiritualist and sectarian movements were closely linked with those of social revolution. Contact with Hussite and Taborite ideas transformed the eschatological Christianity of the time into a gospel of violence, which—together with the appalling social conditions that then prevailed—led to the Peasants' War. One of its apostles was the preacher Thomas Münzer who led the peasants into battle under the sign of the rainbow and was executed in 1525 after the slaughter of the peasant army at Mühlhausen in Thuringia.

One of the great German painters, Jörg Ratgeb, had a similarly tragic destiny. He was born about 1480 at Herrenberg near Stuttgart. Very few of his altarpieces and other paintings remain, apart from the ruined frescoes in the Carmelite Monastery in Frankfurt. He was a highly cultured painter who must have studied in the Netherlands and perhaps also in Italy. In 1508 he was working in Stuttgart in the service of Duke Ulrich of Württemberg. His wife was a serf, and the Duke used this fact to bring pressure to bear on the artist and prevent him from working for anyone else. Ratgeb has been described as an early Mannerist. This is perhaps a just description, if only the formal aspect of his work is taken into account. But his art had more to it than that. It was of a kind found at that time—on the eve of the Peasants' War—only in Germany. It was an art that deliberately renounced knowledge and culture, pictorial brilliance and beauty of colour, choosing to be plain, simple, and folk-like, so that it might speak to the poor, humble, and outcast of the earth.

The most moving legacy of this new art—it was more than just a new "style"—is Ratgeb's *Herrenberg Altarpiece* of 1518-1519 (Staatsgalerie, Stuttgart), whose vast dimensions surpass even those of the *Isenheim Altarpiece*, by which it was clearly influenced. The *Resurrection* combines the spiritual qualities of Mathis' masterpiece with folk tradition. The tomb, consisting of a steep conical rock, is sealed by a stone slab. The resurrected Christ rises up stiffly, resembling a peasant wood-carving. Disks of light circle the hands and feet, with their glowing stigmata, and the upper part of the body. They seem to uphold the figure in a state of levitation. In the left hand is a crystal ball—reminiscent of similar structures in the works of Hieronymus Bosch—that is hovering rather than held. The soldiers are sprawling among a scattered array of colourful objects like tipsy revellers in a folk painting. The picture is so crammed as to suggest a *horror vacui*. The flat simple modelling is reminiscent of a woodcut. The colour is chosen simply to designate the different objects, without any concern for harmony.

This stirring altarpiece is the artist's last surviving work. As the peasant army moved on Stuttgart, the frightened town opened its gates. Delegated as a mediator, Ratgeb went over to the peasants, who made him their captain. After the terrible battle of Herrenberg, in which thousands of peasants lost their lives, he was captured and taken to Pforzheim where he was quartered alive by horses. But the defeat did not help much. After the bloody repression of the Peasants' Revolt, the Baptist movement began to spread from Zurich not only through Germany but through the whole of Europe, confirming what that deeply human sage Sebastian Franck wrote in his *Heretic's Chronicle*, namely that violence never bears fruit if it is not followed by the education of men in what is good and right.

It is not surprising that such a highly subjective and extremist artist as Mathis should be deeply shaken by these events. Not only are they reflected in his work, but they influenced the course of his life as it neared its end. His last painting was the vast *Tauberbischofsheim Altarpiece* on the subject of the Passion, of which the *Bearing of the Cross* and the *Crucifixion* (Staatliche Kunsthalle, Karlsruhe) have survived. Here Mathis has abandoned his differentiated form and high pictorial culture. He wants to penetrate directly to the heart of the matter, and this he does in a disturbing way. The scene showing Christ collapsing beneath the weight of the Cross is set between two town gates (an inner and an outer one) and brought close to the onlooker. The conception of the crowded composition, which had held good from the early Netherlandish painters until Dürer, has been abandoned. Only the figure of Christ is wholly visible, the others are fragmentary. It seems as if there is room for only a few people in the narrow space between the two gates, and as if we were being pushed into this space so that the scene is horribly, chokingly close. The religious persecutions of Mathis' time involved many such scenes, so that the artist was able to draw directly on experience. Mathis' unique illusionist gift makes the figures seem almost modelled in the round in the strange light that streams from somewhere above them.

We are reminded of similar effects achieved at that time by Gaudenzio Ferrari in the Monte Sacro chapels at Varallo by a combination of sculpture and painting. Had Mathis seen something of this kind, or is the effect simply due to a like-minded approach? Ferrari sought to appeal to the primitive instincts of simple folk, to stir them to the depths by making the Lord's suffering and the cruelty of his persecutors as "real" as possible, and Mathis is here pursuing a similar aim. He no longer uses the sophisticated idiom of his earlier altarpieces, which could be appreciated by the educated connoisseur, but abandons the old differentiation, variability, and richness in favour of a "primitive" narrative with an immediate appeal. In this, he resembles Ratgeb: he deliberately refrains from drawing on resources of which he is still fully in possession, as the unique mastery of colour—the soaring blue of the Christ, the glowing carmine-red of the man in the turban—amply demonstrates. The old magical colour is there, but it is used in conjunction with simple, primitive modelling to create a doubly striking effect.

The great change that had come over Mathis is explained by his vicissitudes at the time. He was suddenly dismissed from court service at Mainz and in 1526 took refuge in Frankfurt. Among possessions of his found there after his death were a "Riot List" (a sort of testimony of good character made out by sureties for people suspected of sympathy with the insurgent peasants and the Lutherans) and a nailed-down drawer containing a New Testament and "Lutheran trash"—obviously books he had put there for fear of being persecuted if they were found in his possession. (Aschaffenburg was one of the towns that sided with the peasants.) In Frankfurt, Mathis earned a living by manufacturing soap and doing occasional engineering work. His friend Jacobus Indagine, the astrologer and psychologist, took charge of his working tools when he moved. In 1527 he left Frankfurt and went to the Protestant town of Halle, where he worked as a hydraulic engineer. There he died at the end of August 1528, not as a famed and respected artist like Dürer, but as a "displaced person."

That the search for a *doctrine,* which for Dürer was a constructive, creative force, played a destructive role in the life and work of his contemporaries Jörg Ratgeb and Mathis Gothardt-Neithardt is one of the many paradoxes of the time.

Although both Dürer and Mathis Gothardt-Neithardt were struck down before their time, at the height of their creativeness, the fact that both died in the same year has something historically inevitable about it. With them passed the greatest of all ages of German painting. Admittedly, their pupils and contemporaries continued to be active, but the glow of inspiration had faded and the best surviving artists, such as Burgkmair and Altdorfer, worked on for only a few years—a decade at most—after their death. Reformed Germany had become a barren soil for art. Doctrine had killed the creative spirit—at once impulsive and intuitive, soaring and naive—of the great age. This age had lasted barely half a century. In a small enclave such as the See of Passau it might be possible for a great master of the Danube School like Wolf Huber to maintain the originality of his art right up to the threshold of the age of Bruegel. But the greatest artist next to Dürer and Mathis—Holbein the Younger—left Basel after the devastation of its churches by the iconoclasts and settled in England.

Master of the Angrer Portrait. Portrait of Canon Gregor Angrer of Brixen, 1519. (22⅝×16″)
Tiroler Landesmuseum Ferdinandeum, Innsbruck.

The Formation
of the Character Portrait

I must step forward and for the sake of God's honour
and name incur all men's enmity.

LUTHER, *On Good Works*

Ubi in consilio est odium, ibi caecum est indicium.

ERASMUS, *Colloquia.*

EUROPEAN painting in the fifteenth century produced two great traditions of portraiture. The first, which had originated in France, was developed in the Netherlands by a variety of artists from Jan van Eyck to Michiel Sittow. It was essentially a court art and aimed at the discriminating portrayal of human individuality within the framework of strict conventions. The second was a product of Italy and expressed the new spirit of humanism. Both these traditions came together in Augsburg, the city which produced the most brilliant school of portraiture in Renaissance Germany. Portrait-painting in the Late Gothic period in Germany was overshadowed by religious painting, and the goals that artists in Italy and the Netherlands had set themselves meant nothing to its practitioners. Its achievements were relatively modest, but they paved the way for an understanding of human character—the quality to which the German portraitists of the Renaissance owe their greatness.

As in so many other branches of German art, it was Dürer who laid the foundations. Growing up in the Late Gothic tradition—which he still followed in his first *Self-Portrait* (1493, Louvre) and the early *Portrait of his Father* (1490, Uffizi)—he made the breakthrough to the humanistic portrait with the *Self-Portrait* of 1498 (Prado), after which his work in this domain went on from strength to strength, culminating in the magnificent character studies of the late portrait-engravings. Dürer was a special case, however, and his painted portraits were too few in number to set off a new trend on a European scale. But in Augsburg, the heart of the Swabian region with its long tradition of painting, Holbein the Elder was able to develop his own genius as a portraitist and to lay the foundations for the portraits that would earn his son European fame.

Swabia was particularly receptive soil for the highly developed art of the Netherlands —otherwise neither Holbein the Elder nor Strigel could have achieved their masterly portraits. We must assume that both were acquainted with this art at its source. In Strigel's case there was the added encouragement of royal patronage, which demanded a high level of technical perfection both in form and colour, an ideal to which he was as much committed as Juan de Flandes and Sittow. As the Emperor's court portraitist, Strigel was expected to produce highly polished work—hence the glowing, enamel-like finish of such paintings as the portrait group of *Maximilian and his Family* (Kunsthistorisches Museum, Vienna). The faces are of equal lightness, but delicately modelled by shadows. In the dark interior, the tranquil radiance of this family group produces an almost magical, dreamlike effect. The portrait shows the

Bernhard Strigel (1460-1528).
Portrait of the Emperor Maximilian I and his Family, 1515. (28½×23⅜″) Kunsthistorisches Museum, Vienna.

Emperor with his first wife Mary of Burgundy, his son Philip the Fair, his grandsons Ferdinand of Austria and Charles V, and his grandson-in-law Louis of Hungary. It was presumably painted in Vienna on the occasion of the double wedding in 1515. The captions identifying the figures with members of the Holy Family were added later at the instigation of Cuspinian, into whose possession the picture came and who had a group portrait of his own family appended to it. Strigel was the first to paint real group portraits in this way, elaborating on the old idea of the family altarpiece.

The portraits by Hans Maler of Ulm stem from those by Strigel. Like Strigel, Maler was a pupil of Zeitblom's, as is shown by his early religious paintings, but he must soon have come under Strigel's influence. It was probably on the latter's recommendation that he obtained commissions from Maximilian. This royal patronage was continued by the Emperor's grandson Ferdinand and his wife Anna, and Maler's name often occurs in documents of the period. The London Society of Antiquaries possesses his charming portrait of Ferdinand's sister *Mary of Hungary* (1520).

Maler settled in the mining town of Schwaz in the North Tyrol. There he decorated the church and Franciscan monastery with frescoes and, more important, painted portraits of local plutocrats and officials connected with the wealthy banking house of Fugger, which owned the Schwaz silver mines. These portraits include one of Anton Fugger himself. In their clarity, radiance of colour, and objectivity, they are among the most delightful portraits of the Renaissance. The portraits of the founders of Tratzberg Castle near Schwaz, *Moritz Welzer of Eberstein and his Wife* (1524, Akademie der Bildenden Künste, Vienna), show Hans Maler at the height of his powers.

Since Swabian artists worked there so frequently, the North Tyrol can be considered as forming, to all intents and purposes, a single artistic province with Swabia. One of the most fascinating Tyrolean portrait painters of the Renaissance period was the so-called Master of the Angrer Portrait. Max J. Friedländer has been able to identify a small group of works by the hand of this anonymous artist through their links with the magnificent portrait of *Canon Gregor Angrer of Brixen* (1519, Tiroler Landesmuseum Ferdinandeum, Innsbruck) to which

Hans Maler (traceable 1500-1529).
Portrait of Mary of Hungary, 1520. (18¾×13¾″) Society of Antiquaries of London.

Ambrosius Holbein (probably 1494-after 1519).
Portrait of a Fair-haired Boy, c. 1516. (13¼×10⅝″) Kunstmuseum, Basel.

The inscription on the tablet reads:

PICTA LICET FACIES VI
VAE NON CEDO SED INSTAR
SVM DOMINI IVSTIS NO
BILE LINEOLIS
OCTO IS DVM PERAGIT
PIETH SIC GNAVITER IN ME
D QVOD NATVRAE EST,
EXPRIMIT ARTIS OPVS.

BON· AMORBACCHIVM·
10· J HOLBEIN · DEPINGEBAT·
A· M· D· XIX· PRID· EID· OCT·BR

Hans Holbein the Younger (1497-1543).
Portrait of Bonifacius Amerbach, 1519. (11¼×10¾″) Kunstmuseum, Basel.

he owes his appellation. In this Tyrolean portrait the scale and daring of the composition give an impressive vigour and weight to the personality of the sitter. The strictly frontal presentation lends the painting something of the powerful realism of the Italian portrait busts of the Quattrocento. Canon Gregor Angrer of Brixen (Bressanone) often went to Italy on diplomatic missions, and may have had a say in the strikingly modern form of the picture space, which this master always kept very narrow. The dark colours emphasize the modelling of the face. A connection with the Augsburg school has been surmised, but there are also strong and unmistakable traces of the local Tyrolean tradition. In this mature late work, the Angrer Master shows himself the equal of Burgkmair.

In their complete synthesis of German and Italian styles of portraiture, the Angrer Master and Burgkmair paved the way for the art of Hans Holbein the Younger, who was born at Augsburg towards the end of 1497. A painter of precocious talent, he received his early training from his father, of whose art his own seems to be the direct continuation. By 1515, however, when his father was working on the *Altarpiece of St Sebastian*, Holbein the Younger had already moved to Basel. His brother Ambrosius, who was probably born in 1494, set off on his journeyman's travels in 1514, visiting Constance and Stein am Rhein and turning up in Basel in 1516. There the brothers, too young to set up on their own account, entered the workshop of the painter Hans Herbster as assistants. Thus the great cycle of German art—from the journeyman Dürer to the journeyman Holbein—came full circle in the Swiss city on the Rhine, the most important centre of German humanism.

Of the two Holbein brothers, Ambrosius was the more sensitive and gentle, and he was unable to liberate himself from the dominating influence of his father to the same extent as the more robust and more talented Hans. The power of that influence, the more compelling because of the very high quality of their father's art, is revealed in a series of early works by the brothers which have been attributed to each of the three Holbeins in turn.

They include the fine deep-coloured portrait of *Hans Herbster* in Basel—probably the work of Ambrosius. That the two charming portraits of boys, also in the Basel Museum, are definitely by him has been proved by a note in the Amerbach Inventory. The dark-haired younger boy is set in an architectural framework of pillars with an architrave; this was also used by Holbein the Elder for the *Portrait of a Man* dated 1513 (formerly Lanckoronski Collection). Ambrosius heightens the severity of the architecture by emphasizing the contrasts of light and shade, and this further enhances the delicate translucency and appealing youthfulness of the subject. In their early years in Basel, Ambrosius and Hans the Younger undertook a number of joint commissions such as the two signboards they painted for a schoolmaster in 1516. Another joint effort—in which Hans set the tone and did most of the work—was the remarkable series of marginal drawings, executed in late 1515 and early 1516, in a copy of Froben's edition of Erasmus' *Praise of Folly* belonging to the schoolmaster Oswald Myconius. This brilliant achievement brought the young artists to the attention of the publishers of Basel, especially Froben for whom they did a number of title-pages, borders, and initials. Hans was thus able to develop his genius as an illustrator, which was counterbalanced by his incredible objectivity as a portraitist.

Hans Holbein the Younger (1497-1543). The Corps

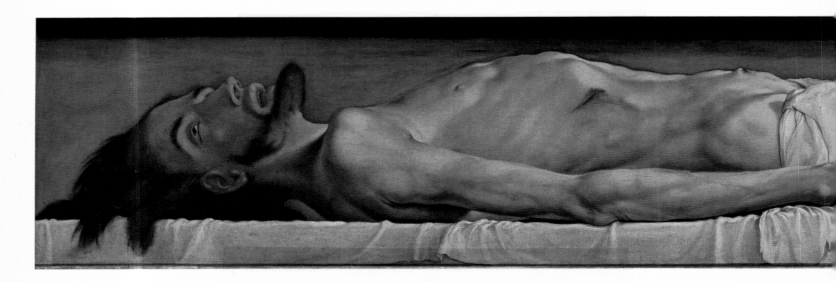

His first fully developed portraits were those of Jakob Meyer, Burgomaster of Basel, and his wife (Kunstmuseum, Basel), painted in 1516. They are in diptych form and were preceded by two careful tinted silverpoint drawings, following a method used by Holbein the Elder in preparing his portraits. Such accomplished portraits could not have been achieved by a nineteen-year-old boy without the support of a notable tradition—this was provided by the works of his father and his uncle. The setting of Renaissance architecture is of a kind found in both Holbein the Elder and Burgkmair—one remembers in particular the latter's 1512 woodcut of Johann Paumgartner. A similar daylight clarity of colour is a characteristic of Hans Maler's portraits. Apt the Elder and his sons, as well as Leonhard Beck and Jörg Breu, had achieved outstanding things in the portrait, and so had the masters working in the Swabian towns, such as Strigel at Memmingen and Schaffner at Ulm. This was a firm foundation for the work of a young painter who, moreover, found in Basel a tradition of portraiture that was very much alive, as is evidenced by the portraits of the notable Meyer zum Pfeil family (Kunstmuseum, Basel). Nevertheless, in their integrity and objectivity, the youthful Holbein's portraits were a brilliant achievement that once and for all set a new standard for truth and naturalness in painting. The architectural incidentals come from that treasury of forms on which the natives of Augsburg could draw so effortlessly and which found particularly full and generous expression in his designs for stained-glass paintings.

Holbein's gift of architectonic invention served him well in dealing with a monumental task he undertook during his stay in Lucerne from 1517 to 1519: the decoration of the façade and interior of the house of Burgomaster Jakob Hertenstein. The practice of decorating façades with paintings was a very common one in Northern Italy, and there, for this type of work, a young artist could expect to find inspiration in abundance. Holbein accordingly visited Milan in the winter of 1518-1519, probably going on to Mantua, since he used motifs from Mantegna's *Triumphal Procession* on the Lucerne façade, and also decorated the room in which he placed a portrait of young Benedikt von Hertenstein (1517, Metropolitan Museum, New York) with a classical triumphal procession.

The experience of Italy must have had the same significance for Holbein as it had for Dürer. He became acquainted not only with the work of Foppa, Bramante, Gaudenzio Ferrari, and Solario, but also with Leonardo's *Last Supper* and with the paintings of his pupils Luini, Boltraffio, and Cesare da Sesto. The classical fusion between southern and northern art is seen in its noblest form in the portrait of the young lawyer and humanist *Bonifacius Amerbach*

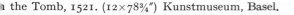
the Tomb, 1521. (12 × 78¾″) Kunstmuseum, Basel.

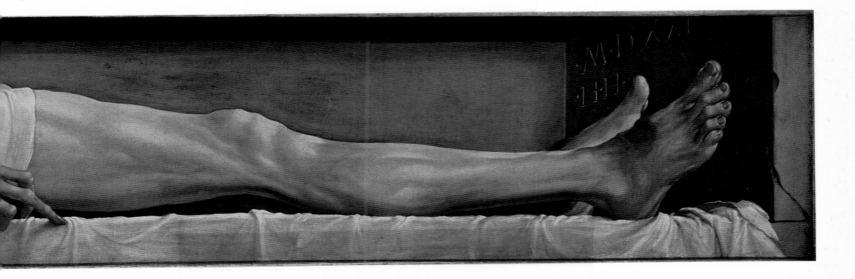

(1519, Kunstmuseum, Basel). This half-length portrait has the slightly slanting composition typical of Holbein. Amerbach is dressed simply and elegantly in a scholar's robes and is shown in front of a fig tree to which is fixed a panel with a Latin inscription. Behind it are snow-covered mountains under a radiant blue sky. A marvellous contrast is made between the southern warmth that enfolds the scholar and the coolness of the distant northern mountains from which he came—like so many sons of German patrician families who were studying in the South. The painting is imbued with that sense of a wider world that the humanists were expressing in science as Holbein was in art. Rational, restrained, cool, and measured on the outside, it is infused with deep human feeling. This portrait proclaims the spirit of a new age.

The works produced by Holbein in the years following his return to Basel from Lucerne show the extent to which he was inspired by his visit to the South. A diptych in monochrome tones of the *Man of Sorrows* and the *Virgin Mary* and a chiaroscuro drawing of the *Holy Kinship* (both in the Kunstmuseum, Basel) show the stimulating effects of his encounter with Lombard architecture. Although the folding altarpiece had lost its importance by Holbein's time, he paid it a final tribute in the *Altarpiece of Chancellor Hans Oberried* painted for the Charterhouse of Kleinbasel (1520-1521); the central panel was destroyed by the iconoclasts, the wings are in Freiburg Cathedral. The figures are dominated by the lavish architecture. For the *Nativity* Holbein used an engraving by Nicoletto da Modena. It is a picture of bold lighting effects, harking back to Baldung's night-piece for the altar of Freiburg Cathedral. The *Epiphany* is set in front of a ruined castle, which is distinctly reminiscent of the Castello Sforzesco in Milan with its culverts and Bramantesque architecture. The portraits of the donors were painted by Holbein the Elder.

The most striking evidence of the influence of Italian painting on Holbein is to be found in the altarpiece of the *Last Supper* (perhaps for Basel Town Hall; Kunstmuseum, Basel) in which the artist was clearly influenced by Leonardo. The intently questioning gesture with which Peter turns to John disposes of any doubt on the matter. In its deeply glowing colour the picture departs from the light Florentine colour-range of Leonardo's fresco and approaches the rich full colour of Lombard painting, as exemplified by the works of Solario and Gaudenzio Ferrari. The eight wing panels in Basel Museum may have served to close off the panel of the *Last Supper*. The brilliant finish of these paintings could not have been achieved without the example of the Lombards. For the cool lighting effects, however, Holbein seems to have drawn on another source—the *Isenheim Altarpiece*, with which he must have been familiar. The way the threatening cloud is carried over from the *Crucifixion* to the *Bearing of the Cross* shows the same striving for unity that we find in Burgkmair's altarpieces. The *Entombment* with its slender figures presages the canons of form of the School of Fontainebleau, on which Holbein had considerable influence through the Biblical woodcuts he published in Lyons. It also suggests that he was familiar with the composition of Raphael's *Entombment* of 1507.

In 1519 Holbein was admitted to the Basel painter's guild, and in 1520 he was granted citizenship of the town. The following years witnessed his most important achievements in the realm of religious painting. In 1521, he painted the *Corpse of Christ in the Tomb*, in 1522 the Solothurn *Virgin and Child*, and towards 1526 the mature masterpiece *The Virgin and Child with the Family of Burgomaster Meyer*. The 1522 *Virgin* (Kunstmuseum, Solothurn), painted for Hans Gerster, the town clerk of Basel, shows the Virgin seated between two saints—a knight (St Ursus?) and a bishop. In the Louvre there is a portrait sketch of a pretty young woman—believed not without reason to be the painter's wife—on which, with slight modifications, the figure of the Solothurn Virgin is based. This shows the new secular spirit that was beginning to enter into painting. Dürer, even when he used models for his religious pictures, raised them to such a transcendental level that we are hardly aware of them as real men and women. Holbein was in no way inferior to Dürer in the statics of picture construction, but his

Hans Holbein the Younger (1497-1543). The Virgin and Child with the Family of Burgomaster Jakob Meyer,
1526 and 1528/1529. (57¾×40⅛") Collection of Prince Ludwig of Hesse, Grand Ducal Palace, Darmstadt.

are actual people who make up the composition of a *Sacra Conversazione* with the highest degree of human reality of which painting is capable. Nor do the closely linked colours carry the painting into a transcendental sphere—on the contrary, they intensify the impression of the tangible and present. Beside the sunny humanity of the Mother of God with her only Son glistens the dark armour of the knight, who is a real protector rather than a symbol. Since Konrad Witz, nobody had painted armour so realistically. Even the Virgin's halo can be taken as the glow of the real morning sun that shines through the arch, making the iron railings cast shadows, rather than the emanation from a divine being. Mathis' *Maria-Schnee Altarpiece* may have served as a model here, but Holbein definitely transformed the supernatural radiance into a natural one.

Jakob Meyer zum Hasen was one of the most influential men in Basel. As an army officer and an envoy, he frequently visited Italy. A banker by profession, he had rapidly made a fortune and risen to the dignity of burgomaster by the time Holbein painted his first portrait of him. In 1521 he was deprived of office, supposedly because of financial transactions, but in reality because he was the leader of the Catholic party in Basel—feeling on religious matters was already running high in the city. In 1526, he commissioned from Holbein a picture of himself and his family under the protection of the Mother of God. As it was intended for the chapel of his country estate of Weiherhaus at Gross-Gundeldingen—an intimate private room too small to hold a full-size altarpiece—the picture was conceived in the form of a *pala*, a devotional work for the Meyer family and a small circle of friends.

The theme is a traditional one—the Virgin of Mercy protecting the faithful under her outspread mantle. The painting, now in the Grand-Ducal Palace at Darmstadt, was thus in the nature of an avowal by the donor of his adherence to the Catholic faith. That the artist was aware of this is apparent even in the preparatory drawings. As was his custom, Holbein made careful preliminary studies from life; three of these—depicting Meyer, his wife, and his daughter—have been preserved (Kupferstichkabinett, Basel). They are large drawings in coloured chalk like those that earned Holbein fame as a draftsman in his maturity. The technique was one he may have learnt directly from Leonardo's followers in Milan and that he must also have come across in Clouet's circle in France in 1524. In the drawing the donor's head is in the same position as in the painting, but in the first he is calmly seated whereas in the second he is kneeling. A similar change was made in the figure of Meyer's daughter Anna. Holbein did not spare his clients the effort of posing for him in accordance with the plan he had established for the picture. One thing, however, is present in both the drawing and the painting: the expression of devout confidence in the donor's face. The painter understood the purpose of the picture and took it objectively and unmistakably into account.

The construction of the painting is rather tightly packed. The niche—in the form of a shell—and its support weigh heavily on the figures, but they also offer them secure protection (this has been misunderstood in the copy in Dresden). In its present form the composition is even more crowded than it was originally, since Holbein touched up the painting at the request of the donor in 1528-1529, after his first sojourn in England. Meyer's son had died in the meantime, and in the new version all the members of his family, both living and dead, are shown united under the protection of the Virgin. Thus Meyer's first wife, who had died in 1511, has been added to the group of women on the right. The daughter, who in the first version was still a child with flowing hair as in the drawing, is now dressed in bridal clothes and has more grown-up features. This masterpiece was thus achieved by co-operation between the painter and those he portrayed. Since his basic material was the human being and his strength as a painter lay in his objectivity in handling this material, it was natural that he should select a

◄ Hans Holbein the Younger (1497-1543). Portrait of Jane Seymour, 1536. (25¾×18¾") Kunsthistorisches Museum, Vienna.

model for his portrayal of the Virgin. In 1526 Holbein painted a diptych showing *Venus* and *Lais* the Corinthian courtesan (Kunstmuseum, Basel); the model for this extremely polished work, with its wealth of reds, golds, and blues, was a society woman called Dorothea von Offenburg. For Holbein her Leonardesque type of beauty was the living embodiment of an ideal, and he chose her unhesitatingly as his model for the figure of the Madonna. Thus the Mother of God has the same lifelike presence as those she protects. As always with Holbein the Younger, the colour is somewhat metallic in quality, ranging from dark gold to steel blue —as far as warmth and harmony of tone are concerned, Holbein the Elder had more influence on Burgkmair than on his son.

Here Holbein set a standard of objective realistic handling that was new in German painting and was attained in Italy only by Raphael and Titian. Holbein the Elder strove for it but the idealism of his art put up a barrier that only the realistic genius of his son could break down. Thus Holbein the Younger came closer to the concepts of the classical High Renaissance, as evolved in Italy, than any other painter in the North, and did so at a time when idealism and poetry were giving way to discipline and a clear-headed critical approach. In this way he became the leading painter of the Late Renaissance in Germany and succeeded during his lifetime in acquiring European stature for German art—something that all his great predecessors had failed to do. Thanks to his controlled and objective approach, his pictures offered a faithful mirror of Man, of his soul and character, and he became the greatest portraitist of all time. That he also had considerable imaginative and narrative powers is shown by his woodcuts for the Bible, his *Dance of Death*, and his frescoes in the Basel Town Hall. By themselves, however, these would never have raised him to the level of Dürer or Mathis. It is his art as a portraitist that puts him in the front rank of German painters.

Through Myconius, Amerbach, and Froben, Holbein was introduced to Erasmus. In 1521, Erasmus had settled permanently in Basel, preferring intellectual freedom and independence to the partisan struggles that threatened to involve him everywhere else. He was particularly attached to Basel because of his friendship with Froben, who had published his writings, in particular the editions of St Jerome and the New Testament that had been mainly responsible for his first visit to Basel. At that time he had laughed heartily at Holbein's marginal drawings for the *Praise of Folly*, which Myconius had shown him. Now the child prodigy had become a well-known artist who had painted Froben and his nephew Amerbach, was busy working on illustrations for the publisher, and was hailed as a rising genius. The great scholar accordingly agreed to sit to him for his portrait. Working with his customary thoroughness, Holbein produced in 1523 his first portrait of *Erasmus* (Earl of Radnor, Longford Castle). It shows the scholar as a half-length figure, standing or seated behind a table, surrounded by his beloved books. His thin hands, of which the artist had made a wonderful silverpoint drawing beforehand, rest on a volume bound in red leather and bearing the title *The Labours of Hercules* in Greek. He is enveloped in a black cloak lined with golden brown mink—for this is the chilly, sensitive Erasmus who considered himself so delicate yet could endure so surprisingly much. The fine, intellectual features with wide, thin lips over which a smile is hovering—half mocking and sceptical, half understanding and forgiving—are those of the ageing Erasmus at the height of his fame, glad to have a haven where he could work in peace after so many vicissitudes. In the religious struggles of the time, Erasmus was a controversial figure. His remarkable philological studies helped lay the theological foundations for the Reformation, whose partisans believed that a return to the cleansed and purified texts of the Holy Scriptures would restore the teaching of Christ to its original purity. In increasing measure his humanism became a religious ethos. His emphasis on justification through faith, his contempt for pomp and ceremony in religious services, and his approval of general rather than private confession showed that he was intellectually in sympathy with the main points of the Lutheran programme. On some questions, such as the possibility of repeated baptism and the prohibition of war and oaths, the ideas of Erasmus even approached those of the Baptists. He spoke out

Hans Holbein the Younger (1497-1543). Portrait of Erasmus of Rotterdam, 1523. (30×20″)
Collection of the Earl of Radnor, Longford Castle, near Salisbury.

Lucas Cranach the Elder (1472-1553).
Portrait of Martin Luther, 1525. (Diameter 4″) Kunstmuseum, Basel.

strongly, in the clearest terms, against the worldliness of the Church and its accumulation of wealth. Thus this truly universal genius anticipated almost all the turnings that the religious thought of the period would take.

This made him many enemies, not only in the Catholic Church to which he remained faithful, but also among the Reformers. Luther, from being an admirer, became his bitter opponent since he could not, in his sublime simplicity, recognize the tolerant and forgiving spirit of Erasmus, who was a great educator rather than a theological genius. These, then, are the features of Erasmus, the author of the *Encomium Moriae* and the *Colloquia*. How much more adequately they are portrayed here than in Dürer's chalk drawing of 1520, significant though this may have been! It was in the very nature of Dürer's art to give his models heroic stature, whereas Holbein coolly analysed them. Most of Holbein's portraits demonstrate the superiority of the artist over the sitter, but all those he painted of Erasmus acknowledge the scholar's absolute intellectual superiority.

The portrait now in the possession of the Earl of Radnor, at Longford Castle, was immediately followed by that in the Louvre. Here we see Erasmus engaged in his favourite occupation—writing. He is carefully weighing his phrases, and the clear-cut profile eloquently expresses his concentration. This is a work of the highest precision and consistency, both in composition and expression—in short, *the* classic humanist portrait, a monument to a great age of thought and scholarship. The distribution of form and space on the picture surface has a calculated, almost mathematical quality that was to be further intensified in Holbein's English portraits. It challenges comparison with Cranach's portrait of Luther (Kunstmuseum,

Basel) painted in 1525. Cranach's simple, honest work gives a faithful likeness of the great religious reformer, bringing out all the hardness of his tough peasant skull, but little of his fiery spirit. It thus has a certain narrowness and small-mindedness that make us regret that Dürer never painted his projected portrait of Luther. Cranach's art had become increasingly provincial in its isolation. This is a far cry from the supremely cosmopolitan Erasmus as reflected in the mirror of Holbein's art. Nevertheless, each of these painters in his own way did justice to his subject. The sincerity of the one and the calculation of the other are eloquent in their contrasting fashion.

It was Erasmus who paved the way for Holbein's visit to England. In a letter to Pirckheimer on June 3, 1524, Erasmus reported that he had sent two portraits of himself to English friends. These were the portrait that is now in the collection of the Earl of Radnor (a present to William Warham, Archbishop of Canterbury) and the profile in the Louvre.

Hans Holbein the Younger (1497-1543).
The Artist's Wife, his Son Philipp and his Daughter Katharina, 1528. (30¼×25⅛″) Kunstmuseum, Basel.

In 1526 Holbein left Basel, armed with letters of introduction from Erasmus to Petrus Aegidius in Antwerp and to Thomas More and other friends of the scholar's in London. His visit to the Netherlands, where he was probably welcomed by Quentin Massys, must have been of some importance to him as an artist. As a result of Erasmus' recommendation to More, a trusted friend to whom he had earlier dedicated the *Encomium Moriae*, Holbein was warmly received in the household of the great humanist. On December 18, More wrote to Erasmus: "Your painter, my dear Erasmus, is a marvellous artist." By the end of the year Holbein had started a portrait group of More's family in the latter's house in Chelsea. This work, which was painted in tempera on canvas, has not survived, but we can form an excellent idea of it from the magnificent single studies at Windsor and from a pen sketch of the whole composition in Basel. The family, ten people in all, were grouped, seated or standing, round More and his father. The setting was an intimate one—an Old English interior with Gothic furniture. When Holbein returned to Basel he brought back the pen sketch as a present from More to Erasmus who, in a touching letter, expressed his thanks and his delight at being reunited with his friends, even if it was only through a picture. The idea of group portraits had originated in paintings showing the Holy Kinship, and was used first in Swabia as can be seen from Strigel's works. Jan van Scorel took it up in his altarpiece at Ober-Vellach in the Austrian Alps, and transposed it after his return to the Netherlands into the corporation portrait. By then, Holbein had already painted the More family, and he must therefore be recognized as the pioneer in this important new branch of the art of portraiture.

In the following year, 1527, Holbein painted a portrait of More alone (Frick Collection, New York), which is noteworthy for the brooding seriousness of the sitter's face: it seems as if—even before he had been raised to the highest office—he had a premonition of his tragic fate. At the same time his features betray a hidden fire, showing that here was a man of unbending integrity, prepared to die for what he thought right. Holbein's objectivity, though often so merciless, always does justice to true human greatness, despite the distancing effect. Through More, Holbein gained entry to the highest intellectual circles of England, which at that time surpassed all other European countries in humanist culture. The religious controversies that were such a disturbing factor in the intellectual life of Central Europe had not yet affected the island. The young King Henry VIII—the hope of all English intellectuals until his Nero-like transformation of his way of life—was the foremost promoter of humanism. "Here the arts are freezing to death," Erasmus had written in the letter of introduction that Holbein brought to Petrus Aegidius from Basel. The noble head of William Warham, Archbishop of Canterbury, is depicted in a painting of the same year (Lambeth Palace, London). This prince of the Church had himself painted in the same posture as Erasmus in the painting the latter had sent him, perhaps with the intention of reciprocating the gift. The intelligent features of Niklaus Kratzer of Munich, Court Astronomer to Henry VIII, appear in a fine portrait now in the Louvre (1528). Kratzer was tutor to More's children and this naturally brought him into contact with Holbein. A spirit of mathematical clarity, cleanliness, and neatness pervades this painting, which must have been a task after Holbein's own heart. The wonderful still life composition of the instruments has been arranged with infinite thought round the figure, which is solidly rendered in surface and depth. The same mathematical clarity, combined with the greatest inner vitality, characterizes the double portrait of Thomas Godsalve and his son John (1528, Dresden).

In 1528 Holbein returned to Basel. The reasons for his journey to England had been mainly economic, but he had stepped out of the increasingly provincial atmosphere of Central Europe into the wider world. Although England could not give him the artistic stimulus he had received from his visits to Italy, France, and the Netherlands, its intellectual climate was nevertheless different—had it not delighted Erasmus, who had made a number of congenial friends there? This atmosphere of intellectual freedom and cosmopolitan openness must have meant a great deal to a portraitist like Holbein. Its effect can be seen in the portraits of the last Basel period (1528-1532) which include, first and foremost, that of his own family—his wife, his son Philipp, and his small daughter Katharina—which is painted in oils on paper (Kunstmuseum, Basel). The figures form a restfully balanced pyramidal composition. We are reminded of similar compositions—showing the Virgin with the Christ Child and St John or St Anne with the Virgin and Child—in the works of the classic Italian and German painters, including Leonardo, Raphael, and Titian, as well as Dürer and Mathis. It is strange that Holbein, who abroad had propagated the style of the Late Renaissance, should have reverted to this simple, harmonious type of High Renaissance composition as soon as he returned home. The expression of the boy, with its mixture of shyness and intensity, recalls the *Isenheim Altarpiece*—which Holbein frequently visited.

Hans Holbein the Younger (1497-1543). Jean de Dinteville and Georges de Selve ("The Ambassadors"), 1533. (81¼×82½")
By Courtesy of the Trustees, National Gallery, London.

Hans Holbein the Younger (1497-1543). Portrait of Georg Gisze, 1532. (37¾×33¾")
Staatliche Museen, Berlin-Dahlem.

This is Holbein's simplest, yet most expressive and deeply human portrait. The painter portrays his family with ruthless objectivity, undeterred by the fact that the picture might be considered as a self-indictment. A sense of gloom and solitude hangs over the family, which had been separated from their husband and father for so long. At this time Protestant iconoclasts were beginning to be active in Basel, and the prospects for an artist there were dim. This may partly account for the despairing expression on the face of Holbein's wife, who can hardly have been in a prosperous condition on his return, otherwise he would not have hastened to secure her material situation by buying her a house.

By now, Holbein was undoubtedly famous. The Town Council of Basel commissioned him to continue the work on the Town Hall frescoes, and the wings of the great cathedral organ must also have been executed shortly after his return. Art-loving citizens commissioned him to decorate their houses—"Zum Tanz," "Zum Kaiserstuhl"—with frescoes. His commissions were now for secular paintings only, for in Basel the Reformation had brought a violent outbreak of iconoclasm. In February 1529, bonfires of religious paintings were set alight round the churches and blazed for two days and nights. What could not be burned was smashed to pieces or whitewashed, as Erasmus noted at the time. Erasmus himself—like many of the university professors and high ecclesiastical dignitaries of the time—left Basel, and moved to the neighbouring Catholic town of Freiburg-im-Breisgau, which was under the sovereignty of Ferdinand of Austria.

It is understandable that such events should make a deep impression on a creative artist, even one so deeply reserved as Holbein. His attitude to the new doctrine was so equivocal that he was summoned before the Town Council to which he excused his absence from the Communion as being due to lack of understanding—"they would have to explain it better to him." Thus the persecution of artists continued—only this time it came from the opponents of those who had persecuted Mathis and Ratgeb. It is thus hardly surprising that in 1532 Holbein again left Basel, which had become a wilderness artistically. In Freiburg he visited Erasmus whom he again asked for letters of introduction. On this occasion he painted the miniature portrait that Erasmus bequeathed with his works of art to Bonifacius Amerbach (Kunstmuseum, Basel). These small portraits on little beechwood panels with turned frames were Holbein's first experiments in a field—the portrait miniature—in which he was later to achieve outstanding things in England. Round about this time, he painted a similar miniature of Melanchthon (Hanover). He may have got the idea from Cranach's miniature portraits of Luther and his wife, painted in 1525, since these came to Basel and Holbein based a woodcut on the portrait of the Reformer.

Holbein disappointed Erasmus by turning his back on his old friends in England and seeking contact with a circle of influential people who were on the whole opposed to them. More's star was on the decline. English society, too, began to be poisoned by religious controversy, and a number of people who had sat for Holbein ended their lives under the executioner's axe. The artist therefore had to be cautious. His ambition to become court painter was not fulfilled until 1535 or 1536. From Erasmus' correspondence with More and Aegidius it is clear that Holbein was once again applying the principles of the Swiss mercenary to his career, that is, seeking to make money abroad and return home with it. At the beginning of his second sojourn in England, his clients came from neither humanist nor court circles, but from the prosperous German merchant community which had its headquarters in the Steelyard in London. Their names were Wedigh, Born, Tybis, Fallen, and Gisze. The great portrait of Gisze (1532, Staatliche Museen, Berlin) is the most important of those Holbein painted at this time. The idea of the Kratzer portrait has here been taken up again and developed in the most delightful way: that of showing a man in his professional environment. It is both a great portrait and a wonderful still life. The instruments, books, and papers scattered on the shelves, ledges, and table, the vase of Venetian glass through which Gisze's shimmering silk sleeves are visible, the Oriental rug—all these are observed with an exquisite care for detail without detracting from the mathematical firmness of the central form. Portraits combined with interiors went back to an old Netherlandish tradition stretching from Van Eyck and Petrus Christus to Massys. Holbein probably harked back to works of this kind he had seen in the Netherlands, but this in no way detracts from the originality of his achievement. Holbein's connection with the merchants of the Steelyard earned him one of the most monumental commissions of his London years: the allegories *The Triumph of Wealth* and *The Triumph of Poverty* for the Steelyard's banqueting-hall. These tempera paintings on canvas again harked back to a youthful impression—that of Mantegna's *Triumphal Procession*.

The extent to which the portrait of Gisze represented something new in the form of a move from an exclusively German to a European tradition of painting is clear when we compare it with the work of an Augsburg master who was roughly a contemporary of Holbein's. Christoph Amberger, born about 1500, became a member of the Augsburg guild in 1530. His portrait of the Nuremberg patrician *Christoph Baumgartner* (1543, Kunsthistorisches Museum, Vienna), which places the subject in a Renaissance room with a window offering a view of a mountain landscape, is—for all its modernity—a synthesis of the manners of Dürer and Burgkmair. There was an abrupt change in Amberger's style when he switched over to Mannerism under the influence of the portrait paintings of Paris Bordone; this development can be seen in the portrait of *Christoph Fugger* (1541, Alte Pinakothek, Munich). Holbein had broken out of the framework of the South German tradition much earlier. He was already approaching a European concept of art when he painted *Bonifacius Amerbach*. Thus, unlike Amberger, he followed an uninterrupted line of development and never became a Mannerist, although in his mature works he is just as representative of the European concept of art as the great Italian and Netherlandish portraitists in the Mannerist style, such as Pontormo, Bronzino, Parmigianino, and Vermeyen. The portrait of *Charles de Solier, Sieur de Morette* (1535, Gemäldegalerie, Dresden) is the German equivalent of Parmigianino's so-called *Malatesta Baglione* in Vienna and Vermeyen's *Erhard de la Marck* in the Rijksmuseum, Amsterdam. It shares their "European" features, but surpasses them both in intrinsic importance, for only Holbein could achieve the artistic aims of the Mannerists with the mastery and ease of the High Renaissance classicists.

What is astonishing is the way in which Holbein managed to extend his range to the monumental portrait, which in Italy only Titian had succeeded in mastering. Holbein was at home in monumental fresco-painting, but it nevertheless required daring to paint the French ambassador Jean de Dinteville and his friend Bishop Georges de Selve (National Gallery, London) life-size and to combine their portraits with a lavish still life that was an encyclopaedia of all the mathematical and astronomical knowledge of the time. All the objects depicted are observed with a precision worthy of Van Eyck. The distorted skull—the emblem of the Dintevilles—seen in perspective is a *trompe l'œil* feature of a kind highly esteemed in Mannerist art. Everything is fitted into the mighty framework of a composition that is as monumental as it is objective.

Holbein appears to have achieved his ambition of becoming court painter through the good offices of the French diplomats. In 1533 and 1534 he painted portraits of officials of the Royal Household, such as the Equerry Sir Nicholas Carew, the Falconer Robert Cheseman, the Treasurer Thomas Cromwell, and others. In 1536 he produced his first portrait of King Henry VIII (Thyssen Collection, Lugano), a forerunner of the monumental mural painting in Whitehall depicting Henry VIII, his father Henry VII, and their wives (the left half of the cartoon has been preserved at Chatsworth). In Holbein's paintings Henry VIII appears in truly regal splendour. He had the reputation of being the best-dressed man of his time and Holbein's portraits of him are above all magnificent costume paintings. Holbein took pleasure in fine clothes, just as he enjoyed giving play to his imagination in the designs for

Hans Holbein the Younger (1497-1543).
Portrait of the Falconer Robert Cheseman, 1533. (23¼×24⅝″) Mauritshuis, The Hague.

jewellery, costumes, utensils, and weapons that, as court painter, he was called upon to produce in the same way as he had designed book decorations and illustrations in the past. While he was not much drawn to the King, he was sympathetic towards the Queen, Jane Seymour. Her quiet, withdrawn nature is revealed most pleasingly in the splendid portrait of 1536 (Kunsthistorisches Museum, Vienna). The wealth of artistically worked jewels, some of which may have been designed by the painter himself, do not detract from the human warmth with which Holbein depicted her—and many other Englishwomen. The portraits of European princesses which Holbein had to paint on the continent when the King, after Jane Seymour's death, was searching for a bride have a cool reserve and courtly aloofness, but the small round miniature portraits—like the drawn portrait studies—are imbued with unreserved naturalism and the greatest human immediacy. In some small roundels, in which he portrays himself painting, the master has handed his own features down to posterity.

Christoph Amberger (c. 1500-1561/1562).
Portrait of Christoph Baumgartner, 1543. (33×24¼″) Kunsthistorisches Museum, Vienna.

ANNO·DÑI·1541·
·ETATIS·SVÆ·28·

Hans Holbein the Younger (1497-1543).
Portrait of a Young Man, 1541. (18½×13¾″) Kunsthistorisches Museum, Vienna.

Lucas Cranach the Elder (1472-1553).
Self-Portrait, 1550. (25⅛×19¼″) Uffizi, Florence.

In his last portraits, produced in the early 1540s, Holbein concentrated wholly on the human figure set firmly against a neutral background like a splendid inscription in clear-cut Roman type; a good example is the compact, fully realized *Portrait of a Young Man* (1541, Kunsthistorisches Museum, Vienna). Nothing is admitted that might distract attention from the portrayal of character, which is expressed in the outline and the posture as well as in the hands and the face. A man is defined by his bearing—no other painter understood and expressed this as well as Holbein did. His world is a cosmos that is inhabited by Man alone, a cosmos in which each individual has his appointed and immutable place. Holbein's portraits are not —like Dürer's or Gothardt-Neithardt's—signposts to an eternity in which earthly individuality will be submerged in universal worship and the experience of salvation, but belong to a fixed order that has always been, and always will be, valid. In his world this is all that counts and there is no more difference between the sacred and the profane, the present and the hereafter.

In the great age of German painting it was the art of the portrait that survived longest. The triviality of the court paintings and the didactic piety of the church paintings fade into insignificance beside the concentrated power and infinite simplicity of the *Self-Portrait* that Cranach painted in his old age (1550, Uffizi, Florence). Here we have a religious ethos embodied in a secular subject. The portrait represents all that remained close to life in German art in the age of Mannerism. Holbein's death from plague in 1543 marked a sudden break. It is difficult to say how he would have developed, had he lived. How long would it have been possible to go on expressing the new concepts of the age by classical means? In Italy, Michelangelo and Titian, working in magnificent isolation, created their own worlds and towered in monolithic independence over the new age. Although Holbein had moved into a wider, more cosmopolitan world, his untimely end was nevertheless bound up with the destiny of German art.

Albrecht Altdorfer (c. 1480-1538).
The Battle of Alexander, 1529. (62⅜×47⅜″) Alte Pinakothek, Munich.

Cosmic Perspectives

ROUND about 1520 Albrecht Altdorfer painted a *Nativity* (Kunsthistorisches Museum, Vienna) that is strangely different from his other Christmas pictures. This is not just because it is a genuine night-piece that, by its thoroughgoing rejection of solidity of form in favour of light values, seems to anticipate the art of Elsheimer and the seventeenth century. The important thing about it is its embodiment of a new concept of space that was to be just as significant for the fine arts as for science. Its fundamental feature is the idea of roundness, of the circle and the sphere. In the "earthly" part of the picture, this appears in a number of objects, both close and distant, such as the rotunda in Lombard Renaissance style, with its round windows and porches, and the circles of light cast on the snow by the angels' lanterns. It is further emphasized in the figures of the children and the utensils, and is found on the cosmic plane in the rising sun which forms a fiery ball set in the centre of a tunnel of clouds. Out of the dark space of the night sky rejoicing angels tumble like sparks or meteorites— small celestial bodies enclosed in their own circles of light, in attitudes unconnected with any notion of "up" or "down." This cosmic sense of space is finally crowned at the top of the picture, where a circular firmament opens in countless atoms of light. Here there are angels that turn to glittering pinpoints as they recede into the farthest distance. The rhythm of these atoms of light is decisive for the colour structure of the whole picture. Not only the clouds in the sky, but the granulation of the frosty soil and the blanket of snow in the foreground are made up of coloured globules.

Here for the first time in painting we find the spherical sense of space that was soon to revolutionize mathematics and the natural sciences. Just about this time Copernicus was working on the manuscript of his *De revolutionibus orbium coelestium*, which—in opposition to the Aristotelian concept of concentric shells with the earth at the centre and the Ptolemaic system of the epicycle—formulated the revolutionary heliocentric concept of a universe in which the earth rotates round the sun. The earth thus ceased to be the heart of the universe. The enclosing shells were shattered, and the sense of being at the immovable centre of things was replaced by one of hovering in the infinity of the universe. In Altdorfer's painting the earth is no longer something unique and exclusive, but exists only in relation to a distant sun suspended in the immeasurable universe. This did not involve any diminution in the religious significance of the cosmic system. To this macrocosm corresponded the microcosm of Man as a being morally responsible in the exercise of his free will. So ended the old astrological dependence on the heavenly bodies, as taught by Renaissance philosophers from Pico della Mirandola to Paracelsus, who wrote in his *Liber de imaginibus:* "And as God himself and *Prima Materia* and Heaven are all three eternal and indestructible, so too is the spirit of Man." The Saviour had taken on insignificant human form and become, as it were, a small glow-worm in cosmic space, but this infinite space existed only in relation to that event. *Virtus*, the creative ethos underlying the whole of life, was the manifestation of the divine in human form.

In art, landscape painting is the mirror of man's conception of the cosmos. The landscape of northern art in the fifteenth century is a terrestrial landscape, seen and experienced in the concave. This approach corresponds to the medieval idea of the cosmos as the inside of a hollow sphere, and is still found in the works of Bosch and his successors, who transformed the terrestrial landscape into the world landscape. The notion of the cosmic sphere is clearly illustrated on the wing of an altarpiece by Bosch (Ducal Palace, Venice) which depicts the *Entry of the Blest into Paradise* as a journey through a deep tunnel that pierces the shell of this sphere. On the outside of the wings of the triptych—*The Garden of Earthly Delights* and *The Creation of the World*—he shows it as a pale crystal ball hovering in a dark void. The world landscape is thus viewed in terms of the inside of a hollow sphere.

When the subjects for the series of historical paintings *The Battles of Antiquity* were distributed among various artists, Altdorfer was assigned the *Victory of Alexander the Great over King Darius of Persia*. He conceived it as an adventure in painting no less daring than the voyages of the contemporary circumnavigators of the globe. The terrestrial struggle is depicted not as a mere duel between two heroes but as a mass event involving the human species—thus pointing the way for the art of Pieter Bruegel. The world landscape is enlarged into the cosmic landscape. The dramatic event taking place on the earth is echoed in the battle between the surging ranks of the clouds, between sun and moon, between light and darkness in the universe. To depict all this in a picture in which the microcosm is transformed into the macrocosm, miniature painting into monumental painting, was a bold undertaking in which Altdorfer succeeded by means of unprecedented concentration. The task he set himself surpassed anything Dürer might have conceived in the way of "finicking work" and, in order to achieve it, the painter gave up the chance of taking office as burgomaster of Regensburg. The fact that, far from failing in it, he produced an absolute masterpiece shows the tremendous intensity of his creative imagination.

Despite the curve of the horizon, the fifteenth-century notion of concave space had not vanished completely from Altdorfer's work. We look down on the earth at our feet as on a huge *mappa mundi*. Lakes and seas, high mountains and deep valleys alternate in a sweeping panorama. But this overall view is not confined to the earth. It stretches to the firmament beyond with its heavenly bodies and atmospheric phenomena on which we also look down as on the curving surface of the hollow sphere of the universe.

The terrestrial horizon had already been treated as a convex curve in the work of Wolf Huber, who saw and experienced space in convexity. This can be seen in his landscape drawings from nature dating from as early as 1510—for instance, the *View of the Mondsee* in the Salzkammergut (Germanisches Nationalmuseum, Nuremberg). In his way of looking at space, Huber was ahead of his time. The convexity persists, even when the terrestrial landscape widens into the world landscape, into the cosmic landscape, as in the later *Allegory of the Cross* in the Kunsthistorisches Museum, Vienna (which unfortunately could not be reproduced, as it is now being restored). Here the curving structure of the globe *upholds*. We find the same thing in Huber's drawings of the 1540s and 1550s. This convex view and experience of space has survived in art right up to the present century.

It is clear that in his conception of the world landscape, as displayed in his later work, Huber was inspired by Altdorfer's *Battle of Alexander*. It is equally clear that the curvature

Albrecht Altdorfer (c. 1480-1538).
The Battle of Alexander (detail), 1529. Alte Pinakothek, Munich.

of the horizon in the *Battle of Alexander* was derived from Huber's convex view of space. But the curvature of Altdorfer's terrestrial horizon does not hold up as firmly and surely as Huber's: it falters and threatens to collapse under the pressure of things and events. Thus Carl Linfert was right in speaking of the "threatening" aspect of Altdorfer's landscapes.

In the *Battle of Alexander*, it seems as though a collision of natural forces were impending. Here the painter gives expression to that "chiromancy," that interpretative power which Paracelsus considered could be applied not only to man's destiny as written in his hand, but also to landscapes, roads, and rivers. The "cipher of nature" clearly confronts us in Altdorfer's works. To him it is still of the semantically visual kind, but it opened the way to the symbolic language of mathematics and physics. Huber's representation of space already comes nearer to the mathematical and physical concepts of modern cosmography. We can see the same thing in other artists who were still at the height of their powers in the middle of the sixteenth century, such as Hermann tom Ring. In Holbein's later English works we find a growing striving for mathematical precision. In the period that followed, this became a prerequisite for the pictorial representation of the cosmos, not only in scientific illustrations but in art. The convex view of space found its ultimate expression in the world landscapes of Pieter Bruegel, which in some of his works such as the *Fall of Icarus* and *Gloomy Day* approach the cosmic. Even with the return to the confined, terrestrial Dutch landscape of the seventeenth century, the convexity remained. The only artists after Bruegel to master the cosmic landscape were Rubens, Seghers, and Rembrandt. In some of his mountain pictures Seghers reverts anachronistically to the concave view of space—hence their threatening quality.

When the artistic spark had died in Germany it was left to Bruegel in the Netherlands to take over the visual mastery of the cosmos and to bring it to a grandiose climax. In Germany, the task begun by the artists was taken over by the independent thinkers in the realms of mathematics and physics, notably the astronomers. It was Kepler who set the crown on the intellectual structure whose foundations had been laid by Dürer and artists of his age.

Select Bibliography

General Index

List of Colour Plates

Select Bibliography

by

EVA BENESCH

SOURCE WORKS

J. G. DOPPELMAYR, *Historische Nachricht von den nürnbergischen Mathematicis und Künstlern...*, Nuremberg 1730. — J. HORMAYR, *Taschenbuch für die vaterländische Geschichte*, Vol. VIII, Vienna 1827, p. 186 ff.: *Memorienbuch Max I.*, Innsbruck, 28 Sept. 1502. — C. VAN MANDER, *Das Leben der niederländischen und deutschen Maler* (German translation with notes by H. Floerke), Vol. I, Munich-Leipzig 1906 in: Kunstgeschichtliche Studien, IV. Folge, edited by T. Frimmel, Vol. I; English edition of VAN MANDER by C. Van de Wall, New York 1936. — P. J. MARIETTE, *Abécédario... sur les arts et les artistes*, edited by P. de Chennevières and A. de Montaiglon, 6 vols, Archives de l'Art français, Paris 1851-1860. — *Des Johann Neudörfer... Nachrichten von Künstlern und Werkleuten... aus dem Jahre 1547*, edited by G. W. K. Lochner, Quellenschriften für Kunstgeschichte X, new edition, Vienna 1888. — H. ROTT, *Quellen und Forschungen zur südwestdeutschen und schweizerischen Kunstgeschichte im XV. und XVI. Jahrhundert, I. Bodenseegebiet, II. Alt-Schwaben und die Reichsstädte, III. Der Oberrhein*, Stuttgart 1933, 1934, 1936, 1938 (6 vols). — J. VON SANDRART, *(Teutsche) Academie der (Edlen) Bau-, Bild- und Mahlerey-Künste*, Nuremberg 1675; edited and annotated by A. R. Peltzer, Munich 1925. — J. SCHLOSSER, *Die Kunstliteratur*, Ein Handbuch zur Quellenkunde der neueren Kunstgeschichte, IV. Buch: *Die Kunsttheorie der ersten Hälfte des 16. Jahrhunderts*, Vienna 1924, p. 226 ff. — Idem, *La Letteratura Artistica*, 2nd and 3rd editions, edited by O. Kurz, Florence-Vienna 1956, 1964, p. 259 ff. — K. SCHOTTENLOHER, *Bibliographie zur deutschen Geschichte im Zeitalter der Glaubensspaltung 1517-1585*, Kommission für Erforschung der Reformation und Gegenreformation, 6 vols, Leipzig 1932-1940. — G. F. WAAGEN, *Kunstwerke und Künstler in Deutschland*, Parts I, II, Leipzig 1843, 1845.

EARLY LITERATURE

H. C. AGRIPPA AB NETTESHEIM, *De incertitudine et vanitate omnium scientiarum & artium*, Cologne 1527. — Idem, *De occulta philosophia*, Cologne 1510. —

(ST AUGUSTINE), *De Civitate Dei* (manuscript); *Aurelij Augustini opus... de Civitate Dei*, J. Froben, Basel 1522. — BOMBAST VON HOHENHEIM, see PARACELSUS. — (ST BRIDGET), *Revelationes Sancte Brigitte*, Nuremberg 1500. — (C. CELTES), *Conradis Celtis... quatuor libri amorum secundum quatuor latera Germaniae...*, Nuremberg 1502. — (NICOLAUS COPERNICUS), *N. Copernici, De Revolutionibus Orbium Coelestium*, Nuremberg 1543. — NICOLAUS DE CUES, *De visione Dei*, 1453. — Idem, *Opera omnia*, Paris 1514, 3 books in 2 volumes. — (ERASMUS, DESIDERIUS), *Enchiridion Militis Christiani...*, T. Martinus, Antwerp 1503; J. Froben, Basel 1518. — Idem, *Familiarium colloquiorum Des. Erasmi Roterodami opus...*, Paris 1527. — *Erasmus Desiderius Encomium moriae, i.e. Stultitiae Laus, Lob der torheit*, facsimile of the Basel edition of 1515 (with marginal drawings by Hans Holbein the Younger), edited by H. A. Schmid, Basel 1931. — (ERASMUS, DESIDERIUS), *Habes iterum Morias Encomiu(m)...*, J. Froben, Basel 1515. — S. FRANCK, *Chronica der Baepst*, 1531, Appendix: *Ketzerchronik*. — (J. GEILER VON KAISERSBERG), *Gayler von Kaysersperg, Das Buch Granatapfel*, Augsburg 1510 (with woodcuts by H. Burgkmair); Strasbourg 1511 (with woodcuts by H. Baldung). — J. DE INDAGINE, *Introductiones Apotelesmaticae... in Chyromantiam, Physiognomiam, Astrologiam Naturalem...*, Strasbourg 1522. — (J. KEPLER), *Ioannis Keppleri Harmonices Mundi*, Linz 1619. — P. MELANCHTHON, *Elementorum rhetoricis*, 1531. — (P. MELANCHTHON), *Ursache/Warumb die gemainde/ und Kirchen Christi/ungegrünten Concilien nit sollen stadt-geben/sonder bey der Bibel/das ist/bey dem Rainen wort Gottes/festhalten und bleyben/* aus Latein Ph. Mel (anchthon), verdeutscht durch IUSTUM IONAM DOCT, Regensburg 1553. — PARACELSUS, *Werke*, edited by J. Huser, Basel 1589 ff. — Idem, *Sämtliche Werke*, edited by K. Sudhoff, Munich-Berlin 1931, 13 vols (*Liber de Imaginibus*, S. X, Ch. XII, p. 382 ff., *Meteora*, Neisse 1566, S. VII, p. 249 ff.). — J. REUCHLIN, *De arte cabalistica*, Hagenau 1517. — W. ROPER, *The Life and Death of Sir Thomas More*, Paris 1626; Oxford 1716. — (HROSVITHA), *Opera Hrosvite illustris virginis et monialis germane gente Saxonica orte nuper a Conrado Celte inventa*, Nuremberg 1501. — C. SCHEURL, *Libellus de laudibus Germanie et ducum Saxonie,*

Leipzig 1508. — *Vita Reverendi patris Dni Anthonij Kressen... per C. Scheurl*, Nuremberg 1515. — JACOBUS SPRENGER, *Malleus maleficarum (Der Hexenhammer)*, Speyer 1490. — *Theologia Teutsch*, Augsburg 1518, first printed edition from a manuscript of 1497 (now in the Stadtbibliothek, Frankfurt); originally written about 1430, probably by Johannes de Francfordia. — (M. VITRUVIUS POLLIO), *Marcus Vitruvius de Architectura*, Rome 1486. — JACOBUS DE VORAGINE, *Incipit prologus sup(er) Legendas sanctoru(m), (Legenda aurea)*, Paris 1475.

GENERAL WORKS

W. ANDREAS, *Deutschland vor der Reformation*, 6th edition, Stuttgart 1959. — E. F. APPELT, *J. Kepplers astronomische Weltansicht*, Leipzig 1849. — E. BLOCH, *Thomas Münzer als Theologe der Revolution*, Munich 1921. — K. BURDACH, *Reformation, Renaissance, Humanismus*, Berlin 1928. — E. CASSIRER, *Individuum und Kosmos in der Philosophie der Renaissance*, Studien der Bibliothek Warburg X, Leipzig-Berlin 1927. — *Der Briefwechsel des Konrad Celtis*, collected and edited by H. Rupprich, Munich 1934 (Veröffentlichungen der Kommission zur Erforschung der Geschichte der Reformation und Gegenreformation, Humanistenbriefe III). — R. W. CHAMBERS, *Thomas More*, The Bedford Historical Series II. London 1945. — W. DILTHEY, *Auffassung und Analyse des Menschen im 15. und 16. Jahrhundert*, in *Gesammelte Schriften*, Vol. II, 5th ed., Stuttgart-Göttingen 1957, p. 80 ff. — DESIDERIUS ERASMUS ROTERODAMUS, *Ausgewählte Werke*, edited by H. Holborn, Munich 1933. — E. GOTHEIN, *Reformation und Gegenreformation*, Schriften zur Kulturgeschichte der Renaissance, Reformation und Gegenreformation, Munich-Leipzig 1924, Vol. II, in particular: *Die Kreuzwunder*, p. 62 ff. — W. GRAF, *Doktor Christoph Scheurl von Nürnberg*, Beiträge zur Kulturgeschichte des Mittelalters und der Renaissance, Vol. 43, Leipzig-Berlin 1930. — J. HUIZINGA, *Erasmus*, London 1924. — Idem, *Europäischer Humanismus: Erasmus*, Rowohlts deutsche enzyklopädie, Hamburg 1958. — N. LIEB, *Die Fugger und die Kunst*, Munich 1952. — S. MORISON, *The Likeness of Thomas More*, London 1963. — H. J. MOSER, *Geschichte der deutschen Musik*, Vol. I, 5th edition, Stuttgart-Berlin 1930. — Idem, *Paul Hofhaimer*, Stuttgart-Berlin 1929. — T. MUENTZER, *Sein Leben und seine Schriften*, edited by O. H. Brandt, Jena 1932. — *Willibald Pirckheimers Briefwechsel I* (Veröffentlichungen der Kommission zur Erforschung der Geschichte der Reformation und Gegenreformation, Humanistenbriefe IV), in conjunction with A. Reimann, edited by E. Reicke, Munich 1940. — L. VON RANKE, *Deutsche Geschichte im Zeitalter der Reformation*, Berlin 1839-1847. — E. REICKE, *Willibald Pirckheimer*, Jena 1930. — A. REIMANN, *Die älteren Pirckheimer. Aus dem Nachlass*, edited by H. Rupprich, Leipzig 1944. — *J. Reuchlins Briefwechsel*, collected and edited by L. Geiger, Tübingen 1875. — G. RITTER, *Die Neugestaltung Europas im 16. Jahrhundert*, Berlin 1950. — A. ROSENKRANZ, *Der Bundschuh 1493-1517*, 2 vols, Heidelberg 1927. — O. SCHOTTENLOHER, *Erasmus im Ringen um die humanistische Bildungsform*, Reformationsgeschichtliche Studien und Texte 61, Münster (Westphalia) 1933. — E. TROELTSCH, *Die Soziallehren der Christlichen Kirchen und Gruppen*, in *Gesammelte Schriften*, Vol. I, Tübingen 1912. — W. WINDELBAND, *Lehrbuch der Geschichte der Philosophie*, Tübingen 1916, part IV, section 29, *Makrokosmos und Mikrokosmos*. — A. WOLF, *A History of Science, Technology and Philosophy in the 16th and 17th Centuries*, Vol. I, London 1935.

HISTORY OF ART

L. B. ALBERTI, *De Pictura*, 3 vols, 1435-1436. — L. BALDASS, *Der Künstlerkreis Kaiser Maximilians*, Vienna 1923. — E. F. BANGE, *Die deutschen Bronzestatuetten des 16. Jahrhunderts*, Denkmäler deutscher Kunst, Deutscher Verein für Kunstwissenschaft, Berlin 1949. — J. BAUM, *Ulmer Kunst*, Stuttgart 1911. — F. BAUMGARTEN, *Der Freiburger Hochaltar*, Strasbourg 1904. — O. BENESCH, *Beiträge zur Oberschwäbischen Bildnismalerei*, Jahrbuch der Preussischen Kunstsammlungen 54, Berlin 1933, p. 239 ff. — Idem, *Österreichische Handzeichnungen des XV. und XVI. Jahrhunderts. Die Meisterzeichnung*, Vol. V, Freiburg im Breisgau 1936. — Idem, *Die Tafelmalerei des 1. Drittels des 16. Jahrhunderts in Österreich*. Die Bildende Kunst in Österreich, Vol. III, p. 137-148, Baden bei Wien 1938. — Idem, *The Art of the Renaissance in Northern Europe. Its Relation to the Contemporary Spiritual and Intellectual Movements*, Cambridge, Mass., 1945, 1947, revised and enlarged edition, London 1965. — Idem, *The Rise of Landscape in the Austrian School of Painting at the Beginning of the Sixteenth Century*. Konsthistorisk Tidskrift XXVIII, 1-2, Stockholm 1959, p. 34 ff. — Idem, *Maximilien empereur gothique et renaissant*, L'Œil, No. 58, Paris, October 1959, p. 16 ff. — Idem, *Meisterzeichnungen der Albertina*, Salzburg 1964 (English edition in the press: *Master Drawings in the Albertina*). — E. BUCHNER, *Studien zur Mittelrheinischen Malerei und Graphik der Spätgotik*, Münchner Jahrbuch der Bildenden Kunst, N.F. 4, 1927, p. 229 ff. — Idem, *Die Augsburger Tafelmalerei der Spätgotik*, Beiträge zur Geschichte der deutschen Kunst, Vol. II, Augsburg 1928, p. 1 ff. — Idem, *Das deutsche Bildnis der Spätgotik und der frühen Dürerzeit*, Denkmäler deutscher Kunst, Deutscher Verein für Kunstwissenschaft, Berlin 1953. — Idem, *Deutsche Malerei der Dürerzeit*, Munich 1959. — J. BURCKHARDT, *Die Kultur der Renaissance in Italien*, 15th edition, Leipzig 1926; *The Civilization of the Renaissance in Italy*, London 1934. — B. BUSHART, *Studien zur altschwäbischen Malerei*, Zeitschrift für Kunstgeschichte, Vol. 22, Heft 1, Munich-Berlin 1959. — C. DODGSON, *Catalogue of Early German and Flemish Woodcuts in the British Museum*, Vol. I, London 1903, Vol. II, London 1911. — M. DVORAK, *Idealismus und Realismus in der Kunst der Neuzeit* (Academic Lecture Course, Vienna 1915-1916, typescript). — Idem, *Kunstgeschichte als Geistesgeschichte*, Munich 1924: *Dürers Apokalypse*, p. 193 ff.; *Schongauer und die niederländische Malerei*, p. 151 ff. — A. FEULNER, *Die deutsche Plastik des 16. Jahrhunderts*, Munich 1926. — O. FISCHER, *Die altdeutsche Malerei in Salzburg*, Leipzig 1908. — Idem, *Geschichte der deutschen Malerei*, Deutsche Kunstgeschichte, Vol. III, Munich 1942, p. 166 ff. — M. J. FRIEDLÄNDER, *Die altniederländische Malerei*, 12 vols, Berlin-Leiden 1924-1935. — T. FRIMMEL, *Verzeichnis einer Wiener Bilder-Lotterie vom Jahre 1670 (21. April)*, Beilage der *Blätter für Gemäldekunde*, Vol. I, 1905-1910, Vienna 1910, p. 147, No. 132. — P. GANZ, *Malerei der Frührenaissance in der Schweiz*, Zurich 1924. — H. GASSER, *Das Gewand in der Formensprache Grünewalds*, Berne 1962. — M. GEISBERG, *Der deutsche Einblattholzschnitt in der ersten Hälfte des XVI. Jahrhunderts*, Munich 1923-1929. — Idem, *Die deutsche Buchillustration in der 1. Hälfte des XVI. Jahrhunderts*, Munich 1930, 1931 (1. und 2. Jahrg.). — K. GIEHLOW, *Kaiser Maximilians I. Gebetbuch*, Vienna 1907. — C. GLASER, *Zwei Jahrhunderte deutscher Malerei*, Munich 1916. — Idem, *Die altdeutsche Malerei*, Munich 1924. — W. HUGELSHOFER, *Schweizer Handzeichnungen des XV. und XVI. Jahrhunderts*, Die Meisterzeichnung, Vol. I, Freiburg im Breisgau 1928. — I. MAYR, *Das Jagdbuch*

Kaiser Maximilians I., Innsbruck 1901. — T. Müller, *Alte Bairische Bildhauer*, Munich 1950. — V. Ober-hammer, *Die Bronzestandbilder des Maximiliangrab-males in der Hofkirche zu Innsbruck*, Innsbruck 1935. — O. Pächt, *Österreichische Tafelmalerei der Gotik*, Augsburg 1929. — R. Pallucchini, *La Pittura Veneta del Quattrocento*, Bologna 1956. — K. T. Parker, *Elsässische Handzeichnungen des XV. und XVI. Jahrhunderts, Die Meisterzeichnung*, Vol. II, Freiburg im Breisgau 1928. — F. Schestag, *Kaiser Maximilian I. Triumph*, Jahrbuch der Kunsthistorischen Sammlungen des Ah. Kh., Vol. I, Vienna 1883, p. 154 ff. — E. Schilling, *Nürnberger Handzeichnungen des XV. und XVI. Jahrhunderts, Die Meisterzeichnung*, Vol. III, Freiburg im Breisgau 1929. — A. Schramm, *Der Bilderschmuck der Frühdrucke. 7. Lienhart Holle... in*

Ulm, Leipzig 1923; XVII: *Die Drucker in Nürnberg, 1. Anton Koberger*, Leipzig 1934; XXII: *Die Drucker in Basel*, II. Teil, Leipzig 1940. — A. Stange, *Deutsche Malerei der Gotik*, Vols VII-X, Berlin 1955-1960. — H. Voss, *Der Ursprung des Donaustils*, Kunstgeschichtliche Monographien, Vol. VII, Leipzig 1907. — J. Graf Waldburg-Wolfegg, *Das mittelalterliche Hausbuch*, Munich 1957. — M. Weinberger, *Nürnberger Malerei an der Wende zur Renaissance und die Anfänge der Dürerschule*, Studien zur Deutschen Kunstgeschichte, Heft 217, Strasbourg 1921. — F. Winkler, *Altdeutsche Tafelmalerei*, Munich 1941 (1944). — H. Wölfflin, *Die klassische Kunst*, 7th edition, revised by K. Escher, Munich 1924. — Idem, *Die Kunst der Renaissance, Italien und das deutsche Formgefühl*, new edition, Munich 1964.

INDIVIDUAL STUDIES AND ARTICLES

Altdorfer, Albrecht: L. Baldass, *Albrecht Altdorfer*, Vienna 1941. — H. L. Becker, *Die Handzeichnungen Albrecht Altdorfers*, Munich 1938. — O. Benesch, *Der Zwettler Altar und die Anfänge Jörg Breus*, Beiträge zur Geschichte der deutschen Kunst II, Augsburg 1928, *Exkurs II: Altdorfer und der "Donaustil"*, p. 268 ff. — Idem, *Altdorfers Badstubenfresken und das Wiener Lothbild*, Jahrbuch der Preussischen Kunstsammlungen 51, Berlin 1930, p. 179-188. — Idem, *Der Maler Albrecht Altdorfer*, Vienna 1939 (4 editions). — Idem, *Altdorfer, Huber and Italian Art*, Burlington Magazine LXXXIX, London, June 1947, p. 152 ff. — E. Buchner, *Albrecht Altdorfer, Die Alexanderschlacht*, Stuttgart 1956. — M. J. Friedländer, *Albrecht Altdorfer*, Berlin 1923. — C. Linfert, *Albrecht Altdorfer, Die Enthüllung der Landschaft*, Mainz 1938. — E. Ruhmer, *Albrecht Altdorfer*, Munich 1965. — H. Tietze, *A. Altdorfer in St. Florian*, Jahrbuch der Preussischen Kunstsammlungen XXXVIII, 1917, p. 94 ff. — Idem, *Albrecht Altdorfer*, Leipzig 1923. — F. Winzinger, *Albrecht Altdorfer, Zeichnungen*, Munich 1952. — Idem, *Albrecht Altdorfer, Graphik*, Munich 1963.

Altdorfer, Erhard: O. Benesch, *Erhard Altdorfers "Schleierfindung des hl. Leopold"*, Kirchenkunst, 7. Jahrg., Heft 5/6, Vienna 1935, p. 109 ff. — Idem, *Erhard Altdorfer als Maler*, Jahrbuch der Preussischen Kunstsammlungen 57, Berlin 1936, p. 157 ff. — C. Dodgson, *Erhard Altdorfer als Kupferstecher und Zeichner*, Mitteilungen der Gesellschaft für vervielfältigende Kunst, Vienna 1911, p. 21 ff.

Apt: K. Feuchtmayr, *Apt-Studien*, Beiträge zur Geschichte der deutschen Kunst II, Augsburg 1928, p. 97 ff. — J. Lauts, *Ein wiedergefundenes Gemälde von Ulrich Apt*, Pantheon XVIII, Munich 1960, p. 57 ff.

Baldung Grien: H. Curjel, *Hans Baldung Grien*, Munich 1923. — O. Fischer, *Hans Baldung Grien*, Munich 1939. — C. Koch, *Die Zeichnungen Hans Baldung Griens*, Denkmäler deutscher Kunst, Deutscher Verein für Kunstwissenschaft, Berlin 1941.

Beck: E. Buchner, *Leonhard Beck als Maler und Zeichner*, Beiträge zur Geschichte der deutschen Kunst II, Augsburg 1928, p. 388 ff.

Breu: O. Benesch, *Der Zwettler Altar und die Anfänge Jörg Breus*, Beiträge zur Geschichte der deutschen Kunst II, Augsburg 1928, p. 229 ff. *Exkurs I, Die Schreinfiguren*, p. 266 ff. — E. Buchner, *Der ältere Breu als Maler*, Beiträge zur Geschichte der deutschen Kunst II, Augsburg 1928, p. 277 ff.

Burgkmair the Elder: A. Burkhard, *Hans Burgkmair d. Ä.*, Meister der Graphik XV, Berlin 1932. — Idem, *Hans Burkmair d. Ä.*, Deutsche Meister, Vol. 13, Leipzig (1934). — P. Halm, *Hans Burgkmair als Zeichner*, Part I, Münchner Jahrbuch der bildenden Kunst, III. Folge, Vol. XIII, 1962, p. 75 ff.

Cranach the Elder: O. Benesch, *Zur altösterreichischen Tafelmalerei*, Jahrbuch der Kunsthistorischen Sammlungen, N. F. II, Vienna 1928, *Die Anfänge Lukas Cranachs*, pp. 77-118. — Idem, *Zu Cranachs Anfängen*, Belvedere 8, Vienna 1929, p. 144 ff. — M. J. Friedländer and J. Rosenberg, *Die Gemälde von Lucas Cranach*, Berlin 1932.

Dürer: O. Benesch, *Die Fürsterzbischöfliche Gemäldegalerie in Kremsier*, Pantheon, Munich 1928, 1. Heft (January), p. 22 ff. — Idem, *Das Kremsierer Dürer-Bildnis*, Pantheon, Munich 1934, 10. Heft (October), p. 299 ff. — Idem, *Zu Dürers Rosenkranzfest*, Belvedere IX, Vienna 1930, p. 81 ff. — E. Buchner, *Die sieben Schmerzen Mariae*, Münchner Jahrbuch der bildenden Kunst, N. F. XII, 1934-1936, p. 250 ff. — W. M. Conway, *Literary Remains of Albrecht Dürer... with Transcripts from the British Museum Manuscripts*, Cambridge 1889. — E. Flechsig, *Albrecht Dürer. Sein Leben und seine künstlerische Entwicklung*, Berlin, Vol. I, 1928, Vol. II, 1931. — M. J. Friedländer, *Albrecht Dürer*, Leipzig 1921. — L. Grote, *"Hier bin ich ein Herr" - Dürer in Venedig*, Bibliothek des Germanischen Nationalmuseums Nürnberg zur deutschen Kunst- und Kulturgeschichte, Vol. 2-3, Munich 1956. — Idem, *Albrecht Dürer*, Geneva 1965. — E. Heidrich, *Dürer und die Reformation*, Leipzig 1909. — L. Justi, *Konstruierte Figuren und Köpfe unter den Werken Albrecht Dürers*, Leipzig 1902. — H. Kauffmann, *Albrecht Dürers rhythmische Kunst*, Leipzig 1924. — Idem, *Albrecht Dürers Dreikönig-Altar*, Wallraf-Richartz-Jahrbuch X,

Cologne 1938, p. 166 ff. — K. LANGE and F. FUHSE, *Dürers schriftlicher Nachlass*, Halle an der Saale 1893. — K. MARTIN, *Albrecht Dürer, Die vier Apostel*, Reclam No. 87, Stuttgart 1963. — J. MEDER, *Dürer-Katalog*, Vienna 1932. — E. PANOFSKY, *Albrecht Dürer*, Princeton N. J. 1948, 2 vols. — Idem, *The Life and Art of Albrecht Dürer*, Princeton N. J. 1955. — E. ROEMER, *Dürers ledige Wanderjahre*, Jahrbuch der Preussischen Kunstsammlungen 47, Berlin 1926, p. 118 ff., 48, Berlin 1927, p. 77 ff. — H. RUPPRICH, *Dürers Schriftlicher Nachlass*, Vol. I, Deutscher Verein für Kunstwissenschaft, Berlin 1956; Vol. II, 1966; Vol. III in the press. — Idem, *Dürers Stellung zu den agnoëtischen und kunstfeindlichen Strömungen seiner Zeit*, Bayerische Akademie der Wissenschaften, Sitzungsberichte, Jahrg. 1959, Heft 1, Munich 1959. — Idem, *Die kunsttheoretischen Schriften L. B. Albertis und ihre Nachwirkung bei Dürer*, Schweizer Beiträge zur Allgemeinen Geschichte, 18./19., Berne 1960/61, p. 219 ff. — V. SCHERER (editor), *Dürer*, Klassiker der Kunst, Vol. 4, Stuttgart-Leipzig 1908. — M. THAUSING, *Dürer, Geschichte seines Lebens und seiner Kunst*, Leipzig 1884, 2 vols. — H. TIETZE and E. TIETZE-CONRAT, *Kritisches Verzeichnis der Werke Albrecht Dürers, Der junge Dürer*, Augsburg 1928. — Idem, *Kritisches Verzeichnis der Werke Albrecht Dürers, II. Der reife Dürer*, 2 vols, Basel 1937, 1938. — R. VISCHER, *Studien zur Kunstgeschichte*, Stuttgart 1886; in particular: *A. Dürer und die Grundlagen seiner Kunst*, p. 156 ff.; *Über Michael Wolgemut*, p. 294 ff. — F. WINKLER, *Die Zeichnungen Albrecht Dürers I-IV*, Berlin 1936-1939. — Idem, *Dürer und die Illustrationen zum Narrenschiff*, Forschungen zur deutschen Kunstgeschichte, Deutscher Verein für Kunstwissenschaft, Vol. 36, Berlin 1951. — Idem, *Albrecht Dürer - Leben und Werk*, Berlin 1957. — H. WÖLFFLIN, *Die Kunst Albrecht Dürers*, Munich 1905; 6th edition, revised by K. Gerstenberg, 1943.

Erhart: G. OTTO, *Gregor Erhart*, Denkmäler deutscher Kunst, Deutscher Verein für Kunstwissenschaft, Berlin 1943.

Görtschacher: E. BUCHNER, *Urban Görtschacher, Ein Kärntner Maler der Renaissance*, Jahrbuch der Kunsthistorischen Sammlungen, N. F. II, Vienna 1928, p. 129 ff.

Gothardt-Neithardt (Grünewald): L. BEHLING, *Die Handzeichnungen des Mathis Gothart Nithart genannt Grünewald*, Weimar 1955. — E. BUCHNER, *Die Bildnisse des Grafen Thomas und Johann von Rieneck von Matthias Grünewald*, Wallraf-Richartz-Jahrbuch, N. F. I, Cologne 1930, p. 170 ff.; cf. also G. VON DER OSTEN, *Zwei Bildnisse von Gabriel Zehender (?)*, Wallraf-Richartz-Jahrbuch XXVI, Cologne 1964, p. 235 ff. (attempted attribution of the two Rieneck portraits). — A. BURKHARD, *Matthias Grünewald*, Cambridge, Mass., 1936. — H. FEURSTEIN, *Zur Deutung des Bildgehaltes bei Grünewald*, Beiträge zur Geschichte der deutschen Kunst, I, Augsburg 1924, p. 137 ff. — Idem, *Matthias Grünewald*, Bonn 1930, Buchgemeinde, Vol. I. — W. FRAENGER, *Matthias Grünewald in seinen Werken*, Berlin 1936. — P. FRAUNDORFER, *Altes und Neues zur Grünewald-Forschung*, Herbipolis Jubilans/1200 Jahre Bistum Würzburg/Festschrift, Würzburger Diözesangeschichtsblätter 14./15. Jahrg., 1952/53, Würzburg 1952, p. 373 ff. — L. GROTE, *Die Erasmus-Mauritius-Tafel von M. Grünewald*, Stuttgart

1957, Reclam. — H. A. SCHMID, *Die Gemälde und Zeichnungen von Matthias Grünewald*, Strasbourg 1911, 2 vols. — W. K. ZÜLCH, *Der historische Grünewald, Mathis Gothardt-Neithardt*, Munich 1938.

Hagnower: W. VÖGE, *Niclas Hagnower der Meister des Isenheimer Hochaltars und seine Frühwerke*, Freiburg im Breisgau 1931.

Herlin: E. BUCHNER, *Die Werke Friedrich Herlins*, Münchner Jahrbuch der bildenden Kunst XIII, 1923, p. 1 ff. — G. A. BURKHART, *Friedrich Herlin-Forschungen*, Erlangen 1912, Beiträge zur fränkischen Kunstgeschichte, Heft II, p. 1 ff.

Holbein, Ambrosius: W. HES, *Ambrosius Holbein*, Strasbourg 1911. — O. FISCHER, *Ambrosius Holbein*, Pantheon XX (1937), p. 306 ff.

Holbein the Elder: L. BALDASS, *Niederländische Bildgedanken im Werke des älteren Hans Holbein*, Beiträge zur Geschichte der deutschen Kunst II, Augsburg 1928, p. 159. — O. BENESCH, *Zu den beiden Hans Holbein*, Zeitschrift für Bildende Kunst 64, Leipzig 1930/31, p. 37 ff. — C. BEUTLER, G. THIEM, *Hans Holbein d. Ä. Die spätgotische Altar- und Glasmalerei*, Schriftenreihe des Stadtarchivs Augsburg, Vol. 13, Augsburg 1960. — E. BUCHNER, *Zum Werk Hans Holbeins des Älteren*, Beiträge zur Geschichte der deutschen Kunst II, Augsburg 1928, p. 133. — C. GLASER, *Hans Holbein der Ältere*, Kunstgeschichtliche Monographien XI, Leipzig 1908. — E. HIS, *Hans Holbeins des Älteren Feder- und Silberstiftzeichnungen*, Nuremberg n. d. — N. LIEB and A. STANGE, *Hans Holbein der Ältere*, Munich - Berlin 1960.

Holbein the Younger: O. BENESCH, *Zu den beiden Hans Holbein*, Zeitschrift für Bildende Kunst 64, Leipzig 1930/31, p. 37 ff. — H. VON EINEM, *Holbeins "Christus im Grabe"*, Akademie der Wissenschaften und der Literatur, Abhandlungen der Geistes- und sozialwissenschaftlichen Klasse, Jahrg. 1960, No. 4, Wiesbaden. — P. GANZ, *Die Handzeichnungen Hans Holbeins d. J.*, Denkmäler Deutscher Kunst, Deutscher Verein für Kunstwissenschaft, Berlin 1937. — Idem, *The Paintings of Holbein the Younger*, London 1950. — O. KURZ, *Holbein and others in a seventeenth-century Collection*, Burlington Magazine LXXXIII, London 1943, p. 280. — O. PÄCHT, *Holbein and Kratzer as Collaborators*, Burlington Magazine LXXXIV, London 1944, p. 138-139. — E. SCHILLING, *Zeichnungen der Künstlerfamilie Holbein*, Basel 1954. — H. A. SCHMID, *Die Werke Hans Holbeins in Basel*, Öffentliche Kunstsammlung Basel, Kleiner Führer Nr. 2, Basel 1930. — Idem, *Hans Holbein der Jüngere. Sein Aufstieg zur Meisterschaft und sein englischer Stil*, 3 vols, Basel 1948, volume of plates 1945. — A. WOLTMANN, *Holbein und seine Zeit*, 2nd edition, Leipzig 1874-1876, 2 vols.

Holbein, Sigmund: E. BUCHNER, *Ein unbekannter Meister der Augsburger Renaissance (Sigmund Holbein?)*, Münchner Jahrbuch der bildenden Kunst, 3. Folge, vol. VI, 1955, p. 153 ff.

Huber: O. BENESCH, *Altdorfer, Huber and Italian Art*, Burlington Magazine LXXXIX, London, June 1947, p. 152 ff. — P. HALM, *Die Landschaftszeichnungen des Wolfgang Huber*, Münchner Jahrbuch der bildenden Kunst, N. F. VII, 1930,

p. 1 ff. — E. HEINZLE, *Wolf Huber*, Innsbruck n.d. — M. WEINBERGER, *Wolfgang Huber*, Deutsche Meister, Vol. II, Leipzig 1930.

Kulmbach: F. STADLER, *Hans von Kulmbach*, Vienna 1936. — F. WINKLER, *Die Zeichnungen Hans Süss von Kulmbachs und Hans Leonhard Schäufeleins*, Denkmäler deutscher Kunst, Deutscher Verein für Kunstwissenschaft, Berlin 1942. — Idem, *Hans von Kulmbach, Leben und Werk eines fränkischen Künstlers der Dürerzeit*, Die Plassenburg, Schriften für Heimatpflege und Kulturpflege in Ostfranken, Vol. 14, Kulmbach 1959.

Laib: L. BALDASS, *Conrad Laib und die beiden Rueland Frueauf*, Vienna 1946.

Leu: W. HUGELSHOFER, *Das Werk des Zürcher Malers Hans Leu*, Anzeiger für schweizerische Altertumskunde, N. F. XXV, 1923, I, p. 163 ff., 1924 II, p. 28 ff., III, p. 122 ff.

Lochner: O. H. FÖRSTER, *Stefan Lochner, Ein Maler zu Köln*, Frankfurt 1938.

Mair von Landshut: W. HUGELSHOFER, *Zum Werk des Mair von Landshut*, Beiträge zur Geschichte der deutschen Kunst, I, Augsburg 1924, p. 111 ff.

Maler: G. GLÜCK, *Hans Maler von Ulm, Maler zu Schwaz*, Jahrbuch des Ah. Kaiserhauses XXV, Vienna 1905, p. 245 ff. — H. MACKOWITZ, *Der Maler Hans von Schwaz*, Schlernschriften Band 193, Innsbruck 1960.

Master of the Angrer Portrait: M. J. FRIEDLÄNDER, *Der Meister des Angrer-Bildnisses*, Der Cicerone 21 (1929), p. 1 ff.; Pantheon 10 (1932), p. 232 ff.

Master E S: M. LEHRS, *Geschichte und kritischer Katalog des deutschen, niederländischen und französischen Kupferstichs: II, Der Meister E. S.*, Vienna 1910.

Master of the Housebook: M. LEHRS, *Geschichte und kritischer Katalog des deutschen, niederländischen und französischen Kupferstichs: VIII, Der Meister des Hausbuches*, Vienna 1932. — E. Graf zu SOLMS-LAUBACH, *Der Hausbuchmeister*, Städeljahrbuch IX, Frankfurt a. M. 1935/36, p. 13 ff. — A. STANGE, *Der Hausbuchmeister*, Studien zur deutschen Kunstgeschichte 316, Baden-Baden - Strasbourg 1958.

Master of the Historia Friderici et Maximiliani: O. BENESCH and E. M. AUER, *Die Historia Friderici et Maximiliani*, Denkmäler Deutscher Kunst, Deutscher Verein für Kunstwissenschaft, Berlin 1957.

Mathis, see Gothardt-Neithardt.

Pacher: J. ALLESCH, *Michael Pacher*, Deutsche Meister 12, Leipzig 1931. — E. HEMPEL, *Das Werk Michael Pachers*, Vienna 1938. — H. SEMPER, *Michael und Friedrich Pacher/Ihr Kreis und ihre Nachfolger*, Esslingen 1911.

Ratgeb: O. BENESCH, *Zum Werk Jerg Ratgebs*, Zeitschrift für Bildende Kunst 61, Leipzig 1927/28, p. 49 ff. — A. BURKHARD, *The Herrenberg Altar of Jörg Ratgeb*, Cambridge, Mass., 1965. — W. FRAENGER, *Jörg Ratgeb, Ein Maler und Märtyrer des Bauernkrieges*, Castrum Peregrini XXIX, The Hague 1956. — B. KURTH, *Ein unbekanntes Jugendwerk Jörg Ratgebs*, Beiträge zur Geschichte der deutschen Kunst, Augsburg 1924, I, p. 186 ff.

— W. K. ZÜLCH, *Jerg Ratgeb Maler*, Wallraf-Richartz-Jahrbuch XII, XIII, Cologne 1943, p. 165 ff.

Riemenschneider: J. BIER, *Tilman Riemenschneider*, Vol. I, Würzburg 1925, Vol. II, Augsburg 1930.

Ring, Hermann tom: E. HÖLKER, *Die Malerfamilie Tom Ring*, Münster 1927.

Schäufelein: E. BUCHNER, *Der junge Schäufelein als Maler und Zeichner*, in Festschrift für M. J. Friedländer zum 60. Geburtstag, Leipzig 1927, p. 46 ff. — M. CONSUELO OLDENBOURG, *Die Buchholzschnitte des Hans Schäufelein*, Studien zur deutschen Kunstgeschichte 340, 341, Baden-Baden - Strasbourg 1964. — F. WINKLER, *Die Zeichnungen Hans Süss von Kulmbachs und Hans Leonhard Schäufeleins*, Denkmäler deutscher Kunst, Deutscher Verein für Kunstwissenschaft, Berlin 1942.

Schongauer: E. BUCHNER, *Martin Schongauer als Maler*, Denkmäler deutscher Kunst, Deutscher Verein für Kunstwissenschaft, Berlin 1941. — M. J. FRIEDLÄNDER, *Martin Schongauer*, Berlin 1923. — M. LEHRS, *Geschichte und kritischer Katalog des deutschen, niederländischen und französischen Kupferstichs: V, Martin Schongauer und seine Schule*, Vienna 1925. — J. ROSENBERG, *Martin Schongauers Handzeichnungen*, Munich 1923.

Sittow: P. JOHANSEN, *Meister Michel Sittow*, Jahrbuch der Preussischen Kunstsammlungen 61, 1940, p. 1 ff.

Stoss: E. BUCHNER, *Veit Stoss als Maler*, Wallraf-Richartz-Jahrbuch XIV, Cologne 1952, p. 111 ff. — M. LOSSNITZER, *Veit Stoss*, Leipzig 1912.

Strigel: G. OTTO, *Bernhard Strigel*, Kunstwissenschaftliche Studien XXXIII, Munich-Berlin 1964.

Vischer the Elder: S. MELLER, *Peter Vischer der Ältere und seine Werkstatt*, Leipzig 1925.

Wydyz (Weiditz): C. SOMMER, *Beiträge zum Werke des Bildschnitzers Hans Wydyz*, Oberrheinische Kunst III, Jahrg. 1928, Freiburg im Breisgau, p. 94 ff., plate 46.

Wertinger: E. BUCHNER, *Monats- und Jahreszeitenbilder Hans Wertingers*, Zeitschrift für Bildende Kunst, 61. Jahrg., Leipzig 1927/28, p. 106 ff.

Wolgemut: F. J. STADLER, *Michael Wolgemut und der Nürnberger Holzschnitt im letzten Drittel des XV. Jahrhunderts*, Studien zur deutschen Kunstgeschichte, Heft 161 and volume of plates, Strasbourg 1913.

MUSEUM AND EXHIBITION CATALOGUES

Museum Catalogues:

Augsburg, *Katalog der königlichen Gemäldegalerie* (I.V. BRAUNE), 1912. — Basel, *Katalog der Öffentlichen Kunstsammlung*, 1946. — Basel, Kunstmuseum, *150 Gemälde, 12.-20. Jahrhundert*, Basel 1964. — Berlin, Staatliche Museen, *Die Gemäldegalerie, Die deutschen und altniederländischen Meister*, Berlin 1929. — Berlin, Staatliche Museen, *Die Gemälde des XIII.-XVIII. Jahrhunderts*, Dahlem 1956; *Verzeichnis der ausgestellten Gemälde des 13.-18. Jahrhunderts im Museum Dahlem*, Berlin 1964. — Cologne, Wallraf-

Richartz-Museum, 1959. — Dresden, *Katalog der Staatlichen Gemäldegalerie* (H. POSSE); *Katalog der Alten Meister*, Dresden-Berlin 1930. — *Die Dresdener Gemäldegalerie* (H. MENZ), Munich-Zurich 1962. — Frankfurt, *Gemälde des Historischen Museums*, Frankfurt am Main 1957. — Frankfurt, Städelsches Kunstinstitut, *Verzeichnis der Gemälde*, 1924. — Innsbruck, Museum Ferdinandeum, *Katalog der Gemäldesammlung*, 1928. — Karlsruhe, Staatliche Kunsthalle, *Alte Meister bis 1800* (J. LAUTS), Karlsruhe 1966 (text volume). — Kassel, *Katalog der Staatlichen Gemäldegalerie*, 1958. — Klosterneuburg, *Katalog der Stiftlichen Kunstsammlungen*, I: O. BENESCH, *Die Gemäldesammlung Klosterneuburg*, 1937. — London, *National Gallery Catalogues*, 1929, *The German School* (Michael LEVEY); *Illustrations*, 1937. — Madrid, *Catalogo del Museo del Prado*, 1933. — Madrid, *Prado, Musei e Monumenti d'Europa* (Manuel LORENTE), 2 vols, Novara 1962. — Munich, *Katalog der Gemäldegalerie des Bayerischen Nationalmuseums* (K. VOLL, H. BRAUNE, H. BUCHHEIT), 1908 *(Kataloge des Bayerischen Nationalmuseums* Vol. 8). — Munich, Alte Pinakothek, *Kurzes Verzeichnis der Bilder* (E. BUCHNER), 1957. — Munich, *Alte Pinakothek* (E. BUCHNER), Munich 1957. — Munich, *Katalog der Alten Pinakothek*, II, *Altdeutsche Malerei* (C. A. ZU SALM), Munich 1963. — New York, The Metropolitan Museum of Art, *A Catalogue of Early Flemish, Dutch and German Paintings* (H. B. WEHLE), New York 1947. — Nuremberg, *Kataloge des Germanischen Nationalmuseums, Die Gemälde des 13. bis 16. Jahrhunderts*, 2 vols, Leipzig 1937. — Paris, Musée National du Louvre, *Catalogue des Peintures, Ecoles Flamande, Hollandaise, Allemande et Anglaise*, 3 vols (Louis DEMONTS), Paris 1922. — Paris, *La Peinture au Musée du Louvre, Ecole Allemande* (Louis RÉAU), Paris n.d. — Stuttgart, *Katalog der Staatsgalerie Stuttgart I, Alte Meister*, Stuttgart 1962. — Stuttgart, *Meisterwerke der Stuttgarter Staatsgalerie* (B. BUSHART), Stuttgart n.d. — Venice, *Gallerie dell'Accademia di Venezia* (S. MOSCHINI), *Cataloghi dei Musei e Gallerie d'Italia*, Vol. I, Rome 1955. — Vienna, *Die Gemäldegalerie der Akademie der Bildenden Künste*, 2 vols (R. EICHENBERGER), Vienna-Leipzig 1927. — Vienna, Kunsthistorisches Museum, *Katalog der Gemäldegalerie* (L. BALDASS), 1938; *Gemäldegalerie*, 2 vols, *Vlamen, Holländer, Deutsche, Franzosen,* (V. OBERHAMMER), 1963. — Vienna, *Führer durch das Erzbischöfliche Dom- und Diözesanmuseum in Wien* (F. DWORSCHAK, H. GÖHLER, J. SCHMIDT), Vienna 1934. — Washington, *National Gallery of Art* (J. WALKER), New York 1963. — Washington, *National Gallery of Art, Paintings and Sculpture from the Samuel H. Kress Collection* (W. E. SUIDA), Washington 1959.

Exhibition Catalogues:

Albrecht Altdorfer und sein Kreis, memorial exhibition for the 400th anniversary of Altdorfer's death (E. BUCHNER), Munich 1938. — *Hans Baldung Grien-Ausstellung*, Staatliche Kunsthalle, Karlsruhe 1959. — *Das Malerwerk Hans Burgkmairs von Augsburg*, Staatliche Gemäldegalerie, Augsburg 1931. — *Die Kunst der Donauschule 1490-1540*, Abbey of St Florian and Schlossmuseum, Linz, May-October 1965. — *Albrecht Dürer-Ausstellung*, Germanisches Nationalmuseum, Nuremberg 1928. — *Meister um Albrecht Dürer*, Germanisches Nationalmuseum, Nuremberg 1961. — *Die Malerfamilie Holbein in Basel*, Kunstmuseum, Basel 1960 (for this exhibition, see also L. BALDASS, *Zeitschrift für Kunstwissenschaft*, XV, Berlin 1961, p. 81 ff.) — *Hans Holbein der Ältere und die Kunst der Spätgotik* (B. BUSHART and others), Rathaus, Augsburg, August-November 1965. — *Maximilian I.-Ausstellung*, Oesterreichische Nationalbibliothek, Graphische Sammlung Albertina, Kunsthistorisches Museum (Waffensammlung), Vienna 1959. — *Martin Schaffner, Maler zu Ulm*, Schriften des Ulmer Museums, N. F., Vol. 2, Exhibition, Ulm 1959.

General Index

Unless otherwise stated, pictures mentioned as being in the following cities are in the leading museum or collection: AUGSBURG, Staatliche Gemäldegalerie; BASEL, Kunstmuseum; BERLIN, Staatliche Museen; FRANKFURT, Städelsches Kunstinstitut; MUNICH, Alte Pinakothek; NUREMBERG, Germanisches Nationalmuseum; VIENNA, Kunsthistorisches Museum, Gemäldegalerie.

List of Colour Plates

THIS VOLUME OF THE COLLECTION "PAINTING - COLOR - HISTORY" WAS
PRODUCED BY THE TECHNICAL STAFF OF EDITIONS D'ART ALBERT SKIRA.
FINISHED THE FIFTEENTH DAY OF AUGUST NINETEEN HUNDRED AND SIXTY-SIX

TEXT AND ILLUSTRATIONS PRINTED BY

SKIRA

COLOR STUDIOS

IMPRIMERIES RÉUNIES, S.A., LAUSANNE

PLATES ENGRAVED BY GUEZELLE & RENOUARD, PARIS

PHOTOGRAPHS BY

Maurice Babey, Basel (pages 17, 21, 30, 33, 34, 42, 46, 49, 52, 53, 55, 56, 62, 66, 72, 105, 107, 108, 111, 112-113, 114, 118, 125, 129, 134, 139, 146, 150, 174, 176, 179), Henry B. Beville, Alexandria, Va. (page 18), Joachim Blauel, Munich (page 141), R. Dobrick, Darmstadt (page 159), John Freeman, London (pages 153, 163), Kurt Haase, Frankfurt (page 27), Hans Hinz, Basel (pages 26, 73, 85, 97-98, 116, 131, 132, 144, 154, 155, 156-157, 164, 165), Stanislas Kolowca, Cracow (page 101), Louis Laniepce, Paris (page 167), Erwin Meyer, Vienna (pages 37, 50, 59, 61, 78, 82, 102, 115, 122, 124, 127, 152, 160, 172, 173), and Walter Steinkopf, Berlin (pages 63, 121, 138, 142, 168). Photographic material obligingly lent by The Art Institute of Chicago (page 126), Scala, Florence (pages 10, 128), Mauritshuis, The Hague (page 171), Staatliche Kunsthalle, Karlsruhe (pages 14, 75, 147), Germanisches Nationalmuseum, Nuremberg (page 69), and Photothèque, Paris (pages 39, 58, 90, 91-92, 93, 96, 99).

The reproduction on page 116 appears by permission of Kunst- und Verlagsanstalt Franz Hanfstaengel, Munich.